• Amida

A

MONASTIC SYRIA

CISTERCIAN STUDIES SERIES: NUMBER ONE HUNDRED TWELVE

THE LIVES OF SIMEON STYLITES

Translated, with an Introduction,
by
Robert Doran

Foreword
by
Susan Ashbrook Harvey

Cistercian Publications
Kalamazoo Michigan

© Translation, copyright 1992 by Cistercian Publications Inc.

Three *Lives* of Simeon (Simon, Symeon) Stylites (The Stylite).
d. 459 AD, translated from the Greek and Syriac.

The work of Cistercian Publications is made possible in part
by support from Western Michigan University to the
Institute of Cistercian Studies.

Library of Congress Cataloging-in-Publication Data

The Lives of Simeon Stylites / translated, with an introduction by
Robert Doran : foreword by Susan Ashbrook Harvey
   p.   cm. — (Cistercian studies series ; no. 112)
   Includes English translations of two Greek biographies by
Theodoret and Antonius, and an anonymous Syriac version.
   Includes bibliographical references and index.
   ISBN 0-87907-412-4 (alk. paper). — ISBN (invalid) 0-87907-
512-7 (pbk. : alk. paper)
   1. Simeon Stylites, Saint, d. 459.   2. Christian saints—Turkey—
Biography.   3. Pillar saints—Turkey—Biography.   I. Doran,
Robert, 1940–   .   II. Theodoret, Bishop of Cyrrhus.   Philotheos
historia.   Chapter 26.   English.   1992.   III. Antonius, monk,
disciple of Simeon Stylites, fl. 470.   Bios kai politeia tou makariou
Symeōn tou Stylitou.   English.   1992.   IV. Neshaneh de-Mar
Shem on Resha de-Abile.   English.   1992.   V. Series.
BR1720.S52L58   1992
270.2′092—dc20
[B]   92-3179
                                                                CIP

Printed in the United States of America

In honor of my mother
Bridget Doran
and
in memory of my father
Cyril Doran

TABLE OF CONTENTS

ACKNOWLEDGEMENTS

This project was completed thanks to the help, assistance and encouragement of many colleagues.

The preparation of this volume was made possible in part by a grant from the Division of Research Programs of the National Endowment of the Humanities, an independent federal agency. I am also indebted to Amherst College for awarding me both a Miner D. Crary Fellowship, which enabled me to inspect the Vatican and British Library manuscripts, and an Amherst College Faculty Fellowship, which allowed me the time to begin the project. Both the Vatican Library and the British Library supplied me with microfilms of the manuscripts, and allowed me access to the manuscripts themselves.

The project moreover was helped by many individuals. Professor Arthur Vööbus kindly sent me a microfilm of his photographs of the new manuscript of the life of Simeon which he discovered at Mardin. Dr Rozanne Elder of Cistercian Publications was patient with my slow progress, and her anonymous readers helped improve my work immensely. Sebastian Brock gave generously of his time and meticulous attention to detail in going over both my introduction and my translation of the Syriac. I benefitted greatly from the colleagueship and judicious suggestions of Susan Harvey, who also graciously allowed me to read her unpublished work. I also want to thank John Strugnell and Peter Brown who read the manuscript and offered encouragement along the way. Finally I thank my wife Susan Niditch, who always rekindled my enthusiasm, and my daughters Rebecca and Elizabeth, who never tired of listening to new stories about Simeon.

FOREWORD

IN THE MID-FIFTH CENTURY AD, a monk named Daniel took leave from his mesopotamian monastery to go on pilgrimage for the further edification of his soul. He had two destinations in mind: the city of Jerusalem, and 'the holy and thrice-blessed Simeon, the man on the pillar, in whose footsteps he felt constrained to follow'.[1] Daniel never did reach Jerusalem. As he travelled towards the site of Simeon on his pillar, he met a group of monks disdainful of the stylite (from the Greek word *stylos*, meaning 'pillar').

'For,' said they, 'it is true that a man even if he were living in your midst might practise a mode of life hitherto unknown and please God, yet never has such a thing happened anywhere that a man should go up and live on a pillar.'[2]

Nonetheless, the monks were persuaded to join Daniel in his quest to see what the holy man was doing and what resulted from his practice.

When they arrived at the place and saw the wildness of the spot and the height of the pillar and the fiery heat of the scorching sun and the Saint's endurance and his welcome to strangers and further, too, the love he shewed towards them, they were amazed.[3]

When Simeon invited the group to climb up the ladder to visit him on the pillar, the formerly scornful monks refused, mortified

---

[1] *The Life of Daniel the Stylite*, 6; translated by N. H. Baynes and E. Dawes, *Three Byzantine Saints* (1948; rpt. Oxford: Mowbray-Crestwood: SVS, 1977) 10. The greek text was edited by H. Delehaye in his volume *Les Saints Stylites*, Subsidia Hagiographica 14 (Brussels: Société des Bollandistes, 1923; rpt. 1962) 1–94.

[2] *The Life of Daniel*, 7; Baynes and Dawes, *Three Byzantine Saints*, 10.

[3] *Ibid.*; pp. 10–11.

7

by their own insolence and by the full realization of what Simeon's life required. But Daniel went up. On Simeon's small platform atop a pillar forty cubits high, exposed to nature and to the sight of all who watched, the earnest monk received the saint's blessing and departed.

In time Daniel too ascended a pillar, strengthened by Simeon's encouragement and by the gift of his tunic upon the saint's death.[4] But where Simeon had climbed his pillar high in the mountains well beyond Antioch, Daniel took his stance at the edge of Constantinople: the very heart of the Eastern Roman Empire. For the next thirty-three years, until his death at the age of eighty-four, Daniel conducted the private and public affairs of the empire from his pillar, fulfilling the work of his master even as the prophet Elisha had inherited the work of his master Elijah.[5] Others would follow. In greater and lesser numbers as the centuries went by, stylites continued this same practice of standing prayer, enacted midway between heaven and earth, up through the late nineteenth century. What Simeon started was a work that endured.

As Daniel's story shows, Simeon the Stylite was a haunting presence in the world of his own day, even as he continues to be for those who study his life now. The short entries referring to Simeon in Daniel's hagiography mark the three aspects of his career repeatedly affirmed in all the primary sources we have about him. First, Simeon's capacity for severe self-mortification was problematic even for his contemporaries, especially his fellow monastics. His was a model that disturbed as much as it inspired. Second, Simeon's labors, however horrifying to watch or to endure, clearly inspired awe rather than revulsion. One result was that Simeon himself became the focus of an extraordinary pilgrimage movement, as people throughout the known world of his day flocked to his pillar for all manner of succour—for healing, counsel, judgements, teaching, inspiration, or simply to see the wonder of this man's work. Finally, Simeon's impact on his world was not due to his shock value or his celebrity status; like Daniel, those who confronted the stylite were moved above all by the profound constancy of his life of prayer. In the end, it was

---

4   *Ibid*, ch. 21–22.
5   2 Kgs 2.

Simeon's spirituality, not his athleticism, that won him disciples and imitators and that forced his detractors to ponder the nature of his vocation.

No writings by Simeon survive to us. We do not know why he climbed his pillar, why he stayed there, or what he thought he was doing. We do, however, have writings by those who saw him, by the disciples who served him, and by those who chose to follow his religious vocation. With no access to Simeon's own mind, and with his motivation at best obscure to us, we can only try to make sense of what Simeon did by listening to how his contemporaries made sense of him. Most important among the sources are the three hagiographies gathered and lucidly translated in the present volume by Robert Doran, interrelated yet distinct in their interpretations of the saint and his ascetic calling. In the introduction to the translations, Professor Doran places Simeon and these texts into the richly textured religious tapestry of the late antique mediterranean world. Indeed, only when seen in the full context of his inherited world can Simeon's actions be assessed. The value of this volume is the manner in which it opens that world to us, with clarity and depth.

Whatever one may think of Simeon's asceticism, one thing is clear: his contributions to society were concretely constructive, and belie the apparent 'uselessness' of a life of self-mortification. In effect, this holy man ran an extensive social service network from the top of his pillar. When a poor cucumber farmer, the widowed father of children, found his field sabotaged by village bullies he came to Simeon, seeking not only help for his livelihood but justice for what he had suffered (*Syriac Life*, section 39). When a corrupt civic official in Antioch imposed a tripled tax on leather workers who used red dye, a guild of three hundred men, they came to Simeon's pillar (*Syriac Life*, 56). Many such stories about Simeon survive to us, as do those of his work with the sick, his intervention for the poor, his pacifying role in the heated ecclesiastical politics of his day or in the delicate foreign policy between the byzantine emperor and the unruly bedouin arab tribes to the east. Here is how his disciples described Simeon's work:

> How many oppressed were delivered from their op-
> pressors at his word. How many bonds were torn up

through the efforts of the saint. How many afflicted
were relieved from their coercers. How many slaves
were freed and their documents torn up before the
saint. How many orphans and widows, by our Lord's
design, were brought up and nourished through the
saint's stance only his Lord knows. (*Syriac Life*, 77, Doran's translation)

Still, it is also clear that this was not Simeon's original goal.
Simeon left home to seek the religious life, not to change other
people's lives. Those who saw Simeon attest that he sought first
and foremost to live a life of prayer, of worship. While his followers
did not flinch from depicting the harshness of his vocation, they
are unanimous in presenting Simeon as someone who united his
body and soul in a life of devotion to God. When people saw his
devotion and the particular form it took, they flocked to him in
droves. At his pillar they sought to be helped and to help others
in turn. Simeon did not pursue this role; it was granted to him
by the people of his day. Why?

Simeon's physical separation from society—in the wilderness,
on his pillar, forty cubits in the air—was essential to the work
he did on society's behalf. He was literally in the world yet not
of it. Furthermore, because of the extremity of his physical location, he required a personal following to take care of him as well
as to put his work into effect. His separation was two-fold: first
by where he actually was and second by a community of followers who mediated between the saint and the people seeking his
aid. Simeon, the holy one, was in no way part of the ordinary.
People could see and tangibly know that separation. This is the
basic meaning of the word 'holy' or 'sacred': that which is set
apart. Simeon lived his devotion to God set apart quite literally
from all that the world contained; he belonged only to God. His
judgement, his words, his actions, his commands were seen to
have no other source and no other purpose. In acknowledgement
of the sacredness of Simeon's location, people did what he told
them to do: taxes were remitted, unjust policies were righted, food
was distributed. A life of devotion, an ascetic life, had necessary
consequences in Simeon's world. The holy one by definition—by
the life of devotion to God—was called to serve all in need.

What we must not forget is that when Simeon's contemporaries looked at the harshness of his life, they saw the beauty it symbolized no less than the suffering it required. Theodoret of Cyrrhus believed that Simeon lived the life of angels, standing in ceaseless prayer midway between heaven and earth. For the disciple Antonius, the worm that fell from a festering wound in Simeon's leg became a priceless pearl. And the writers of the Syriac life saw Simeon as the new Moses on the new Mount Sinai dispensing the new Law; he was transfigured before his disciples as Christ was once transfigured on Mount Tabor; he stood on his pillar as incense on an altar, his prayer rising heavenward.

When we look at Simeon from our modern point of view, we see a brutal life of self-inflicted pain. When his contemporaries looked at him, they saw a life transformed, a man transfigured, a world redeemed. This was not a mass hallucination. They saw these things because they saw them concretely enacted: Simeon lived the life he did and it did not kill him; at his pillar the sick were healed, the hungry were fed, the down-trodden were championed. To be meaningful, a symbol must be true to the world it addresses. The world of late antiquity, and especially the fifth-century byzantine east, was a harsh reality at best. Wars, famine, drought, illness, and deep economic crisis formed the fabric of daily life. Ethereal, disembodied symbols would not speak to many in such times. But a man who confronted the plain reality of his world—a suffering, cruel reality—, who took that reality into his own body and lived it as it was; who knew what it meant to be hungry and weary and sick, and who took that as his chosen life; a man who sought justice for the oppressed in this life as well as in the next: this was a man whose symbolic meaning changed before the viewers' very eyes. A worm was not a worm: it was a pearl. A pillar was not a torture chamber: it was an altar. Simeon the Stylite rising heavenward like incense was not a victim of ascetic zeal: he was a living icon of the transfigured Lord. People knew this. They knew what Simeon lived and what he did by means of his life.

Simeon's body bore the truth of the world he saw: the sufferings, the terror, the weariness, and the radiance of transfigured grace. His body presented that truth to his witnesses not as a metaphor but as a genuinely changed reality. Through him, health was given to the sick, food to the hungry, justice to the oppressed and peace to the soul. Jolted, humbled, and moved, the people of his day responded. Some, like the monk Daniel, joined his way. Others, like the writers whose texts are gathered in this volume, told the story so that the work of his prayer would not be forgotten.

Susan Ashbrook Harvey

Brown University

ABBREVIATIONS

Ant   The Life by Antonius, as translated in the present volume.

B   The British Manuscript of the Syriac Life of Simeon Stylites

HR   *Historia Religiosa*, by Theodoret of Cyr as translated by R.M. Price. Theodoret of Cyrrhus, *A History of the Monks of Syria*. Cistercian Studies Series, 88. Kalamazoo, MI: Cistercian Publications, 1985.

M   The Mardin Manuscript of the Syriac Life of Simeon Stylites

Syriac   The Syriac Life of Simeon Stylites

V   The Vatican Manuscript of the Syriac Life of Simeon Stylites

INTRODUCTION SIMEON STYLITES

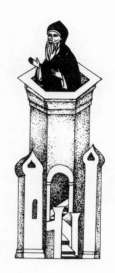

S IMEON STYLITES HAS BEEN A SIGN of contradiction: for some his standing on a pillar was an extravagant example of the morbid phenomenon of Syrian asceticism;[1] for others he has been a saint to be admired and imitated.[2] This book presents the three primary accounts of the life of Simeon: the account by Theodoret, bishop of Cyrrhus; the Syriac life; and the life by Antonius.

As one would expect, each biography gives a different portrait of the saint as each author chooses different incidents and anecdotes to illustrate that ideal of holiness that he wishes his readers to imitate. One can also abstract from the three accounts the basic story line of Simeon's life. In what follows, I have first presented a short sketch of Simeon's career, his role in the society in which he lived, and I have hinted at the religious symbolism at play in Simeon's standing on a pillar. Secondly, I have made some suggestions why each author composed his biography in the way he did, and have analyzed those narratives in common among the three biographies.

---

[1] T. Nöldeke *Sketches from Eastern History* (Beirut: Khayats, 1963) 206–225.

[2] See the list of Stylite imitators that I. Peña, P. Castellana and R. Fernandez (*Les Stylites Syriens* Milan: Franciscan Printing Press, 1975) have uncovered as well as the admiring tone of H.G. Blersch, *Die Säule im Weltgeviert*, Sophia: Quellen östlicher Theologie 17 (Trier: Paulinus, 1978).

Simeon's Life

Simeon was born towards the end of the fourth century in the village of Sisa near Nicopolis on the border between Cilicia and Euphratensis. The details of his childhood are sketchy: his parents are said by the Syriac life to have been believers and to have had Simeon baptized (Syriac 1). All three accounts agree that Simeon tended his parents' flocks (Syriac 1; *HR* 26.2; Ant 2). He was uninstructed in the faith and by chance entered a church one Sunday: he experienced a conversion, which included a vision at a nearby martyrion, and thereafter sought God alone. Theodoret notes that Simeon spent two years with nearby ascetics before moving to the monastery at Teleda (*HR* 26.4), while the Syriac life mentions only that Simeon lived a life of prayer and austerity (Syriac 8) before entering that monastery. There he spent around ten years before being asked by the abbot and community to leave. He travelled back north until he came to the village of Telanissos/Telneshe. After spending three years on the nearby summit living in a small domed hut (*HR* 26.7; Syriac 28.44), he installed himself within a circle of stones out in the open air (*HR* 10; Syriac 44; Ant 12). After some time, Simeon mounted the first of three increasingly higher pillars, on which he took his stance of continual prayer. The final pillar, forty cubits or about sixty feet in height, had a platform on top about six feet square. There, exposed to all the elements, Simeon stood and prostrated, healed and harmed until his death in 459, when he was over seventy years old. His fame stretched from Britain to the Persian empire, and pilgrims flocked to his pillar from all parts and strata of late antique society.

It is hard to pin down the exact dates for Simeon's career as all three accounts of Simeon's life provide different chronologies. The chronology for Simeon's life differs in the three accounts.

	HR 26. 5,7,10	Ant. 12.28	Syriac 110
Teleda	10 yrs.	3 yrs.[3]	9 yrs.
Telneshe			
Domed Hut	3 yrs.	none	

[3] H. Delehaye *Les Saints Stylites* (Bruxelles: Société des Bollandistes, 1923) xvi.

Open Air	?	4 yrs.	10 yrs.
Small columns	?	7 + 15 yrs.	7 yrs.
Large Columns	?	21 yrs.	30 yrs.

The height and number of the columns also varies.

HR 26. 12	Ant. 12.17	Syriac 110
6 cubits[4]	4 cubits	11 cubits
12 cubits		17 cubits
22 cubits	30 cubits	22 cubits
36 cubits	40 cubits	40 cubits

There seems no way one can reconcile these data, but the general outline emerges. Simeon died in 459.[5] Both Antonius and the Syriac author agree that the total length of time Simeon spent in the areas around Telneshe was forty-seven years, so that he would have arrived there in 412. The Syriac life thus has Simeon enter Teleda around 403, and this agrees with Theodoret who wrote his life in 444 and expressly states that Simeon had lived twenty-eight years in the open air. If one then subtracts the time Theodoret says Simeon spent in a domed hut (three years) and the ten years he spent at Teleda, one has Simeon entering Teleda in 403.

Simeon thus lived around Telneshe for fifty years. One can detect from the Syriac life how his fame grew first through miracles done for local people: the miracle for Maris of Telneshe (Syriac 29); for the daughter of the chief of Beth Laha, about three miles from Telneshe (Syriac 33); for the deacon who lived about three miles from the enclosure (Syriac 90). Gradually the influence spread—to the low-lying country (Syriac 91), to the Plain of Antioch (Syriac 34), to Aleppo (Syriac 39; 89)—before branching out to the whole world. Telneshe was on one of the major commercial routes, from Cyrrhus in the north to Apamea in the

---

[4] A cubit is an ancient measure of length derived from the fore-arm, about eighteen inches.

[5] A.M. Festugière [*Antioche Païenne et Chrétienne. Libanius, Chrysostome et les moines de Syrie* (Paris: Boccard, 1959) 377- 386] argues that the version of Simeon's death found in Antonius is to be preferred.

south. As such it would be readily accessible to pilgrims and to those needing miraculous cures.

His Role in Society

Amidst all the discrepancies in detail, one can observe in the Life features of that daily work-load of mediation that Peter Brown pointed to so brilliantly—'what men expected of the holy man coincides with what they sought in the rural patron'.[6] Simeon defends the oppressed, and often one can glimpse the interaction between various social groups. The guild of skin-dyers at Antioch came to Simeon for help against new taxes imposed on them (Syriac 56); two young men in Antioch who did not want to undertake financially crippling positions on the town council sought his help (Syriac 60).[7] Simeon is instructed by Elijah not to show favoritism to the rich, but 'publicly and even-handedly to rebuke all men, whether rich or poor' (Syriac 43). The Syriac life speaks of the halving of the percentage charged on loans (Syriac 77). In a letter from Panir one finds the same attention to regulating day-to-day matters and mediating disputes (Syriac 131). As Theodoret says:

> He can be seen sitting in judgement and handing down proper and just sentences. These and similar activities are dealt with after three in the afternoon, for he spends the whole night and the day up till three p.m. in prayer. After three p.m. he first delivers the divine teaching to those present and then, after receiving the request of each and effecting some healings, he resolves the quarrels of the disputants. Around sunset he then begins his conversation with God. (HR 26.26).

Simeon was, however, much more than a rural patron. His pillar became a pilgrimage center, and supplicants came with all kinds of problems: personal problems of sickness and pain, of a wife's infertility, of sin and transgression; social problems in Antioch were

---

[6] Peter Brown, 'The Rise and Function of the Holy Man in Late Antiquity', *Journal of Roman Studies* 61 (1971) 87.

[7] On the duties and burdens of council office, see A.H.M. Jones, *The Later Roman Empire 284 - 602* (Oxford: Blackwell, 1964) 2: 748–760.

mediated at his shrine, and slaves were manumitted. Villages as a whole sent delegations to Simeon for advice on plagues and attacks by unusual beasts. At such times, processions of singing choir boys might attend the pillar, as in the narrative of the great drought (Syriac 75). In August was celebrated some special commemoration at the pillar to which, the Syriac life relates, thousands would come. The manuscript of the Syriac life in the British Library connects this feast with a miracle wrought by Simeon to overcome drought by a miraculous rainfall, and this may well have been the occasion for the feast. Certainly many thronged to celebrate this festival and supplicate Simeon on the occasion of the earthquakes around Antioch in 459. Simeon's advice on such occasions was usually that the villages or towns concerned keep a vigil for three days, celebrate the Eucharist, and to stop plagues and pests by using *ḥnana*, dust from his shrine mixed with water from the area. A high imperial official, Dionysius, came for help on his embassy to Persia (Syriac 84). Simeon intervened dramatically with Theodosius II to prevent Christians from having to restore a synagogue to the Jews and pay retribution to them (Syriac 121); he is said to have corresponded with the emperors and told them what was fitting for their rule (Syriac 77; 106). Theodoret succinctly stated the world-wide influence of Simeon:

> As they all come from every quarter, each road is like a river: one can see collected in that spot a human sea into which rivers from all sides debouched. For it is not only inhabitants of our part of the world who pour in, but also Ishmaelites, Persians and the Armenians subject to them, the Iberians, the Homerites, and those who live even further in the interior than these. Many came from the extreme west: Spaniards, Britons and the Gauls who dwell between them. It is superfluous to speak of Italy.

One can visualize from an incident of drought the procedure—priests from various villages would lead their followers on pilgrimage, as school boys antiphonally chanted the *Kyrie Eleison*. The long dusty walk of at least several miles and then the trek up the mountain during a drought was no small effort for these young boys and their teachers.

In all of this, the position of Simeon reminds one of the importance of oracle shrines in the second and third centuries C.E. They
too were 'a marriage bureau and a career service, a medical surgery
and a farmers' bulletin'.[8] Apollo at Claros advised cities in Asia Minor how to ward off raiding barbarians, how to banish plagues and
reverse drought. To escape a plague, the citizens of Hierapolis in
Asia Minor had to offer sacrifices to various gods and to set up images of Clarian Apollo as an archer all around the city gates. After
this 'boys and girl musicians [should] go together to Claros, with
hecatombs and glad libations'.[9] Slaves were manumitted at Delphi
and other sanctuaries, as they are in Simeon's presence (Syriac 77;
81). The best attested oracle centers are at Claros and Didyma in
Asia Minor,[10] but others are found in Syria and Mesopotamia: at
Heliopolis and Hierapolis in Syria, the oracle of Zeus Casios (=
Baal Zaphon) near Antioch, of Zeus Belus at Apamea;[11] at Dura
Europos, Palmyra, Edessa and Harran.[12] At Mallus in Cilicia Pausa-
nias knew of an oracle of Amphilochus—'the most trustworthy of
my day' (Paus 1.34.3)—where the oracle worked through dreams
during incubation. Closer to where Simeon set up residence was
the famous shrine of Apollo at Daphne in Antioch.[13] Other Christian holy men before Simeon had been consulted on such issues.
Theodoret's own mother had consulted Macedonius as to how
she might conceive (*HR* 13.16); James of Nisibis had turned back
marauding hordes (*HR* 1.11–12). Christians had also attempted
to close down oracles. The bones of martyrs were buried at the
shrine of Apollo in Daphne and are said to have dried up the
oracle's spring; Emperor Julian's attempt to revive it ended in

---

[8] Robin Lane Fox, *Pagans and Christians* (New York: Knopf, 1987) 214.

[9] Lane Fox, *Pagans and Christians,* 234. For the text of the inscription, see
M.L. West, 'Oracles of Apollo Kareios. A Revised Text', *Zeitschrift für Papyrologie
und Epigraphik* 1 (1967) 183–187.

[10] See H.W. Parke, *The Oracles of Apollo in Asia Minor* (London: Croom
Helm, 1985).

[11] A. Bouché-Leclercq, *Histoire de la divination dans l'antiquité* (Paris: Leroux,
1879–82) 3: 229–270; 396–411.

[12] H.J.W. Drijvers, *The Religion of Palmyra* (Leiden: Brill, 1976) 13; H.J.W.
Drijvers, *Cults and Beliefs at Edessa* (Leiden: Brill, 1980) 65–73.

[13] Bouché-Leclercq, *Histoire de la Divination* 3: 266–269; G. Downey, *A
History of Antioch in Syria from Seleucus to the Arab Conquest* (Princeton: Princeton
University Press, 1961) 82–86; 387–388.

farce. In Asia Minor, Thecla is said to have taken up residence at the shrine of the oracle of Sarpedonios and promptly taken over the function of the shrine.[14] At Heliopolis in Syria a Christian wrote in the guise of the Sibyl.[15] Frequently Theodoret notes how monks set up residence in former pagan shrines and drove out the demons.[16] When the Christian Emperors forbade consulting oracles,[17] the great oracle centers closed at least to public view, although Harran remained a major center of paganism well into the fifth century.[18] In the main, however, Christianity was re-defining the religious map of the ancient world. With the public closing of the oracle centers, the religious need for oracular help still remained and Christian holy men provided it. Simeon became the star attraction. Atop a lonely mountain with a spectacular view stood the wild-looking, unkempt, skin-clad voice of God. He did not speak in verse, nor did responses come through dreams. I am not suggesting a literal imitation of oracle centers, but he fulfilled the function of the oracle.[19] Questions would be put to him. Did the questioners bellow them out over the noise and hubbub of the crowd and Simeon shout back his answer (*HR* 26.14), or were the questions relayed through his faithful guardian on the ladder? Theodoret pictures him giving a sermon each day from atop his pillar, certainly good exercise for the lungs. Most probably distinctions were made between more private, intimate requests, for example, those concerning barrenness or Dionysius' embassy to the Persians, and public claims for assistance against plague or drought.

Simeon was thus seen as a powerful healer by both Christians and non-Christians and to choose Simeon to be one's healer/ physician brought into play an inter-personal dependence that

---

[14] Basil of Seleuceia, *De Vita sanctae Theclae* 2: 282; PG 85:565–568. For a discussion, see H. Delehaye, 'Les recueils antiques de miracles des saints', *Analecta Bollandiana* 43 (1925) 49–57.

[15] Paul J. Alexander, *The Oracle of Baalbek. The Tiburtine Sibyl in Greek Dress* (Washington: Dumbarton Oaks, 1967).

[16] For a survey, see G. Fowden, 'Bishops and Temples in the Eastern Roman Empire A.D. 320–435', *Journal of Theological Studies* 29 (1978) 53–78.

[17] *Codex Theodosianus* 16.10.7.

[18] J.B. Segal, *Edessa 'The Blessed City'* (Oxford: Clarendon, 1970) 104–105.

[19] For a discussion of the continuity and changes between pre-and post-Constantine, see Lane Fox, *Pagans and Christians*, 663–681.

would lead to profound changes. Healing and conversion went
hand in hand.[20] What is fascinating about Simeon, however, is
that not only individuals but whole villages bound themselves in
such a way. When some unusual beasts attacked people in Lebanon
and there was no respite, the villagers turned to Simeon for help
(Syriac 62–63). Simeon at first rebuffed them, telling them to go
to their idols for help. Although this retort goes back to Isaiah
(Is 41:21–29; 42:17), the oracle center of Heliopolis in Syria (=
Baalbek) lay between the Lebanon and the anti-Lebanon, an oracle consulted from afar and by written requests and which Trajan
had consulted (Macrobius *Saturn.* 1.23.10–20). When the people
persisted in their clamour for help and other bystanders interceded as well, Simeon relented if they left their error and turned
to God their maker and made a covenant to become Christians.
The village near Gindaris also had a covenant with Simeon and
they broke one of its laws (Syriac 64). On learning of the dis-
obedience Simeon became furious at them and cast them out of
his presence: they prostrated themselves before the entrance to his
enclosure and besought those going in and out to ask for mercy.
Only after three days of such public humiliation did Simeon let
them enter his presence again. They made a covenant in writing that they would never again transgress. We actually possess
a copy of such a covenant, from the village of Panir, appended
to the Vatican manuscript (Syriac 130–133). It occurs in a letter
from the priest of the village Cosmas, together with the deacons,
lectors, and all the congregation as well as the procurator and leading citizens (*veterani*). The use of the term *veteranus* suggests that
Panir was originally a military colony, as was Qatura, a village
not far from Telneshe.[21] Simeon is addressed as the father and
lord of the village, and the opening salutation is a panegyric of
Simeon's accomplishments. The letter then gives details of con-
duct that Simeon laid down for the village and to which they
subscribe: both Friday and Sunday were to be kept as holy days,
and regulations pertaining to just business dealings were set forth,

---

[20] A. Rousselle, 'Du sanctuaire au thaumaturge: La guérison en Gaule au IVe
siècle', *Annales* 31 (1976) 1085–1107.

[21] G. Tchalenko, *Villages antiques de la Syrie du Nord* (Paris: P. Geuthner,
1953) 1:189–194.

as were rules as to who may and who may not be in the community. Finally the group agreed to all these provisions and swore by God and Christ and the Spirit and by the victory of the Emperors. They would excommunicate anyone who disobeyed, and the threat of death would hang over such a person according to the word of Simeon. If they kept Simeon's commandments and laws they would be helped. Here in this letter are contained all the formal elements of a treaty/covenant form which goes back to the Hittite treaties of the fourteenth/thirteenth centuries B.C.E. Included are the stipulations, what is required of the vassal state, the laws imposed, the list of divine witnesses—in this case not only the Trinity but also the Victory of the Emperors (which perhaps reinforces the suggestion that Panir was a military colony), the blessings and curses. This covenant treaty form has a long history in the Old Testament; what is startling is to see it used here in the context of a covenant between *Simeon* and the village. The villagers are not entering the covenant which is the Church, but are entering into a covenant with Simeon. Gindaris exemplifies what happened when there was a breach of treaty: it had to be entered into again by both parties. Such treaties were presumably deposited at Simeon's enclosure. Again in this instance, Simeon seems to have taken the place of deities in the Near Eastern world: the village community was making a covenant with its lord/protector. This is not to say that Simeon was deified, simply that again one sees how Christian holy men in the fifth century were redefining the map and language of late antique society.

Syriac Christianity

The figure of Simeon must also be considered against the backdrop of early eastern Christianity. Our knowledge of this fascinating period in Church history is sketchy, but eastern Christianity does appear to have had profoundly ascetic, anti-worldly tendencies.

When one reads through the *History of the Monks of Syria* by Theodoret, one cannot help but marvel at the inventiveness of these monks in devising contorted tortures for themselves, and at the renunciation of civilization that shines through. They lived like animals on the mountains, eating grass or uncooked food, subject to all weather in the open air. If they built a shelter for themselves, it was one that they could not possibly stand up in. If Levi-Strauss had wanted to invent models for his dichotomy between nature and society, he could not have done better. The extravagance of these monks forces one to ask where it came from, what type of Christianity it represented?

> The rise of Syriac-speaking Christianity is bafflingly obscure, and the earliest literary works help us little. They are too difficult to date, to place, or to interpret historically... We have as yet no satisfactory social history of the people in Mesopotamia and Adiabene who produced this literature.[22]

Even given this daunting outlook, what strikes one most from the surviving literature is the sense of alienation so pithily captured in the saying of the Gospel of Thomas 42: 'Become passers-by'. Aphrahat exhorted his listeners in the Sixth Demonstration, written in 337: 'Let us be strangers to the world, even as Christ was not of it'.[23] In the Odes of Solomon 17:6, the psalmist says, 'All who saw me were amazed, and I seemed to them like a stranger'. The heroes were the wandering apostles of the apocryphal Gospels: in the *Acts of Thomas* the portrait that emerges is of one who travels from town to town breaking up marriages and preaching a doctrine of sexual abstinence.[24] The same holds true for the stories surrounding Paul and Thecla in Asia Minor.

Within the Syriac-speaking church existed committed ascetics, male and female, who were called the *bnay Qyāmā* and *bnat Qyāmā*, 'sons and daughters of the Covenant'. Much of the extant early Syriac Christian literature was written for such covenanters, to the extent that it was thought that celibacy or marital abstinence were required of those to be baptized. R. Murray has shown, however, that such vows were demanded of the members of the covenant 'on the occasion of [clearly adult] baptism, when, in terms drawn

[22] Robert Murray, 'The Characteristics of the Earliest Syriac Christianity', *East of Byzantium: Syria and Armenia in the Formative Period*, eds. N. Garsoian *et al.* (Washington: Dumbarton Oaks, 1982) 4–5.6.

[23] *Patrologia Syriaca* 1:241,16–17.

[24] On the notion of 'stranger' in the *Acts of Thomas*, see A.F.J. Klijn, *The Acts of Thomas* (Leiden: Brill, 1962) 165–166.

from the call to Holy War in Deuteronomy 20, they were solemnly adjured to choose between marriage and celibate vows',[25] and no conclusion can be drawn about the laity. In this covenant are those who live in a state of virginity and those in holiness or consecration, the state of married persons who renounce intercourse. Such covenanters were also called the *īhīdāyā*, those who are single.[26]

The monasticism that developed out of such a Christian milieu was so extreme that so renowned a scholar as A. Vööbus has suggested that the decisive impulse came from Mani, the founder of Manichaeism.[27] The father of Mani was a Christian, a member of an extremely ascetical baptist group which renounced sex and wine.[28] Mani attempted to develop a universal religion with elements from Zoroastrianism and Buddhism as well as from Christianity and his success can be gauged from the fact that members of his church could be found from China to Africa.[29] Mani's religion was profoundly dualist, with a cosmic battle between the realms of light and darkness.[30] Vööbus' position has been soundly criticized by A. Adam,[31] and scholars are concluding that both the dualism of Mani and the antitheses of Marcion seem to have found a ready home in Syriac Christianity because it was itself grounded in the radical statements of the Gospels themselves, in a thorough commitment to the imitation of Christ.[32]

---

[25] R. Murray, 'East of Byzantium' 7.

[26] George Nedungatt, 'The Covenanters of the Early Syriac- speaking Church', *Orientalia Christiana Periodica* 39 (1973) 206- 207.

[27] A. Vööbus, *History of Asceticism in the Syrian Orient*, Corpus Scriptorum Christianorum Orientalium 184 (Louvain: Secretariat du CSCO, 1958) 1.158–169.

[28] A. Henrichs and L. Koenen, 'Ein griechischer Mani-Codex', *Zeitschrift fur Papyrologie und Epigraphik* 5 (1970) 141–149. Cf. R. Cameron and A. Dewey, eds, *The Cologne Mani Codex* Texts and Translations SBL 15 (Missoula: Scholars, 1979).

[29] See G. Widengren, *Mani and Manichaeism* (New York: Holt, Rinehart and Winston, 1945).

[30] Still the best discussion is Hans Jonas, *The Gnostic Religion* (Boston: Beacon, 1958).

[31] A. Adam, 'Rezension von A. Vööbus: History of Asceticism in the Syrian Orient' *Gottingische Gelehrte Anzeigen* 213 (1960) 127- 145.

[32] See the excellent article by Sebastian Brock, 'Early Syrian Asceticism', *Numen* 20 (1973) 1–19.

Foxes have holes, and birds of the air have nests; but the
Son of Man has nowhere to lay his head. (Mt 8:20/Lk
9:58; G Thom 86)

Do you think that I have come to give peace on earth?
No, I tell you, but rather division; for henceforth in the
house there will be five divided, three against two and
two against three; they will be divided, father against
son and son against father, mother against daughter
and daughter against her mother, mother-in-law against
her daughter-in-law and daughter-in-law against her
mother-in-law. (Lk 12:51–53; G Thom 16)

If the Christian ascetic was alienated from this world, it was so
he/she could be at home in another, that is, with the angels. As
Aphrahat said, 'Whosoever adopts the likeness of angels, let him
be a stranger to humans'.[33] Sebastian Brock has pointed out how
the interpretation of Lk 20:35–36 was developed in the Syriac
tradition which translated these verses as

Those who have become worthy to receive that world
(i.e. the kingdom) and that resurrection from the dead,
do not marry, nor can they die, for they have been
made equal with the angels, [and being] the sons of
the resurrection [they are] like the sons of God.[34]

The ascetics have left human society for the company of angels.

The world of monastic communities in which Simeon moved
was deeply influenced by Syriac Christianity. As spearheads of the
monastic movement Theodoret names James of Nisibis and Julian Saba. From Julian's monastery at Gullab, north-east of Edessa,
came James the Persian and Agrippa to the monastery at Teleda
founded by Ammianus and then headed by Eusebius. Agrippa suc-
ceeded Eusebius, and so brought the influence of eastern Christianity to this monastery. The monastery that Simeon entered
was an offshoot from this monastery at Teleda (*HR* 26.4). Mar

---

[33] The Sixth Demonstration *Patrologia Syriaca* 1:248,25–26. I have used the
translation of the *Nicene and Post-Nicene Fathers of the Early Church* (Oxford:
Parker, 1898) 13:364.

[34] S. Brock, 'Early Syrian Asceticism' 5–6. On this topic of the angelic life,
see S. Frank, *Aggelikos Bios* (Münster: Aschendorff, 1964).

Bas, the early official supporter of Simeon, came from Edessa (Syriac 28).

As P. Canivet suggested, the rule followed at these various off-shoots was no doubt that followed in the monastery of Julian Saba.[35] There seem to have been prayers in common (*leitourgiai*) at fixed times. Apart from this one could go and pray in whatever way one wished (*HR* 4.5).[36] Theodoret tells us, for example, how Ammianus would read the Scriptures and Eusebius would then expound it to him (*HR* 4.6). The monks at Teleda certainly celebrated the Eucharist in common. No mention is made of work for the community; some founders—as Marian and Theodosius—insisted that the monks provide for themselves, others insisted that the monks should live from gifts given, as did Bas. The Syriac life states that Simeon and his brother Shemshi gave most of their inheritance to the monastery (Syriac 9–15), and the abbot certainly had some money to give Simeon when he was forced to leave (Syriac 26). But there were eighty mouths (or one hundred twenty, according to Syriac 25) and, even though the monks did not eat much, some gardening and tilling may have been required. Eusebius, co-founder of Teleda, *ordered* his companions to eat every day, even though he himself ate only every three or four days (*HR* 4.5). Antonius 6 says this was still the case in Simeon's time, while Theodoret (*HR* 26.4) states that the other monks ate every three days.

One must not imagine the monastery at Teleda like an imposing medieval monastery. It was a much simpler affair. Like the houses of the poor, the monastery would have been circled by a wall of stones, about a man's height. Festugière has nicely reconstructed the scene for us:

> Every Syrian monastery contained—besides the church, the common cemetery, a small enough house for the abbot or for guests—one of several buildings for common use: refectory, chapter-room where the

---

[35] P. Canivet, *Le monachisme syrien selon Théodoret de Cyr*, Theologie historique 42 (Paris: Beauchesne, 1977) 169. On the notion of a rule, see O. Hendriks, 'La vie quotidienne du moine syrien oriental', *L'Orient Syrien* 5 (1960) 293–330; 401–431.

[36] Canivet, *Le monachisme syrien*, 169–170.

superior instructed his monks and, as M. Tchalenko has
said, 'work-rooms': by this one primarily understands
the bakery, the kitchen and doubtless all the work-
places that a large community would require, a forge, a
shoemaker, a room for weaving, etc. Everything stops
one from thinking that these buildings served to house
the monks. They had to lodge in some *kellia*, sometimes grouped around the monastery. . . . They were
made of very poor materials, with the result that nothing of them remains.[37]

So one sees in the Syriac life mention of a forge (Syriac 22),
of a gate to the monastery (Syriac 9), and of a common refectory
(B 520) as well as common prayers. The monastery at Teleda which
Simeon entered, therefore, had certain rules (Syriac 25) under
which Simeon, albeit reluctantly, lived for around ten years and
which must have greatly influenced his own habits. One certainly
sees him following prescribed prayer hours such as prayers at 3 in
the afternoon, a time later to become that part of the monastic
Divine Office called none, (*HR* 26.26) and questioning people
about biblical heroes (Syriac 44).

Clearly, however, Simeon was not content to live under such
constraints. The whole thrust of Syrian monasticism was, after all,
towards the ideal of anachoretism rather than cenobitism.[38] After
leaving Teleda he entered a small monastery and lived alone in a
small domed hut. The previous occupants of the monastery, an
old man and a young boy, no doubt did not require such rules as
those observed at the large community at Teleda.[39] Rather than
a monastery, in fact, one might even call it simply the place of
ascetics for the village of Maris as often a village liked to have its
own holy man present. Simeon moved from this mode of life to
living on the summit in a small domed hut, then to life in the open
air and finally to life on a pillar. In all this Simeon was following

---

[37] Festugière, *Antioche* 327.
[38] Vööbus, *History of Asceticism* 1.150–157. Cf. Canivet, *Le monachisme syrien*
208.
[39] There is no need to see in this a wish of the Syriac composer to put a
monastery in the village when there was not one (Canivet, *Le monachisme syrien*
173).

the same anti-societal impulses that led the first founders of Syrian monasticism to live far from the haunts of men and to survive off the land like animals on what was given by God.[40]

The Pillar

Simeon chose a novel way of fleeing men. Theodoret speaks of it as an entirely new phenomenon. Yet it was so appealing that an impressive number of stylites followed.[41] Cult objects featuring the saint appeared in Rome and Gaul during Simeon's lifetime (*HR* 26.1).

What was there about this mode of life which triggered such a response? The very novelty of the spectacle has sent scholars scurrying for precedents, and one was found in a cult practice at the temple of Atargatis (or Derceto or Aphrodite) in Hierapolis, about ninety miles distance from Telneshe. The practice is described in Lucian of Samosata's *De Dea Syria* from the middle of the second century CE.

> The site itself, where the sanctuary is built, is a hill. It lies right in the center of the city and double walls surround it. One of the walls is ancient, the other is not much older than we are. The entryway of the temple faces the north and its height is about 600 feet. In the gateway stand the phalli which Dionysus set up; they are 1800 feet high. A man climbs up one of these phalli twice each year and lives on the tip of the phallus for a period of seven days. This reason is given for the ascent. The populace believes that he communes with the gods on high and asks for blessings on all Syria, and the gods hear the prayers from nearby. Others think that this, too, is done because of Deucalion, as a memorial of that disaster when men went to the mountains and the highest of the trees out of terror at the flood. Now, these explanations seem unbelievable to me. I think that they do this as well for Dionysus. I make the conjecture for these reasons: Whoever erects phalli to Dionysus sets

---

[40] Vööbus, *History of Asceticism* 1: 150–157.
[41] See the growing list in I. Peña et al, *Les Stylites Syriens*, 61–84.

on them wooden men—for what reason I will not say.
At any rate, it seems to me that the man climbs up in
imitation of this wooden man. Many come and deposit
gold and silver, others deposit bronze, which they use
as coin, into a large jar which sits in front and each
person says his name. Someone else stands by and calls
up the name. The climber receives it and makes a prayer
for each person. As he prays, he shakes a bronze device
which sounds loud and sharp when it is moved. He
never sleeps. If sleep ever does overtake him, a scorpion
climbs up, wakes him and treats him unpleasantly. This
is the penalty imposed on him for sleeping. They tell
holy and pious stories about the scorpion. Whether
they are accurate, I am unable to say. It seems to me
that one thing that contributes greatly to wakefulness
is the fear of falling. This is enough said about the
Phallus-Climbers.[42]

Such a parallel has rightly been seen as unlikely to have been the
conscious impulse towards Simeon's ascent. Behind both lies the
general sense of an ascent to heaven,[43] but one should also recall
that in the near vicinity of Telneshe the plain of Dana was domi-
nated by three pagan temples situated on top of three mountains.[44]
At the southern end of the plain of Qatura on which the village of
Telneshe stood rose the summit of Sheikh Barakat on top of which
was the temple of Zeus Madbachos, Zeus of the Altar, and Sela-
manes, and it would have been clearly visible from Simeon's pillar.
One might also note that only men could gather round the saint's
pillar. Women were clearly excluded, as in the account of the visit
of Simeon's mother in Antonius, and could communicate with
the saint only through male messengers. Evagrius also mentions
that women were excluded and that men would dance around

---

[42] *De Dea Syria*, 28–29. The translation is that of H.W. Attridge and R.
Oden, *The Syrian Goddess*, Texts and Translations, SBL 9 (Missoula: Scholars,
1976).

[43] Delehaye, *Les saints stylites*, lcxxvii.

[44] Georges Tchalenko, *Villages Antiques de la Syrie du Nord* (Paris: Geuthner,
1953) 1: 105–109.

the pillar.[45] Male dominance would be readily symbolized by the phallic-like pillar, a clear symbol of fertility. These resonances are also found in the iconography of Simeon.[46] One cannot deny that such symbolism was present in the area;[47] and David Frankfurter has strongly argued for the continuity between Simeon's pillar and traditional modes of religious expression.[48] One must, however, seek the specific impulse for Simeon's actions in his christian tradition.

Delehaye asserted that the impulse for Simeon was completely fortuitous, following Theodoret's reason that Simeon simply wanted to get away from the pestering crowd (*HR* 26.12).[49] For Delehaye, the pillar is incidental and Simeon belongs properly to the 'stationary' saints. Delehaye noted that, before mounting the pillar, Simeon had determined to remain standing. This was no novelty, but a form of asceticism known to Gregory Nazianzenus and to Palladius, who speaks of an Adolius of Tarsus who remained motionless on the Mount of Olives. John of Constantinople and St Domnica did likewise, and St Auxentius stood on a stone praising the Lord.[50] The Syrians in particular seem to have practiced *stasis*: Theodoret (*HR* 27.1) mentions seven others, and distinguishes two kinds—some are always standing, others sit part of the day. Delehaye thus places Simeon squarely within a tradition of stationary saints. That tradition itself still remains unexplained. Why was standing upright considered one of the marks of a holy man? Certainly, it is a remarkable feat of mortification, but does that satisfactorily explain why so many adopted it, persisting even when ulcers appeared or when a staff had to be used for support? What resonances did standing have in the culture? Finally, getting away from the crowd may be a reason for standing on a pillar of

---

[45] *Ecclesiastical History* 1.14.

[46] G.R.H. Wright, 'The Heritage of the Stylites', Australian *Journal of Biblical Archaeology* 1 (1970) 82–107.

[47] As H.J.W. Drijvers, 'Spätantike Parallelen zur altchristlichen Heiligenverehrung unter besonderer Berücksichtigung des syrischen Stylitenkultes' in *Aspekte frühchristlicher Heiligenverehrung*, Oikonomia: Quellen und Studien zur orthodoxen Theologie 6 (Erlangen: Universität Erlangen, 1977) 54–76.

[48] David T.M. Frankfurter, 'Stylites and *Phallobates*: Pillar Religions in Late Antique Syria', *Vigiliae Christianae* 44 (1990) 168–198.

[49] Delehaye, *Les saints stylites*, clxxxi; cf. Festugière, *Antioche*, 310, n.1.

[50] Delehaye, *Les saints stylites*, clxxxi–clxxxiii.

six cubits, but it does not explain why Simeon kept increasing the height till he reached 36/40 cubits.

A specifically Christian impulse may be at hand. The stylized iconography of the Stylites, with outstretched arms above a pillar, presents a cross-like image. And here surfaces the thrust towards the *imitatio Christi* so strong in Syrian asceticism.[51] This imitation of Christ is not solely focused on the suffering of Christ, although Simeon's sufferings are innumerable. The iconography is triumphant and standing with arms outstretched, cross-like, is the attitude of prayer in Syriac Christianity.[52] The attempt to stand constantly is the attempt to pray always (Mk 11:25; Lk 18:1[53]; Azariah at *LXX* Dn 3:25), to resemble those who stand before God, as Elijah had (1 Kgs 17:1; 18:15), as Joshua is described in Sir 46:3, and as the tribe of Levi had been set aside to stand before the Lord to minister to him and to bless his name (Dt 10:8; 18:5.7). More significantly, this metaphor of a servant or courtier standing in the presence of the king was extended to the angelic court.[54] Gabriel stands in the presence of God (Lk 1:19) as do the seven angels (Rev 8:2), the two olive trees and the two lampstands (Rev 11:4), and the hosts of angels (2 Es 8:21). In an apocalyptic text like 1 Enoch 39:12–13, Enoch describes the heavenly court:

> Those who do not sleep bless you, and they stand be-
> fore your glory and bless and praise and exalt, saying:
> *Holy, holy, holy, Lord of Spirits.* And there my eyes saw
> all those who do not sleep standing before him and

---

[51] See the fine analysis of the iconography of Simeon in Drijvers, 'Spätantike Parallelen', 69–73. On the notion of *imitatio Christi*, see H.J.W. Drijvers, 'Die Legende des heiligen Alexius und der Typus des Gottesmannes im syrischen Christentum' in *Typus, Symbol, Allegorie bei den östlichen Vätern und ihren Parallelen im Mittelalter*, Eichstatter Beitrage 4 (Regensburg: Pustet, 1981) 187–217.

[52] Canon 20 of the Council of Nicea states: 'Since there are some who kneel on Sunday and during the season of Pentecost, this holy synod decrees that, so that the same observances may be maintained in every diocese, one should offer one's prayers to the Lord standing.'

[53] Note how the injunction in Lk 18:1 is followed shortly in Luke's Gospel by the parable of the Pharisee and the Publican, both of whom pray standing (Lk 18:9–14).

[54] F.M. Cross, *Canaanite Myth and Hebrew Epic* (Cambridge: Harvard University Press, 1973) 37 and 37, n.1, has shown how the term of 'standing' refers to the divine council where the heavenly monarch is accompanied by his courtiers.

blessing and saying: *Blessed are you, and blessed is the name of the Lord for ever and ever!*

Here emerge again the themes we noted in early Syrian asceticism. The name of the Covenanters, *bnay Qyāmā*, contains the root 'to stand', and Robert Murray has linked this group with the imitation of the angels.[55] The stationary saints, among them Simeon, must be viewed as those who sought to incarnate the richness behind the phrase 'those standing before the Lord'. Here one must recall that, in the Syriac life, Simeon mounts a stone only because he sees a vision of an angel pointing out to him how he should pray (Syriac 112). This narrative stems from the symbolic world we have been sketching.

When Simeon is requested by the crowds not to shut up the door of his enclosure or at least to come down from his pillar a little because they fear he might die from a frightful wound on his foot, Simeon replies:

> Far be it from me all the days of my life that I should break the covenant/cease the standing (*'btl qym'*) that I have convenanted/stood (*'qymt*) to my God. I will do what I have to do, and let my Lord do what he will.

Here it is said that Simeon has made a special covenant with God, to stand on his pillar.

The other area of importance for understanding the significance of Simeon's asceticism comes from the recently discovered corpus of Gnostic literature found at Nag Hammadi. Within this corpus, Michael Williams has shown the importance of the term 'to stand'.[56] The Gnostics are called 'the immovable race' (*hē asaleutos genea*, just as it is said of Atolius of Tarsus that he remained *asaleutos*, 'motionless'). Williams has shown how, from Plato on, 'to stand' is commonly used for the stability of the transcendent realm which does not participate in the flow of becoming, and he has also linked this to descriptions of spiritual heroes, Socrates as well as the stationary saints, who physically stand when caught up

---

[55] Robert Murray, *Symbols of Church and Kingdom. A Study in Early Syriac Tradition* (Cambridge: CUP, 1975) 13–14.

[56] Michael Williams, *The Immovable Race: A Gnostic Designation and the Theme of Stability in Late Antiquity* (Leiden: Brill, 1985).

in contemplation. What is also interesting is that in several of the Nag Hammadi tractates, immovablility is achieved by means of a visionary ascent in which one 'stands' in the transcendent realm. In the tractate *Zostrianos*, Zostrianos leaves this world behind and travels to a light-cloud. He then ascends through stages of the Transmigration which really exists, the Repentance which truly exists, and the Self-begotten. At each stage he is baptized. In the Self-begotten he is baptized five times and each time the formula involves a 'standing'.[57]

This combination of ascent plus standing seems important. An ascent to the heaven by stages is, of course, a common shamanistic experience, as Mircea Eliade has well documented.[58] When speaking of the Mediterranean world of Late Antiquity, one has to remember the centuries-long tradition that one ascended to heaven by physical motion across the planetary spheres.

> Among the ancient Egyptians the firmament was conceived as being so close to the mountains of the earth that it was possible to climb up to it with the aid of a ladder. Although the stars had been relegated to an infinite distance in space, the ladder still survived in Roman paganism as an amulet and as a symbol. Many people continued to place in tombs a small bronze ladder which recalled the naive beliefs of distant ages; and in the mysteries of Mithra a ladder of seven steps, made of seven different metals, still symbolized the passage of the soul across the planetary system.[59]

Such astral conceptions lie behind the depiction of the righteous in late Jewish writings as like the stars of heaven.[60]

It is here, I feel, that we begin to enter the symbolic world in which Simeon's asceticism would appear as holy and numinous.

---

57 James M. Robinson, ed., *The Nag Hammadi Library* (San Francisco: Harper & Row, 1977) 370–371. See also the tractate 'The Three Steles of Seth', *Nag Hammadi Library*, 367, and 'Allogenes', *Nag Hammadi Library*, 449.

58 Mircea Eliade, *Shamanism and Archaic Techniques of Ecstasy* (Princeton: Princeton University Press, 1964) 181–214.

59 Franz Cumont, *Astrology and Religion Among the Greeks and Romans* (New York/London; Putnams, 1912) 184.

60 Dn 12:3; 1 Enoch 104:2.6; Assumption of Moses 10:9.

Not that Simeon was a gnostic or that he consciously said to himself, 'How can I symbolize divinity?' But on his successive pillars, Simeon has physically played out the 'flight of the soul towards heaven', as Theodoret remarks in so Platonic a phrase (*HR* 26.12), and the angelic life of constant worship. As Evagrius wrote:

> This man, endeavouring to realize in the flesh the existence of the heavenly hosts, lifts himself above the concerns of earth, and, overpowering the downward tendency of human nature, is intent upon things above: placed between earth and heaven, he holds communion with God, and unites with the angels in praising him; from earth, offering his intercessions on behalf of humans, and from heaven, drawing down upon them the divine favor. (*Ecclesiastical History* 1.13)

All of this is graphically illustrated in the petition which Simeon is said to have prayed frequently:

> Lord, powerful God, do not force me into the power of mortals and I should dismount from my place here and people see me on the ground. But grant me that on this stone, on which I stood at your command and order, I may complete the days of my life. From it receive the soul of your servant according to your Lordship's will. (Syriac 110)

Here one notes the sense that Simeon has escaped the power of men. As Simeon says to the bishops who wanted him to come down so that they could attend to his injured foot,

> Please pray for me and I have confidence in our Lord Jesus Christ that he will not loosen his hold on his servant so that it should come to pass that he would come down from his station. For he knows that I have handed over my life to him. I have no need of herbs and medicines nor the help of mortal men—sufficient for me is the healing that comes from him. For he has authority like a good master over the creation of his hands to rule and to possess. (Syriac 50)

On the pillar Simeon found his place; from it, like a monk in his monastery, he must not move. His body is not his, it is God's. God, who has taken him out of the reach of mortal men, will provide for him and lift him finally to heaven.

Sources

Three Lives of Simeon exist: one by Theodoret, bishop of Cyrrhus, who wrote it while the saint was still alive; one by 'Antonius', a work of unknown date and provenance; and a Syriac life dated to 473, a little before the massive construction of a martyrion in honor of Simeon which Tchalenko has suggested was begun in 476 and completed in 490 on the initiative of the Emperor Zeno under the influence of Daniel the Stylite.[61] The three Lives in fact overlap very little. That in itself is remarkable: the episodes in common are found in the narrative prior to the saint's entry to his enclosure at Telneshe. Antonius and the Syriac life also agree in the narrative of the saint's funeral procession. After briefly pointing out some features of the three lives, I will then comment on the synoptic episodes.

THEODORET

Theodoret was one of the main actors in the theological drama of the early fifth century. Born towards the end of the fourth century[62] to a wealthy family living in Antioch,[63] Theodoret was well educated. At the age of eighteen he entered the monastery of Gandaris.[64] He was elected bishop of Cyrrhus in 423.

Theodoret was an early supporter of Nestorius against the attacks of Cyril of Alexandria, and wrote a refutation of Cyril's theses against the Antioch-trained bishop. Much involved in the ensuing polemic, Theodoret was finally confined to his diocese by Theodosius II in 449 and later the same year deposed by the Robber Council at Ephesus. Reinstated two years later, he led a

---

[61] Tchalenko, *Villages antiques*, 226–233.

[62] The date of birth is not known exactly. Canivet (*Le monachisme syrien* 39) suggests 393.

[63] His mother tongue seems to have been Syriac: see Canivet, *Le monachisme syrien*, 38–39.

[64] Canivet, *Le monachisme syrien*, 59–60.

quiet life until his death c. 458. Besides the exegetical and doctrinal works that Theodoret wrote,[65] he wrote a *Church History* covering the period 323 to 428, to continue the history of Eusebius.[66]

Theodoret was especially qualified to write about Syrian monasticism. His mother was devoted to the monks who dwelt around Antioch; Theodoret's birth itself was seen as the result of the intercession of the monk Macedonius and Theodoret considered as consecrated to God's service from birth.[67] As bishop, he made it his duty to visit and become acquainted with the cenobites and the solitaries who inhabited his diocese.[68] He himself continued his monastic style of living even after his consecration as bishop.[69] The *Historia Religiosa* is the result of this personal experience and involvement in Syrian monasticism, and was written in 444.[70] Within this work is currently found the life of Simeon, although there are strong arguments that this chapter may have been intended to circulate separately. As Susan Harvey states:

> Theodoret himself treated it with marked difference to the others in his collection: he is here at his most hagiographical. His style is more inflated, his rhetoric more stylized, his use of hagiographical *topoi* more pronounced. The overall tone is that of panegyric.[71]

In her analysis of this chapter taken independently, Susan Harvey has shown how well Theodoret crafted his work to articulate Syrian spirituality in classical Greek forms.

---

[65] For a list of Theodoret's works, see J. Quasten, *Patrology* (Antwerp: Spectrum, 1960) 3:538–554.

[66] For a discussion of this work, see Glenn Chestnut, *The First Christian Histories*, Theologie historique 46 (Paris: Beauchesne, 1977) 200–206.

[67] HR 13.16.

[68] Canivet, *Le monachisme syrien*, 62–63.

[69] Canivet, *Le monachisme syrien*, 62.

[70] Canivet, *Le monachisme syrien*, 31–35. In current editions the work has thirty chapters, and the life of Simeon is the twenty-sixth. P. Devos ('La structure de l'Histoire Philothée de Theodoret de Cyr. Le Nombre de Chapitres', *Analecta Bollandiana* 97 [1979] 319–335) has argued convincingly that originally the work contained twenty-eight sections, of which the life of Simeon was the twenty-fourth.

[71] Susan Ashbrook Harvey, 'The Sense of a Stylite: Perspectives on Simeon the Elder', *Vigiliae Christianae* 42 (1988) 378.

> His most striking assumption is that body and soul are
> at odds with one another, in a battle of wills that forms
> the central focus for Simeon's career in this text. . . In
> Simeon we are presented with a life of true philosophy
> by means of physical discipline, in pursuit of the higher
> virtue of the soul.[72]

While Theodoret uses the language of Plato and Aristotle,[73] Harvey shows he has a theological agenda: to show how Simeon, by disciplining his body to fly heavenward (*HR* 26.25), has made it truly human, 'the place where God's grace is revealed'.[74]

Within the context of the complete *Historia Religiosa*, however, a different emphasis comes to the fore. Theodoret discusses first the monks who have died (chs. 1–20), then those still living. After lives of men (1–28) come lives of women (29–30). Canivet has well perceived that Theodoret had several purposes in mind in writing the *Historia Religiosa*. His explicit contrast of his heroes with those of Greek drama and epic as well as with philosophers aims at setting new models for Christians to imitate and admire. The monks Theodoret selected show great reverence for the clergy: Zenon is only with difficulty forced to bless Theodoret because Theodoret is a lector while Zenon only a lay person (12.4); Simeon the Stylite has Theodoret as bishop bless the crowd (26.14). Theodoret also has his Syrian monks help the clergy extinguish heresy: Julian Saba intervened to help the churches of Antioch and Cyrrhus in the conflicts at the time of Valens (2.15–22); James' prayer helped Theodoret in his mission to the marcionite villages (21.15–18); Simeon the Stylite is pictured as writing to the emperor and to other high dignitaries to defend the interests of the church (26.27).

Before Theodoret was elected bishop and after he had died, Simeon was standing on one of his pillars. When Theodoret wrote his life of Simeon, Simeon still had fifteen years to stand on his main column. In 434, at the behest of Simeon and two other monks, James and Baradatos, Theodoret met his patriarch John of

---

72 Harvey, 'The Sense of a Stylite', 379.
73 Canivet, *Le monachisme syrien*, 259–290.
74 Harvey, 'The Sense of a Stylite', 380.

Antioch and was reconciled to him after breaking off communion with him. Simeon was thus a major figure throughout Theodoret's whole career.

It may seem obvious to say so, but one has to recall when reading Theodoret's account of Simeon that it is one of the last biographical sketches in his *History*, as 'the last five chapters are not found in the same order in the manuscript tradition'[75] and P. Devos has clearly shown that chapters twenty-one through twenty-six make a remarkable literary unity.[76] These chapters in fact form the second section of Theodoret's work: chapters one through twenty are consecrated to monks who have died, the rest to monks who were alive when Theodoret wrote.

Set within this framework, Simeon's life is given resonances which it does not have when viewed separately. One should not be surprised that Simeon's miracles are duplicated elsewhere: sterility is also healed by Macedonius (13.16) and James (12.9); oil blessed by Polychronios expands (24.7); Macedonius has the power to see the future (13.15); sailors called on the God of Theodosius to help them in danger and to calm tempests (10.4). Miracles tend to follow a recurring pattern.

Even in his asceticism Simeon seems to be no innovator. Zebinas, Polychronios, and Damian stand all night (24.4–5). Marion (15.1), Eusebius (18.1), James (21.3), Limnaios (22.2), John (23.1), Moses, Antiochus, and Antonius (23.3) all live in the open air at the mercy of the elements. So do the woman saints Marana and Cyra (29.2). As for ingenuity in self-torture, nobody could outdo Baradates who built a wooden structure not quite big enough for his body and so was obliged always to be bent and cramped. As the box was not well-made he was still at the mercy of the rain and the heat of the sun (27.2). In the introduction to the life of Baradates, Theodoret states that there were many who had decided to have neither grotto nor cave nor tent nor shack but to endure unprotected both the freezing cold and the burning heat. 'Some of these, for example, stand continually, others divide the day between sitting and standing. Some, confined in a small enclosure, refuse contact with the crowd; others, without any such obstacle,

---

[75] Canivet, *Le monachisme syrien*, 84.
[76] Devos, 'La structure', 325–327.

can be seen by whoever so wishes' (27.1). Simeon was one of many similar holy persons for Theodoret—what was new is that he was standing *on a column* (26.12).

Theodoret justifies this new and paradoxical spectacle by recourse to the examples of Jeremiah, Hosea, and Ezechiel (*HR* 26.12), examples which are also found in the Syriac life. But one should note the different emphasis (see below). The Syriac life stresses that Simeon acted on God's command, and so the list of biblical exemplars is followed by a narrative recounting the visions of Simeon which led him to stand on the high pillar: the pillar is to awaken *the world* from the heavy torpor of its inhabitants. Theodoret believes/accepts (*hyolambano*) that this standing could not have occurred without divine dispensation (*HR* 26.12), though he first insists that Simeon only did it to get away from the pestering crowd. Theodoret's stress falls on God's use of the pillar as a ploy to entice people to come. After so explaining Simeon's pillar, Theodoret gives accounts of the conversion of Ishmaelites as well as miracles worked by Simeon among the Arabs. In fact, Theodoret only recounts miracles worked among the Arabs—a Saracen paralytic (*HR* 26.16), an Ishmaelite queen (*HR* 26.21). While professing that what Simeon performed daily surpassed narrating (*HR* 26.21), Theodoret by his selection and arrangement of miracles and conversions has made the standing on a pillar almost a gimmick to attract the child-like barbarians. The laudatory account of people streaming to him to be healed occurs before he began standing on a pillar (*HR* 26.11). Note, for example, that the pillar is described as a novelty to attract sight-seers, the sight-seers in question being the Ishmaelites. Then come two accounts of how such converts behave. 'They hurled themselves in a rather *barbarous* manner' to gain a blessing from Theodoret. Theodoret is only saved from being stripped like a rock star by Simeon's making them scatter with a cry. Theodoret's comment, Simeon 'has sent such a ray of divine knowledge into the minds of the barbarians' is condescending. This episode is followed by another where the tribes bicker and fighting breaks out *in the barbarian way*—it is only stopped by Simeon's intervention, when he calls them dogs. These are the kind of people that Simeon's pillar-standing converts, according to Theodoret. While Theodoret thus praises Simeon and his endurance, he does appear ambiguous on the subject of his

standing on the pillar. Theodoret seems unable to decide whether
to symbolize the pillar as the flight towards heaven (*HR* 26.12)
or to see it as accidental, caused by the importuning crowd (*HR*
26.12). It brought people flocking and converting, but was that
altogether a good thing? Theodoret seems unimpressed by the
converts.[77]

Theodoret knows that Simeon is renowned throughout the
world (*HR* 26.1) and that he has performed, and will in the future perform, many miracles. What Theodoret emphasizes is not
this quality but the inner character of man—his endurance (*HR*
26:22), humility, and sweet-temperedness (*HR* 26:25).[78] These are
the lessons Theodoret wishes to impress on his readers and, in so
doing, perhaps to reinforce the proper distinction to be made between bishops and monks. The monks are admirable examples of
piety, but they remain subordinate to the clergy—Simeon obeys
the advice of the ecclesiastical dignitary Meletius (*HR* 26:10), and
he also sends the Ishmaelites to Theodoret for his priestly blessing
(*HR* 26:14).

When reading Theodoret's life of Simeon in its current context,
therefore, one must keep in mind the voice of the narrator: it is
a bishop conscious of his position as shepherd of God's flock and
not yielding that position to any other.[79]

ANTONIUS

When we turn to the life of Simeon written by Antonius, we
encounter a different narrator's voice. Here speaks the intimate
disciple, revealing special insight into his master's life. Such inside
knowledge is what one often looks for in biography, and ancient
biographers did not hesitate to supply it by casting themselves in
such disciple roles. The Gospels all had to be written by intimates,

---

[77] Ramsay MacMullen, *Christianizing the Roman Empire (A.D. 100–400)*
(New Haven: Yale University Press, 1984) 1–3, uses the conversion of the Arabs
by Simeon as an illustration of how superficial such conversions were.

[78] In many ways Theodoret here seems to follow the rules for an encomium.
For a brief discussion of this biographical genre, see P.L. Schuler, *A Genre for the
Gospels* (Philadelphia: Fortress, 1982) 34–57.

[79] For an analogous treatment, see the discussion of Athanasius as author in
Michael A. Williams, '*The Life of Antony* and the Domestication of Charismatic
Wisdom' in *Charisma and Sacred Biography*, Michael A. Williams, ed., JAAR
Thematic Studies 48:3–4, pp. 23–45.

or at least from notes by intimates, just as Mark's Gospel is said to derive from Peter. The Life of Mani is said to be by his disciple. This claim of access to inside knowledge allows the biographer to develop intimate details of the saint's death, as occurs in section 28. Perhaps as alleged intimate the biographer also felt free to develop dialogue, as in Simeon's conversion (2–3), and his sojourn in the monastery (4–11), but ancient historians usually felt no modern compunction in supplying correct speeches to fit the occasion.

The First Section

The life by Antonius divides easily into three sections: Simeon's life before the column (1–12); miracles wrought by Simeon (13–21); his death and burial (28–33). In the first section, Antonius' chronology and order of events differs from those both in Theodoret and the Syriac versions, but these variations are only what one would expect in traditional tales. The basic thrust remains the same: Simeon on his conversion entered a monastery but because of his severe austerities, he was forced to leave. The biographer stresses explicitly Simeon's similarity to David as shepherd (as Theodoret had done), and to Job in his endurance; in his description of Simeon before the abbot and his brethren (7), the silence of Simeon recalls the silence of Jesus before the Sanhedrin (Mk 14:61; Mt 26:63). The abbot suffers from a dream about Simeon as the wife of Pilate did about Jesus. The description of Simeon's parents in Antonius is different from the Syriac where they die before Simeon leaves to enter the monastery: in Antonius they ceaselessly seek the saint with tears while unbeknownst to them he is in the monastery—a reminiscence of Mary and Joseph seeking Jesus in the temple (Lk 2:44–50)? This allusion to the parents prepares for the miracle of his mother in section 14. In the description of the changing relationship between Simeon and his parents one finds symbolized the passage from social structure to marginality. Simeon is lost to them, as if dead to them, and his mother, no matter how hard she tries, is not to see him and talk with him again in this life. The earthly familial relationship is dissolved, and Simeon has formed a new community around himself. It is only when physically dead herself that the mother can join it and she smiles at doing so. The time Simeon spends in the monastery, the time framed by the references to the parents, is a time of initiation, full of references to death and rebirth. When Simeon first enters the monastery he refuses to reveal who his parents are (4). Simeon's first action in the monastery is to wrap himself as in a shroud with a rope which putrefies his flesh and attracts worms (5–6). Simeon wishes to die from the wound and, in quoting Ps 50:7, explicitly rejects his human parentage.

Simeon is healed of this wound and is asked to leave the monastery. Again one should note the description of relationship. On his exit from the monastery, the abbot calls Simeon his son: the abbot assumes the teacher role vis-à-vis Simeon. When Simeon is brought back from his second attempt at dying, this time in a reptile-ridden well, the abbot begs Simeon to teach him (11). The roles have been reversed.

Within this first section of the life of Simeon, therefore, the biographer has chosen those incidents in Simeon's life that highlight his removal from the ordinary social realm and his transference to a position of eminence over even monastic authority. He is found among the wild beasts, where no one would dare to travel (11). In Telneshe he stands open to the elements and eats no cooked food (12). The first section thus intends to show his status as that of an intermediary and as such he performs healings.

The Second Section

His intermediary status is immediately underlined at the beginning of the second section, when Simeon insists on distinguishing himself from God: one must not say 'Simeon healed me', but 'God healed me'; one must not lie or take an oath by God, but one can take an oath by Simeon. Simeon stands between humankind and God. We see this new status highlighted by a story of Simeon's mother, and then a series of miracles that Simeon performed.

The biographer has chosen seven miracles to describe Simeon's activity. Taken separately, several of these narratives are traditional tales. Within this series, the first six group themselves into pairs: the affair of the pregnant hind is followed by the story of the apparently pregnant woman (15–16); the description of the worm-ridden thigh of the saint is followed by the encounter with the Saracen king wherein a worm from the saint's wound is changed into a pearl (17–18); the healing of the wounded dragon is fol-

lowed by the conversion of the robber-chief (19–20). In the first
pair, men attack a harmless animal and in punishment become like
animals; an animal invades a woman making her pregnant and like
vegetation as her face becomes green like grass. Both break-downs
of categories are righted by Simeon. In the final pair, a dragon, an
animal apparently inimicable to humankind, is cured by Simeon
and harms no one; and a famous robber-chief, a human dragon,
is converted by Simeon. In the middle pair, worms eating on the
putrefied flesh of the saint's thigh are put back in their place by
followers of the saint as he says to the worms, 'Eat what the Lord
has given to you'. Animals apparently antagonistic to man are seen
as having their rightful place in creation. From proximity to the
saint a worm becomes the instrument of healing a Saracen chief
and becomes a pearl, a desired object for humans (18). In each of
the pairs, then, there is an animal followed by a human encounter.
Simeon restores each to its rightful sphere by not allowing a mixing
of human and animal (15–16); he heals both people and animals
(19–20), and through him animals help heal people (18). Simeon
thus spans both the animal and the human worlds and this intermediary role is strikingly portrayed in the seventh and final miracle
of the second section. In this miracle, Simeon provides abundant
water for both people and animals who come to the enclosure. At
the saint's prayer, a cavern full of water is found and they construct
seven outlets for the water. The number seven here signifies fullness, wholeness, abundance, and no doubt that significance also
lies behind the choice of seven incidents for this second section.
Simeon brings wholeness to the creation, and one notes how, at
his death, not only do men, women, and children weep but the
screeching of birds also shakes the whole mountain. All creation
mourns.

The Third Section

The narrative of the saint's death and the transference of his
body to Antioch follows the same basic outline as in the Syriac
versions, although particular emphasis is laid on the presence of
his disciple Antonius at his last moments and on a vision given
to Antonius which prefigured the death of Simeon (on this, more
below). The biographer seems to give an important detail as to
where Simeon was first laid—in the church called Cassianus—

before being transferred to the main basilica after thirty days. This narrative, but not the Syriac life, reveals that attempts to take relics of the saint were unsuccessful. When the bishop of Antioch attempts to take a hair from his beard he is prohibited (29) and the biographer returns to this theme in the last paragraph of his work (33). Here one detects another emphasis on wholeness—Simeon cannot be divided, for he is the source of wholeness and unity.

The biographer has attempted to portray the holy man as cosmic intermediary who unites in himself the world of humans and animals and heals it.

THE SYRIAC LIFE

Sources

The Syriac life of Simeon is the longest of the three lives. Previously it was known in only two recensions, the primary representatives of which are Vatican MS 160 (V) and the British Library MS Add 14484.[80] The untiring research of the late Professor Arthur Vööbus uncovered three more manuscripts, one at Damascus, one at Mardin in Eastern Turkey, and one at Aleppo.[81] Professor Vööbus estimated that these three new manuscripts are very similar, and kindly allowed me to study his photograph of the Mardin manuscript. The Mardin manuscript is a recension of the Syriac Life of Simeon different from both V and B. Some comparison of these three recensions is in order, and I have provided in Appendix A a table whereby the incidents of the life can be found in the corresponding recensions as well as in the edition of the V text by Assemani.

An opening address, not present in V, is found in both B and M.

---

[80] Vööbus, *History of Asceticism*, 209.

[81] A. Vööbus, 'Discovery of New Manuscript Sources for the Biography of Simeon the Stylite', *After Chalcedon. Studies in Theology and Church History offered to Professor Albert van Roey*, eds. C. Laga *et al.*, Orientalia Louvaniensa Analecta 18 (Louvain: Peeters, 1985) 479–484.

B	M
To our brothers and *sons* and friends, children of the holy catholic Church, we make known to you in our writings the heroic exploits of the man *of God*, who loved *Christ*. He began laboring in the vineyard *of our Lord* from daybreak till dusk all the days of his life. He persuaded the obstinate, and he finished his struggle with glory. His Lord took him to himself to give him the *excellent* reward of his *labor* in the place of the consummation (*šwlmh*) of life eternal—the blessed Mar Simeon.	To our *fathers* and brothers and friends who are in Christ, children of the holy Church, we make known to you in our writings the heroic exploits of that *wonderful* man who loved *God completely*. He began laboring in the vineyard of *Christ* from daybreak till dusk all the days of his life. He persuaded the obstinate, and he finished his struggle with glory. His Lord led him to himself so as to give him the reward of his *labors* in that place where his life has a beginning but its end (*šwlmh*) is not attained. This then is the blessed Mar Simeon who was pastor to a flock from his youth and who entrusted himself into the hands of Christ and to whom there were followers in the entire world.

B and M have the same concluding paragraph except for a few minor changes, an ending not found in V. M also has the same, more chronological, sequence of miracles as B rather than the order of V. The sequence of events in sections 89 to 106 belongs chronologically to the early part of the saint's life as they involve people who live nearby and miracles performed through dust rather than a special mixture of dust, oil, and water called *ḥnana* which was used for healing. The visions reported in this sequence also belong to the early life of the saint and provide detail why he was led to stand on a stone. In general, then, M and B have the same order of events: 1–36; 89–106; 77–88; 38–76. There are, however, some significant differences in detail. At B 544,6,[82] at the beginning of section 106, after the quotation from the apostle, M narrates the visions of Satan and the healings which are found

---

[82] For an explanation of these numbers, please see footnote 1 of Appendix A.

at B 549,2–555,3—visions and healings not found in V. Then M follows these healings with the quotation, 'Blessed is that servant on whose account the name of his Lord is praised' which is found at B 545,13, at the beginning of 77. M thus does not contain a reference to letters sent by and to kings. Here V in sections 106.77 has the account as in B if in different order. M has the same order as V with section 79 following 78, whereas B places after 78 the visions of Satan and healings. Again, in the midst of section 114, M has intercalated sections 121–123, different from both V and B which at this point agree. In the series of disputes between Simeon and the monks which runs from sections 17 to 22, moreover, one finds some episodes in B and M which are not present in V, (see Appendix B.2), but M has a sequence of events closer to V than to B.

M

¶17 1. Test which ends in death of a monk by vomiting blood
¶18 2. Simeon's practice of fasting
     3. Simeon forced to sit at refectory table, but does not eat
     4. Simeon gets up at night and hangs a stone around his neck
     5. Accusations of the brethren and their plans to drive Simeon away
¶18 6. Simeon lives in the wood-pile
¶19 7. General accusations of brethren
¶20 8. Simeon stands on a round piece of wood
¶21 9. The hard rope incident
¶22 10. The poker incident

If one orders the series according to M, there are ten events. Of these, V has ¶¶ 1, 2, 6, 7, 8, 9, 10—all in the same order as M. B has all the events except ¶7, but the order in B is 1–4, 8, 5, 6, 10, 9. There is thus similarity and yet difference. One might say that M has followed the order of V and simply inserted events from B, but one should note a clear difference in word usage in the narration of these events.

B	M
Again, when the brethren finished the service of the night and lay down to rest, *he would hang a stone on his neck* all the time his companions were resting. When it was time for them to arise, he would untie the stone from his neck and would arise with them for service.	Then after *the service of the night* when *the brethren* were *resting*, he had a *stone and all the time his companions* were sunk in sleep he *would hang* it *on his neck* until they *were rising to the service* of dawn and secretly he would cast it from him and no one was aware.

One might also notice that in the description of Simeon in ¶1, V and M are identical in order and word-choice, while B has a different order of Simeon's good qualities (see the Syriac Life, footnote 7).

Again, notice how the first vision ends at ¶5.

V	B	M
'*Be strong and act bravely.*' *When* they had *said these things to him, they disappeared and ascended. This is the first vision that appeared to the blessed one as he shepherded the flock.*	'*Be strong and act bravely.*' *When* he had *said these things to him, he disappeared and ascended.*	'*Be strong.*' *He ascended. This is the first vision that appeared to blessed* Mar Simeon *as he was shepherding the flock.*

There is no simple explanation for the connections between these three versions of the Syriac life of Simeon. The almost identical wording used in narrating individual events helps one at times to reconstruct the faulty text of one version. So, for example, I have been able to reconstruct the opening lines of V from the text of M, and have recognized the loss of several lines in v through haplography at ¶77.

One might bring into the comparison the Georgian life of Simeon (G), which P. Peeters characterized as an ancient witness that one could not afford to neglect.[83] G has the same general order as B and M, and includes the miracles and visions found in these

---

[83] Peeters, *Le tréfonds oriental*, 115–116.

manuscripts and not in V. There are, however, some interesting correspondences between G and V and M.

1) G has ¶20 between the incidents of ¶18 and ¶21 as in M and V, but not B, whereas both B and G omit ¶19 while M and V do not.

2) G has the same order as M and V for ¶21 and ¶22, ·while B relates them in inverse order.

3) G, V and M include ¶55, while B does not.

4) V and B have ¶103 follow ¶102, whereas G and M have the reverse order.

5) Both G and M agree in following the quotation from Paul at B 544.5–6 with the description of the battles against Satan at B 549.11. G omits all that lies between, whereas M after the healings then narrates what is found in B 545.13 up to B 548.20. Omitted in both G and M are the references to letters from Kings; omitted in G, M and V are B 548.21–549.11.

6) B and V place ¶121–123 in the same position, whereas G places this narrative after ¶76 and M in the midst of ¶114.

7) B, V, and M all have ¶127 follow ¶126, whereas G has ¶127 before 126. In this, G has the same order as Antonius 31–32.

8) G differs in its placement of ¶81 from B, V, M.

9) ¶¶45–481; 65–66; 74; 109; 114; 120–121; 124 are omitted only in G.

G thus seems to lie closer to M than to B or V as regards its arrangement. This survey of G also confirms that the tradition could allow for re-arrangement of particular episodes. There is thus some kind of fixed way of telling the life of Simeon which nevertheless allows at times for variations in word choice and sentence order. One can never therefore reconstruct the *urtext* of the life. Variation in the order of narration can also occur, although the major difference between B and M on the one hand and V on the other is unusual. There is no doubt that B and M preserve the proper chronological order: ¶89 explicitly states that Simeon was standing on the ground at the time this event occurred; the miracles following in ¶¶90–92 are local miracles when the saint's name was just beginning to be known; the self-imposed imprisonment at ¶93 is a new decision of the saint; no one is lodging near the saint in ¶100; Mar Bas is still present in ¶101; Simeon learns how he is to pray in ¶98;

and he first sets up a stone to stand on in ¶102. Only after all this
does news of Simeon spread to the world (¶104). These narratives clearly belong to the early part of Simeon's life. I am equally
convinced, however, that the re-arrangement in V is by design.
To explain the arrangement in V as by chance or mistake would
require that four folios, depending on the hand and the size of the
manuscript, be misplaced. Such a possibility is rendered unlikely
by the presence in V of a sentence at the end of the narrative
block, ¶¶1–36, which is strikingly similar to the opening sentence
at the beginning of ¶107.

37   Deeds such as these and greater *than these our Lord per-*
       formed by the hands of the blessed one.

107   these glorious deeds and signs then and ten times more
       than these our Lord performed by the hand of the blessed one.

The use of such a connecting sentence, also used at ¶74 to link
events, suggests that the composer of V is deliberately re-arranging
his material.

The Choice of V

Since one cannot reconstruct an original text for the Syriac Life
of Simeon, I have chosen here to translate V. My reasons are as
follows:

1. There is no published edition of M.
2. The critical edition of B by Bedjan has been translated into
   English and German.
3. The only previous 'translation' of V is the rather free Latin
   version by Assemani in 1748. While Assemani's edition is
   in the main correct, there are some notable mistakes which
   I have corrected through studying the original manuscript.
4. V provides the colophon which dates this version to 17 April
   473. Soon after the death of the saint, a fairly fixed tradition
   of the miracles, visions, and life of the saint must have been
   available. Perhaps catenae of miracles, such as one sees in the
   collections of those who opposed the saint (¶¶55–57), those
   done in far-off places, on the sea and among the Gentiles
   (¶¶66–73) as well as visions and the apologia for the saint's
   mounting a pillar which is already present in Theodoret
   were available to be combined. This final composition had
   a pre-history of which we can catch glimpses.

5. V clearly departs—I think intentionally—from a strictly chronological account, and provides an interesting example of how free hagiographers felt themselves with their material.

6. M seems to be aware of the Antonius tradition. At ¶53, M specifies that the names of the two disciples who served Simeon were Marcellus and Antonius (fol. 21, col 2, lines 16–17). One of these is especially favored according to M: he who placed his hand upon his eyes when he died (fol 21, col 2.14). At ¶117 both disciples place their hands on Simeon's eyes in all three manuscripts, but in Antonius 38, Antonius takes hold of Simeon's dead hand and places it on his own eyes. M might thus seem to know and reflect the life of Antonius and to have incorporated it into his account. One might also mention how both B and M supply names for the three elders of Telneshe to whom Simeon announces that his brother will die (¶105). Such a specification is often an indication of later composition.

The Character of the Work

Vööbus characterized the Syriac life as 'a long panegyric, a *neshana*, victory, or praise'. It is this; the position of Simeon is magnified. Certainly, no one of the ancient, middle, or modern times had ever done anything like Simeon (Syriac 45; 108). His fame goes out through all the world (Syriac 77–78; 106; 111; 114) and he has correspondence with the emperor and other leaders (Syriac 49; 77; 106). But Simeon is also said to have surpassed the apostles Peter and Paul in the miracles he performed (Syriac 65), and the apostles are called his brothers (Syriac 42). He is likened to Job (Syriac 48) and to the prophets Elijah (Syriac 42–43; 75) and Samuel (Syriac 75). He is made equal to Moses (Syriac 41) and, in fact, to all the prophets (Syriac 111). Through Simeon 'the holy church was exalted by him and the horn of Christianity lifted up' (Syriac 114). In the visions which describe Simeon's career, Simeon builds the Church and is commissioned to be head, overseer and steward of God's flock (Syriac 3–4); he is compared to a tree which grows up strong and bears much fruit, from whose roots water spouts forth and birds come and eat of the fruits (Syriac 105). In this last comparison, images from Genesis (2:9), Ezechiel

(47:1–12), Revelations (22:1–2), and the Parable of the Mustard
Seed (Mt 13:31–32; cf. Dn 4:10–12) are combined. Simeon is
clearly portrayed as another founder of the Church.

What is even more remarkable is the way Simeon is compared
to Jesus. Frequently John 14:12 is quoted: 'Truly, truly I say to
you, he who believes in me will also do the works that I do; and
greater works than these will he do, because I go to the Father.'
Such an application to miracles performed after Jesus seems to be
a commonplace in the exegetical tradition.[84] What is surprising is
the inclusion of a comparison with Jesus in describing the monastic
customs and exercises (Syriac 108–110). A list is given of those
who fasted forty days: Moses, Elijah, Daniel, and then Jesus. After
this list comes the comment:

> If then, as we said before, our Lord performed these
> glorious acts and signs by the hands of these warriors,
> men of renown, by their fasts of forty days, what can
> we say about the blessed Mar Simeon? No one knows
> how to describe fully the practices of his ascetic life.

The section on Jesus is introduced in a different way from that in
which Elijah and Daniel make up the list, and the phrase 'these
warriors, men of renown' seems inappropriate to Jesus while per-
fectly apt for Moses, Elijah, and Daniel. I suspect that this section
on Jesus may have been added later where the emphasis on Jesus'
having a 'body of Adam, subject to hunger and thirst, to weariness
and sleep' would be part of an argument against the followers of
Eutyches who denied the consubstantiality of Jesus' flesh with human flesh.[85]

---

[84] See, for example, the commentaries on John's Gospel by Theodore of
Mopsuestia and Cyril of Alexandria, as well as the homilies on John's Gospel by
John Chrysostom.

[85] See R. Draguet, 'La Christologie d'Eutyches, d'après les Actes du Synode
de Flavien, 448', *Byzantion* 6 (1931) 441–457. One might compare the statements
of Nestorius (as found in Nestorius. *The Bazaar of Heraclides*, trans. G.R. Driver
and L. Hodgson [Oxford: Clarendon, 1925] 62–66], where the temptations of
Jesus are explicitly recounted as proof of Jesus' having a human nature, with those
of Timothy of Alexandria against the Eutychians, found in Zachariah of Mitylene,
The Syriac Chronicle 4.12. This section in the Syriac life does not necessarily
mean that it is Chalcedonian. One should note that the sanctuary of Simeon
was not monophysite until after 517 (P. Peeters, 'Hypatius et Vitalien', *Annuaire
de l'Institut de Philologie et d'Histoire Orientales et Slaves. Mélanges Henri Gregoire*

The Syriac life is also, however, an apologia for Simeon's novel asceticism of standing on a pillar. It has three reasons why Simeon stood on a pillar:

> 1. It seemed fitting and good to the Lord to send his servants to preach and teach in a way fitting and right for each age (Syriac 111).
> 2. A vision was given to Simeon wherein an angel showed him how to pray (Syriac 112).
> 3. Another vision showed Simeon how the final pillar should be constructed (Syriac 113).

I have argued elsewhere that the author of V placed by design at the end of the narrative the chronological account of Simeon's standing on a stone together with the apologia for standing on a pillar.[86] In this way he prepared the reader to accept this aspect of the saint's asceticism. The composer first established that Simeon was a man sent by God to his people, then he recounted how Simeon stood on a pillar.

This hint of debate surrounding Simeon leads us to the last facet of the Syriac life that I would like to discuss. In it one finds suggestions of parties and politics, of insiders and outsiders. Simeon only tells his vision to those who served him—'furthermore he did not tell everyone who served him but only those whom he loved and trusted' (Syriac 40; 46). Simeon has two special disciples who seem to have been with him almost from the beginning (Syriac 76). To these two Simeon entrusts his followers on his deathbed, commanding the two to love one another and setting the two over their companions (Syriac 117). Special mention is made of one disciple, however, the one who loved him (Syriac 53; 113; 116). This phrase seems to be taken from the Beloved Disciple of the Gospel of John, but it does refer to a disciple of Simeon who,

---

10 [1950] 27 and note 1). It is also interesting that Theodore of Mopsuestia, in his Commentary on the Gospel of Matthew regarding the temptation of Jesus (Mt 4:2), states that the devil thought Jesus to be like Elijah and not God and so boldly tempted him (PG 66:705), while Cyril of Alexandria on the same passage (PG 72:372) in his Commentary on Matthew speaks, not of Jesus' humanity, but of the motivation behind the devil's petition.

[86] R. Doran, 'Compositional Comments on the Syriac Lives of Simeon Stylites', *Analecta Bollandiana* 102 (1984) 35–48.

in the vision of the ladder towards heaven (Syriac 41), is to take Simeon's place.

Besides these hierarchies within Simeon's followers, one also sees relationships to others being set up, particularly to Simeon's first monastery at Teleda. The vision of the death of Shemshi, Simeon's brother (Syriac Life, ¶105), shows that there is to be no companion/rival to Simeon: 'It does not need a companion. It alone is sufficient both for insiders and outsiders.' Shemshi was a member of the monastery at Teleda. When Simeon is forced to leave Teleda, the abbot apologises for dismissing Simeon and prophecies that Simeon will be a protector and supporter of Teleda. In fact, this abbot is said on his deathbed to entrust the monastery to Simeon (Syriac 25)—a testament which does not seem at all known to Theodoret (*HR* 26.5), whose account of why Simeon left the monastery was furnished by the then head of Teleda who gives a different slant from that of the Syriac life.

If one sees reflected in these episodes the relationships among those various monasteries in which Simeon lived at the time the biography was being written, then the struggles within monastic groups at that time seems clear. The disciple whom Simeon loved would stand for the group at Qal'at Simeon, the second disciple for that monastery at Telneshe, Shemshi and the abbot for Teleda. The monastery at Qal'at Simeon claims priority over Telneshe and also hegemony over Teleda. The accounts in the Syriac life of the monks at Teleda harassing Simeon place this monastery in the worst possible light.

Synoptic Comparison

With this we come to the question of how these three lives of Simeon inter-relate. This opens a host of problems, and one, at least, requires further investigation. We have already noticed how the lives give basically the same outline of Simeon's life: his early life as a shepherd; his conversion; his early asceticism; his entrance at Teleda; his removal to Telneshe; and finally, on his death, the re-moval of the saint's body under escort to Antioch. Apart from this general frame, however, there are almost no narratives in common among the three. In stark contrast to the Synoptic Gospels, these lives evidence extremely independent development, and make one ponder what this says about the control over the tradition the Synoptic Gospels show. Lietzmann, Delehaye, Peeters, and Festugière have all pointed to the traditions at Telneshe as the base for the three lives.[87] This may be true for the general lines of Simeon's life, but the actual narration of the life was clearly under little or no control.

There are, in fact, only four narrative episodes in common: Simeon's first conversion; the cord which Simeon wound round his waist while still at Teleda, an episode found in all three lives; the apology for stylitism found in Theodoret and the Syriac; and the funeral procession to Antioch, found in Antonius and the Syriac life.

THE FUNERAL PROCESSION

During Simeon's funeral procession, a man possessed by an evil spirit who lived in a cemetery rushes towards the coffin and is healed (Ant 31; Syriac 127).

Antonius	*Syriac*
When they were about five miles from the city in a place called Merope, the mules stood still and would not budge. There, an extraordinary mystery happened, for on the right of the road stood a tomb and a certain man stayed in it.	During his funeral procession also his Lord manifested a great exploit through him so that all who saw it were astonished, and he made known the gift of healing given to him by God as his labors deserved. For a man in whom dwelt an evil spirit had
Now this is what the man had done: he had loved a married woman twenty years before, but could not possess her, and the woman died and was laid in that tomb. Then, so that the hater of good might gain the soul of	lived among the tombs for many years. The cemetery was close by the road near a town named Maru.

---

[87] Lietzmann, *Das Leben,* 215; Delehaye, *Les saints stylites,* viii; Peeters, *Le tréfonds,* 95; Festugière, *Antioche,* 351–357.

that man, he went to the tomb, opened up the tombstone, and had intercourse with the dead body. He immediately became deaf and dumb, and was held fast to the tomb and could not leave that place. Travellers-by would notice him sitting on the steps of the tomb and each, for God's sake, would offer something to him, some water,some food.

When, by the will of God, the venerable corpse came by on that day and the carriage and the crowd stood still, the man who neither spoke nor heard came out of the tomb crying out and saying, 'Have pity on me, holy one of God, Simeon.'

When he reached the carriage, what had restrained him was immediately taken away and his mind was restored.

All who saw what happened glorified God, and that place shook from the shouts of the people. The man cried out, 'Today I have been saved by you, servant of God, for I had perished in sin.'

Everyone who travelled to and fro along that road saw him. His ability to speak intelligently was taken away, and his understanding removed. He roared all the time and paced back and forth at the entrance of the cemetery. He did not recognize anyone, and no one dared approach him from fear and because of the sound of his roaring.

When he saw the saint's body passing by on the chariot—as if heaven's mercies shone on him, as if it were for this that he had been reserved—he left the cemetery where he dwelt and ran at full speed and threw himself on the coffin in which the saint's body lay.

The moment he reached the coffin, the demon fled and the evil spirit which had consumed him left him. His reason returned and he understood and recognized everyone. The bond of his tongue was loosened and he opened his mouth and gave thanks and praise to God.

Wonder seized everyone and this scripture was fulfilled, 'He has shown his people the power of his works.' He followed the saint and entered the city with him. He spent many days in the church rejoicing and giving thanks and praise to God.

This healing of a deaf and dumb man follows the basic pattern of a miracle and one can note immediately expansions and divergences between the two accounts. Antonius tells why the man was possessed; the Syriac shows scripture being fulfilled. People approach the man and give him food and drink in Antonius; in the Syriac life no one dares approach him. Such a healing also belongs to the general narrative pattern which describes the arrival of relics in a town. As Peter Brown has noted, the translation of relics was the time for emphasizing the concord and unity of the Christian community; no one should be held away from the ceremony.[88] In both the Syriac life and Antonius one notes an emphasis on the numbers of people coming to greet the corpse and rejoice. Brown points out that it was precisely at the festival of the saint whose relics are present that miracles of healing and exorcism occur. It is to this general pattern that Simeon's funeral procession should be related, rather than to dependence of one story on another.

The Apologia

The second common pericope is the list used as an apologia for Simeon's standing on a pillar. The list is found in Theodoret (*HR* 26.12) and the Syriac life (111).

The elements in common are listed here:

Theodoret	*Syriac*
A. God ordered Isaiah to walk naked and without shoes.	A. He had Isaiah walk before him naked and pass by barefoot.
B. Jeremiah to put a girdle round his loins and in this way pronounce his prophecy to the unbelieving, and at another time to place a wooden collar round his neck and later on an iron one,	B. He commanded Jeremiah to put on his neck the yoke and its collar.
C. Hosea to marry a prostitute and again to love an adulterous woman of evil life.	C. He said to Ezekiel, 'Shave your chin and your head with a razor, and put baggage on your shoulder. Breach the wall and go out as though one departing.'

---

[88] Brown, *The Cult of the Saints*, 90–100.

D. Ezekiel to lie down on his right side for forty days, and one hundred fifty on his left, to dig through a wall and flee, portraying in himself the captivity, and another time to sharpen a sword to a point, shave his head with it and divide the hair four ways and assign a part here, a part there, without listing it all.

D. To Hosea a holy prophet he commanded, 'Take a harlot as your wife'.

Such lists of scriptural examples are common, particularly in early rabbinic literature.[89]

One can see from this list how Theodoret has brought into play his knowledge of scripture: he provides an extra example of weird behavior from both Jeremiah and Hosea, and, whereas the Syriac list has mixed the events of Ezechiel 5:1 and 12:3–4 into one command, Theodoret has properly separated them. One suspects that Theodoret is drawing on a simpler enumeration and rectifying it.[90] Yet one should also note that the Syriac composer has altered the function of the list. Whereas for Theodoret the list of examples chosen neatly proves that God ordered these strange sights to stir men's interests, the Syriac composer has expanded the list to include Adam, the sons of Seth, Noah, Abraham, Moses, and Elijah. The function of the list is now not to provide a proof for unusual behavior, for the Syriac composer does not want Simeon's behavior to be classed as weird, but by the repetition of Abraham, Moses, and Elijah, to place Simeon within God's normal pattern of action: 'Thus to each and everyone of his servants at the right time he commanded him how to

---

[89] A. Wünsche ('Die Zahlensprüche im Talmud und Midrasch', *ZDMG* 65 [1911] 57–100; 395–421; 66 [1912] 414–459) provides a catalogue of such pericopes.

[90] See W. Sibley Towner ('Form-Criticism of Rabbinic Literature', *JJS* 24 [1973] 101–118; *idem.*, *The rabbinic 'enumeration of scriptural examples'. A study of a rabbinic pattern of discourse with special reference to Mekhilta d' R.Ishmael* [Leiden: Brill, 1973]) for an analysis of such rectification at work in traditional literature.

behave . . . Whoever obeys and keeps and does his will is kept and magnified and becomes famous.' In the Syriac life, then, Simeon is placed, not simply among the spectacular prophets, but in the line of all God's heroes. By this one can see how both Theodoret and the Syriac composer have embellished this list, a list which Lietzmann properly connects with the traditions at Telneshe.[91]

The Conversion

The narrative of Simeon's conversion also has elements in common. (See table on pages 60–62.)

All versions give different reasons for Simeon's going to Church; Antonius and the Syriac composer have Simeon hearing Paul, Theodoret the words of the Gospel. Antonius and the Syriac composer emphasize Simeon's ignorance. Theodoret and Antonius have made this into a dramatic scene with dialogue and a significant conversion ending. The Syriac composer seems more impressed with Simeon's unusual habit of offering storax[92] to God—which would fit his emphasis on Simeon's being chosen by God to live apart from men. The very fact that it is one of the few narratives in common among the three lives, and that Theodoret heard it from Simeon's own lips, attests to its importance.

---

[91] Lietzmann *Das Leben* 215–218.
[92] Storax is a fragrant gum resin. See the Syriac Life, n.4.

Antonius 2

On the Lord's day, he would enter the church at the time the oracles of God [are read] and joyfully listen to the holy scriptures although he did not know what it was he heard. When he had come of age, impelled by the word of God he came one day into the holy church. On hearing the [words of the] apostle read aloud, he asked an old man, 'Tell me, father, what is being read?' The old man said to him, 'It is about control of the soul.' Holy Simeon said to him, 'What is control of the soul?' The old man replied, 'Son, why do you ask me? I see that you are young in years, but possess the understanding of an old man.' Holy Simeon said to him, 'I am not testing you, father, but what was read sounds strange to me.' The old man said

Theodoret 26:2–3

Once when there was much snow and it was necessary for the sheep to remain inside, Simeon took advantage of the rest and went to the divine temple with his parents. I heard the story from his own sacred mouth:

he said he heard the Gospel message which blesses those who weep and mourn but names wretched those who laugh; which calls enviable those who keep their soul pure; and all the other sayings linked with these. Then he asked one of the bystanders what one should do to gain each of these. He suggested the solitary life and sketched for him that consummate philosophy.

Syriac 2

As he and his brother were the heirs, he was of necessity forced to return to the house of his parents. When he noticed the villagers were going to the church on Sunday, he went along with them.

When he heard the epistle being read, he asked those beside him, 'Whose writings are these, and what is in them?' They answered him, 'These are the writings of God who dwells in heaven, and the words of God are in them.'

to him, 'Self-control is the soul's salvation, for it shows the way to enlightenment and leads to the kingdom of heaven.' Holy Simeon said to him, 'Teach me about these things that you mention, honored father, for I am uneducated.' The old man said to him, 'Son, if one fasts unceasingly to God, he will rightfully grant all one's prayers—that is, one prayer at the third hour, likewise at the sixth, ninth, twelfth and so on, just as it is done in the monasteries. So, my son, if you know what you have heard, reflect on these things in your heart: for you must hunger & thirst, you must be assaulted and buffeted and reproached, you must groan and weep and be oppressed and suffer ups and downs of fortune; you must renounce bodily health and desires, be humiliated and suffer much from men, for so you will be comforted by angels. Now that you have all these things, may the Lord of glory grant you good resolve according to his will.' When he heard this, holy Simeon went out of the church and came to a deserted area. He put himself face down and, taking neither food nor drink, wept for seven days as he prayed to God.

When he had received the seeds of the divine word and carefully hidden them in the deep furrows of his soul, he said that he ran to the nearby chapel of the holy martyrs. There he planted his knees and forehead against the ground and besought him who wished to save all human beings to guide him to the perfect path of piety.

He was greatly astounded and amazed in his mind and on the next Sunday he again went and entered the church and listened attentively and diligently with all reverence to the holy scriptures.

The Cord:

The final narrative episode in common between the three lives is from the time when Simeon is still in the monastery at Teleda.

Syriac 21	Theodoret HR 26.5
Once he took a rope harder than wood and fastened it upon his body.	I heard the present leader of the flock recount how once [Simeon] took a rope made out of palm leaves—it was exceedingly rough even to the touch—and tied it round his waist. He did not put it on the outside but planted it on his skin and bound it so tightly as to wound the whole part which it encircled. When he
After a long time, as his body grew it thrust through the bands of that rope. After a further long time the abbot came to know of it, but Simeon would not consent to unfasten it except under duress.	had spent more than ten days in this way and the wound had become more painful and was dripping blood, someone on seeing him asked the cause of the blood. When [Simeon] said nothing was wrong, his fellow combatant forcibly stuck in his hand, discovered the cause, and informed the superior. Immediately rebuking and exhorting and denouncing the cruelty of the act, he with difficulty untied that bond, but he could not persuade [Simeon] to apply any medicine to the wound. When they saw him doing other things of this kind, they ordered him to leave that training-ground out of fear that he would cause harm to those of weaker physical condition but who might attempt to strive for what was beyond their powers

The episode as narrated in Antonius is lengthy, and I will not reproduce it here, but direct the reader to Antonius 5–7.

The Syriac life is the shortest and this is only one of many
episodes told to show how the monks at Teleda were jealous of
Simeon and would not let him follow his zeal for God. As a
narrative it leaves many problems unanswered: how long did he
have the rope on? where did he get the rope? how did the abbot
come to know?

Theodoret has given a much more circumstantial narration,
which he heard from the contemporary abbot of Teleda. Here
too it is presented as one of many incidents which caused friction
between Simeon and the leaders of the monastery. Theodoret
gives a time-span, more than ten days, and tells exactly how the
abbot came to know of the rope. Simeon's wound in Theodoret,
while painful, does not seem to be of the same order as the wound
in the Syriac life where the body grows around and through the
rope so that the rope, when finally taken off, is covered with flesh
and blood.

Antonius has a much fuller version of the story and presents it
as the single incident which causes Simeon to be sent from the
monastery. Antonius tells where Simeon got the rope (from the
monastery well) and gives a time-frame (more than a year). He
explains how the abbot came to know of it—not, as in Theodoret,
by seeing dripping blood, but through smell. Simeon's flesh has so
putrefied under the rope that worms dropped off it. Antonius has
skillfully woven together the report of Simeon's fasting and this
incident so that complaints about the fast lead to a complaint about
the smell. Antonius enjoys dialogue and a fascinating conversation
between the abbot and Simeon displays, of course, Simeon's wisdom. Antonius—unlike Theodoret—has Simeon helped a little by
doctors, a factor which only heightens the reader's sense of the
enormity of the wound.

In comparing these three narratives, one has the sense that the
Syriac is an abbreviated version, but not of Theodoret, because
of the difference in the description of the wound. Theodoret's
account seems to reflect the story from the viewpoint of Teleda—
the wound was not so grievous as might be expected and the lack
of medicine was due to Simeon's obstinacy.[93] The incident did

---

[93] For the role of medicine in monasteries, see Canivet, *Le monachisme syrien*
127–142.

not last a long time but it, along with other incidents, showed the leaders of the monastery that Simeon was unsuitable for cenobitic life. It was not the jealousy of the other monks that drove Simeon out, but Simeon's own unsuitability. This last point is in marked contrast to the thrust of the Syriac life, and possibly is Teleda's answer to Telneshe's hostility.

At this point, one should note the extreme primitiveness of Antonius' account. Simeon's whole body is covered by the rope; his bed is full of worms and his flesh putrid. Simeon longs to die in this way. One recalls how initiates into shamanism undergo symbolic death,[94] and this, combined with the anthropological bent we have noted above in our analysis of the life by Antonius, would suggest that Antonius has deliberately chosen to highlight this incident as a rite of passage from the cenobitic to the solitary life at Telneshe.

The narratives in common between the lives come down, then, to these four: the funeral procession; the apologetic scriptural enumeration in favor of stylitism; the conversion of Simeon; and a narrative of his 'conversion' from the cenobitic to this special calling. From this convergence we must assume that these last two had a profound influence on Simeon and led him to his tireless, all-consuming search for God.

Conclusion

Simeon had many followers in his mode of living, but perhaps one of the best testimonies to him is the tone these lives take about him. Simeon lived in the height of the controversy over nestorianism and monophysitism, but he himself resolutely stood for the interests of the Church councils. He tried to persuade Theodoret to accept the compromise solution of John of Antioch and Cyril of Alexandria,[95] which Theodoret eventually did. So it is fitting that the very different authors of these lives do not attempt to enlist him in party polemics, as later writers

---

[94] Eliade, *Shamanism* 33–66.
[95] See M. Richard, 'Théodoret, Jean d'Antioche et les moines d'Orient', *Mélanges de Science Religieuse* 3 (1946) 147–156.

did,[96] but show forth Simeon as friend of God and protector of the oppressed.

Texts Used

The editions I have chosen to translate are the following:

Antonius: H. Lietzmann, *Das Leben des heiligen Symeon Stylites*, Texte und Untersuchung zur Geschichte der altchristlichen Literatur 32.4. Leipzig: Hinrichs, 1908. 20–78. I have folowed the text-critical suggestions of A.J. Festugière *Antioche Païenne et Chrétienne. Libanius, Chrysostome et les moines de Syrie*. Paris: E. de Boccard, 1959. 370–388.

Theodoret: P. Canivet and A. Leroy-Molinghen, *Théodoret de Cyr, Histoire des Moines de Syrie*, 2 vols. Sources Chrétiennes 234, 257. Paris: Editions du Cerf, 1977–79.

Syriac: I have used a microfilm of the Vatican manuscript itself, as well as viewing it directly. I have also consulted the edition of S.E. Assemani *Acta sanctorum martyrum et occidentalium* II. 268–398. Rome: Collini, 1748. This edition was re-printed in 1970 by Gregg International Publishers Ltd.

---

[96] See C.C. Torrey, 'The Letters of Simeon the Stylite', *Journal of the American Oriental Society* 20 (1899) 260–273.

The Life
of
Saint Simeon
Stylites
By
Theodoret
Bishop of Cyrrhus

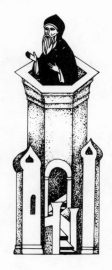

N OT ONLY ALL THE SUBJECTS of the Roman government know the famous Simeon, the great marvel of the world, but even the Persians, the Medes and the Ethiopians. His fame has reached the Scythian nomads and taught his love of labor and his love of wisdom.[1] Now although I have the whole world, so to speak, as witnesses to his indescribable struggles, I feared his story might seem to those who come after like a tale wholly devoid of truth. For what took place surpasses human nature, and people are accustomed to measure what is said by the yardstick of what is natural. If something were to be said which lies outside the limits of what is natural, the narrative is considered a lie by those uninitiated in divine things. However, since the earth and sea are full of devout people who, educated in divine things and taught the gift of the all-holy Spirit, will not disbelieve what I am about to write but will surely believe, I shall write my story eagerly and confidently. I shall begin at the time he was honored with his heavenly calling.

---

[1] *Philosophia* often means the monastic life. Since Theodoret here parallels the word to *philoponia*, however, I have chosen to translate it in its root meaning. For a discussion of *philosophia* in Theodoret, see Canivet, *Le monachisme syrien*, 273–275.

2. There is a village called Sisa in the border country between our country and that of Cilicia.[2] There he was born, and
was first taught by his parents to shepherd animals, so that in
this respect he might be likened to those great men: Jacob the
patriarch, Joseph the chaste[3], Moses the law-giver, David the
king and prophet, Micah the prophet, and the inspired men like
them. Once when there was much snow and it was necessary
for the sheep to remain inside, Simeon took advantage of the
rest and went to the divine temple with his parents. I heard the
story from his own sacred mouth: he said he heard the Gospel
message which blesses those who weep and mourn but names
wretched those who laugh, which calls enviable those who keep
their soul pure; and all the other sayings linked with these.[4] Then
he asked one of the bystanders what one should do to gain each
of these. He suggested the solitary[5] life and sketched for him that
consummate philosophy.

3. When he had received the seeds of the divine word and
carefully hidden them in the deep furrows of his soul, he said
that he ran to the nearby chapel of the holy martyrs. There he
pressed his knees and forehead against the ground and besought
him who wishes to save all men to guide him to the perfect path
of piety. After he had spent a long time this way, a sweet sleep
came upon him and he had the following dream: 'I seemed to be
digging foundations', he said, 'and then I heard someone standing there tell me that I had to deepen the ditch. I deepened it as
he ordered and then attempted to rest awhile, but he again commanded me to dig and not to stop work. After commanding me
to do this a third and a fourth time, he finally said that it was deep
enough, and ordered me to build from now on without trouble
as if the toil was over and the building would be no trouble.'

---

2 Sisa lay in the territory of Cyrrhus, in the region of Nicopolis.

3 For this meaning of *sōphrōn*, see *HR* 9.12, 15.6. The reference is to Joseph's
refusal of Potiphar's wife's advances (Gen 39:7–12). Philo (*On Joseph* 40) also
speaks of Joseph's *sōphrosynē*.

4 A mixture of Lk 6:21.25 and Mt 5:4.8.

5 *Monadikos* Cf. Theodoret, *Comm in Ps 24:12*: *polloi kai diaphoroi tēs eusebeias
hoi bioi monadikos kai koinōnikoi, erēmikoi kai politikoi*: The styles of the pious life
are many and varied—the solitary and that in community, life in the desert or
in the town.

The events can testify to this prediction, for what took place was beyond nature.[6]

4. Rising up he went to lodge with some nearby ascetics.[7] He lived with them for two years but then, as he eagerly desired a more perfect virtue, he went to the village of Teleda which we mentioned above, where the great and divine men Ammianus and Eusebius established their training-ground for ascetics. However, the inspired Simeon did not go there, but to the other one which was its offshoot: Eusebonas and Abibion, after they had taken advantage of the teaching of the great Eusebius, had built this other school of philosophy. Throughout their life they were alike in mind and manner, exhibiting, as it were, one soul in two bodies, and they made many also love this way of life. When they had died in good repute, the excellent Heliodorus assumed the leadership of the community. He was sixty-five years old and had spent sixty-two years within [the community], for he was nurtured by his parents for three years and had then entered the flock without ever having seen anything that happens in the world. He said that he did not know the shape of pigs or cocks or any such. I myself saw him frequently, and I marvelled at the simplicity of his character and admired exceedingly the purity of his soul.

5. This consummate athlete of piety came to him and spent ten years contending. Although he had eighty fellow combatants, he outdid them all. While the others took food after two days, he remained without food the whole week. The superiors could not stand it: they quarreled continually with him and called his actions a breach of discipline, but they could not persuade him by what they said nor could they curb his zeal. I heard the present leader of the flock[8] recount how once [Simeon] took a rope made out of palm-leaves—it was extremely rough even to the touch— and tied it around his waist. He did not put it on the outside but planted it on his skin and bound it so tightly as to wound

---

[6] Artemidorus of Ephesus states that dreams of building a memorial are good omens (*Oneirocritica* 2.61).

[7] Not necessarily in a monastery. See Canivet, *Le monachisme syrien*, 50–59.

[8] I agree with Canivet and Price in translating this sentence. Festugière thought that there was also a reference to Simeon and so would translate 'I heard from his own lips and from the present leader of the flock'.

the whole part which it encircled. When he had spent more than ten days in this way and the wound had become more painful and was dripping blood, someone on seeing him asked the cause of the blood. When [Simeon] said nothing was wrong, his fellow combatant forcibly stuck in his hand, discovered the cause, and informed the superior. Immediately rebuking and exhorting and denouncing the cruelty of the act, he, with difficulty, untied that bond, but he could not persuade [Simeon] to apply any medicine to the wound. When they saw him doing other things of this kind, they ordered him to leave that training-ground out of fear that he would cause harm to those of weaker physical condition who might attempt to strive for what was beyond their powers.

6. So he left and came to the more uninhabited parts of the mountain. There he found a cistern, waterless and not too deep, and he lowered himself down into it and sang hymns to God. After five days had gone by, the superiors of the training-ground repented and sent out two men with orders to search for him and bring him back. So going around the mountain they asked some men grazing animals if they had seen anyone of [Simeon's] complexion and appearance. When the shepherds pointed out the cistern, they at once shouted down it many times, but finally brought a rope and drew him up with a great deal of trouble, for the way up is not as easy as the way down.

7. After spending a short time with them, he went to Telanissos, a village lying at the foot of the summit on which he now stands. He found there a small hut and spent three years confined in it. Always eager to grow richer in virtue, he wanted to endure forty days without eating like the divine men Moses and Elijah. He tried to persuade the excellent Bassus, who at that time used to make visitations of many villages as he was in charge of the priests in each village,[9] not to leave anything inside and to seal the door with clay. When [Bassus] pointed out the difficulty of the

---

[9] Bassus was a *periodeutēs*, a priest entrusted with the supervision of churches in a rural area. On the office, see H. Leclercq, 'Périodeute', *DACL* 14/1: 369–379, and the observations of Canivet, *Théodoret de Cyr*, 2:173 n.2. For the difficulty in defining the precise relationship between a *periodeutēs* and a *chōrepiscopos*, see R. Amadou, 'Chôrêveques et périodeutes', *L'Orient Syrien* 4 (1959) 233–240.

undertaking and counselled him not to make suicide out to be a virtue—for it is the greatest and foremost of crimes—he said, 'Well then, father, leave me ten loaves of bread and a pitcher of water. If I see that my body needs nourishment, I will partake of them.' It was done as he proposed: the food was left behind, and the door sealed with clay. At the end of the forty days, that excellent man of God Bassus came and removed the clay. When he was inside the door, he found both the total number of loaves as well as the pitcher full of water, but [Simeon] himself prostrate, breathless, unable to speak or move. Asking for a sponge, he soaked and rinsed his mouth with it and then offered to him the symbols of the divine mysteries. Revived by these he raised himself up and took a moderate amount of nourishment—wild lettuce, chicory, and the like—which he chewed into small pieces and so passed them into his stomach.

8. Overcome with astonishment, the great Bassus went back to his own flock and told them this great marvel. Now he had more than two hundred disciples, whom he did not permit to have either beast or mill-stone,[10] or to accept any money offered to them. They could not go outside the gate either to buy what was necessary or to see some acquaintance, but they had to remain inside and receive the food sent by divine grace. The disciples keep this rule up to the present and, even though their numbers have increased, have not transgressed the precepts given to them.

9. But I will return to the great Simeon. From then till the present, a time-span of twenty-eight years, he remains without food during Lent. Time and practice have reduced much of the pain. For his custom was to stand during the first days and sing hymns to God; then, when his body did not have the strength to keep on standing because of the lack of food, he would sit and discharge the divine liturgy. During the last days he would even lie stretched out, for, as little by little his strength waned and declined, he was forced to lie half-dead. But when he stood on the column, he refused to come down and thought of another way to stand: he fastened a beam to the column and attached himself

---

[10] Festugière (*Antioche* 393, n.4) suggested *moulēn* = mule rather than *mulēn* = mill-stone. But did not Bassus reject any help except what came from God, namely, no flocks for food and no millstones for wheat?

to the beam with ropes and spent Lent this way. Later, as he had fuller benefit of grace from on high, he did not even need this support, but he stands throughout Lent without taking food but strengthened by his zeal and by divine grace.

10. As I said, he spent three years in that hut and then occupied that famous summit where he ordered a circular wall to be made and had a chain twenty cubits long made out of iron. He fastened one end of it to a huge rock and attached the other to his right foot, so that even if he wanted to he could not leave the confines. He remained inside, keeping heaven always before his eye and forcing himself to contemplate what lies beyond the heavens, for the iron fetter could not hinder the flight of the mind. But when the excellent Meletius, a sound man of brilliant intellect and endowed with astuteness and who was charged to make a visitation of the region of the city of Antioch,[11] told him that the iron was superfluous since right reason sufficed to place rational fetters on the body, he yielded and accepted the counsel obediently, and bade a smith be called and ordered him to take off the fetter. Now when a piece of hide which had been applied to the leg so that the iron would not maim the body also had to be ripped apart as it had been sewn together, it is said that one could see more than twenty large bugs hiding in it. The excellent Meletius also said that he saw it. I have mentioned it here to point out the great endurance of the man. For he could have easily squeezed the piece of hide with his hand and killed all of them, but he put up patiently with all their annoying bites and willingly used small struggles as training for greater ones.

11. As his reputation spread everywhere, all hurried to him— not just those in the neighborhood, but also those who lived many days' journey distant. Some brought those with weakened bodies, others sought health for the sick, others were entreating that they might become fathers, and what they could not receive from nature they begged to receive from him. When they received it and their prayers had been heard, they joyfully returned and, by proclaiming the benefits they had obtained, they sent back many more

---

11 Meletius was a *chōrepiscopos*. Canivet (*Théodoret de Cyr* 2:181, n.4) states that since this event occurred after 416, the bishop of Antioch would be Alexander. On the role of the *chōrepiscopos*, see Amadou, 'Chórêveques et périodeutes'.

with the same demands. As they all come from every quarter, each road is like a river: one can see collected in that spot a human sea into which rivers from all sides debouche. For it is not only inhabitants of our part of the world who pour in, but also Ishmaelites, Persians and the Armenians subject to them, the Iberians, the Homerites, and those who live even further in the interior than these.[12] Many came from the extreme west: Spaniards, Britons, and the Gauls who dwell between them.[13] It is superfluous to speak of Italy, for they say that he became so well-known in the great city of Rome that small portraits of him were set up on a column[14] at the entrances of every shop to bring through that some protection and security to them.

12. As the visitors came in increasing numbers and they all tried to touch him and gain some blessing from those skin garments,[15] he thought at first that this excess of honor was out of place, but then he found it annoying and tedious and therefore devised the standing on a column. First he had one hewn of six cubits, then one of twelve, after that one of twenty-two, and now one of thirty-six,[16] for he longs to soar to heaven and leave this earthy sojourn. I myself cannot accept that his standing occurred without divine dispensation. So I appeal to fault-finders to bridle their tongues and not allow them to wag at will, but to consider how frequently the Master has contrived such things for the good of the

---

[12] The territory of the Iberians lay between the Black Sea and the Caspian Sea; that of the Homerites was in the south-west of Arabia.

[13] Several sixth century texts mention Simeon: *History of the Franks* 8.15, 10.24, and *The Glory of the Confessors* 26, both by Gregory of Tours. In the *Life of Genovefa* 27, traders are said to have brought a letter from Saint Geneviève to Simeon.

[14] Reading with Canivet *anastēlōsai* rather than *anastēsai*. For a discussion of such images, see J. Nasrallah, 'Couvents de la Syrie du Nord portant le nom de Siméon', *Syria* 49 (1972) 127–159.

[15] Elsewhere, Theodoret speaks of the healing powers of the cincture of Peter the Galatian (*HR* 9.15) which someone stole from Theodoret's own mother. According to the Syriac Life 114, Simeon wanted to be buried in this garment; in the life of Daniel the Stylite, Daniel received it as a gift from the dying Simeon. This latter narrative smacks of the literary motif of the famous man's successor exemplified in the story of Elijah and Elisha at 2 Kgs 2:12–15.

[16] On the various heights given for the column in the various lives, see the Introduction, p. 17. A cubit is the length of a forearm, about eighteen inches.

indifferent. He ordered Isaiah to walk naked and without shoes;[17] Jeremiah to put a girdle round his loins and in this way pronounce his prophecy to the unbelieving, and at another time to place a wooden collar round his neck and later on an iron one;[18] Hosea to marry a prostitute and again to love an adulterous woman of evil life;[19] Ezechiel to lie down on his right side for forty days and one hundred and fifty on his left, to dig through a wall and flee, portraying in himself the captivity, and another time to sharpen a sword to a point, shave his head with it, and divide the hair four ways and assign a part here, a part there, without listing it all.[20] The Ruler of the universe ordered each of these things to be done so that by the strangeness of the spectacle he might gather those who would not be persuaded by speech nor give an ear to prophecy and so dispose them to hear the divine oracles. For who would not be amazed to see a man of God walking about naked? Who would not have wanted to learn the reason for the phenomenon? Who would not have asked why the prophet dared to cohabit with a prostitute? So, just as the God of the universe providentially ordered each one of those done for the good of those living carelessly, so he arranged this extraordinary novelty to draw everyone by its strangeness to the spectacle and make the proferred counsel persuasive to those who come. For the novelty of the spectacle is a reliable guarantee of the instruction, and whoever comes to the spectacle departs instructed in divine affairs. Just as those whose lot it is to rule people change the patterns on the coins after a certain period of time, sometimes imprinting the forms of lions, sometimes of stars and of divine messengers, at other times trying to make the gold appear more valuable by an unusual coin-type, so too the sovereign of the universe puts like coin-types these new and manifold modes of life onto piety and moves to praise the tongues not only of those brought up in the faith but also of those laboring under disbelief.

13. Words do not testify that these things have this character, but the facts themselves shout it out. For it was the standing on the column which enlightened the many myriads of Ishmaelites

---

[17] Is 20:2.
[18] Jer 13:1, 27:2, 28:13.
[19] Hos 1:2, 3:1.
[20] Ez 4:4–6, 12:4–5, 5:1–4.

enslaved in the deep darkness of impiety.[21] Because this brilliant lamp, as if placed on a lamp-stand, sent off rays in every direction, like the sun. One could see, as I said, Iberians, Armenians, and Persians coming to gain the benefit of divine baptism. The Ishmaelites, who came in bands of two or three hundred at a time, sometimes even of a thousand, with a shout repudiate their ancestral error; they smash in front of that great luminary the idols revered by them and renounce the orgies of Aphrodite—for originally they had adopted the worship of this demon. They partake of the divine mysteries, accepting laws from his sacred mouth and saying farewell to their ancestral customs, as they refuse to eat wild asses and camels.[22]

14. I myself was an eye-witness of these events and I have heard them renouncing their ancestral impiety and consenting to the gospel teaching. Once I underwent a great danger: he had ordered them to approach and receive from me the priestly blessing, telling them that they would reap the greatest profit from it. They all ran up together in a rather uncivilised way, some pulled at me from in front, some from behind, some from the sides; those in back climbed on the others and stretched out their hands; some pulled at my beard, others grabbed at my garments. I would have suffocated from their ardent approach if he had not cried out and dispersed them all. Such benefit has welled up from the column at which

---

[21] Canivet believes the rest of this paragraph to be an insertion because it breaks the continuity of the account.

[22] For a discussion of the conversion of the Arab tribesmen of the Syrian desert, see J.Trimingham, *Christianity among the Arabs in Pre-Islamic Times* (New York: Longman, 1979). Ramsay MacMullen has suggested that 'Aphrodite' here refers to the Arab goddess Allat (*Christianizing the Roman Empire* [New Haven: Yale University Press, 1984] 2–3), rather than the Syrian goddess Atargatis. R.M. Price suggests that renouncing camel meat 'shows that Syrian Christians respected the prohibition in Deut 14:7' (Price 174, n.20). Asses, of course, were also non-kosher. However, this scene is similar to the one in the Syriac Life 77, where the Arabs are described as those 'who did not know what bread is but ate of animal flesh'. Rather than a reference to a particular Deuteronomic prohibition, one should perhaps see that for the author embracing Christianity meant a move from savagery to culture. Cf. Ammianus Marcellinus *Res gestae* (14.4.1) (LCL). One should also note the narrative in section 18, interpolated into the text, where an Ishmaelite makes a vow not to eat any animal food, a frequent form of asceticism. The renunciation of the flesh of camels and wild asses may be a first step towards such asceticism.

mockers love to scoff, such a ray of divine knowledge has it sent down into the minds of the barbarians.

15. I know another such instance by them. One tribe begged the divine man to utter a prayer and blessing for their leader; but another tribe which was present opposed this, saying that a blessing ought be offered not on his behalf but in favor of their own leader, since the former was utterly unrighteous while the latter hated unrighteousness. An intense debate and dispute, typical of barbarians, ensued and finally they rushed at one another. I spoke at great length, exhorting them to remain calm since the divine man could certainly bestow a blessing on both. But these said that that man ought not obtain it, while those tried to withhold it from the other. By hurling threats at them from above and calling them dogs, he, with difficulty, quenched their quarrel. I have told this as I wished to point out the faith which inspired them, for they would not have acted like fools against one another if they had not believed that the blessing of the inspired man had immense power.

16. On another occasion I saw a noteworthy miracle. Someone came in—he too was a tribal leader of the Arabs[23]—and begged the divine person to help a man who on the road had become paralysed in the limbs of his body. He said the man had suffered the disease at Callinicum, an important citadel. When he had been placed in the center, [Simeon] ordered him to repudiate his ancestral impiety. When he obeyed willingly and fulfilled the order, he asked him if he believed in the Father and the only-begotten Son, and the Holy Spirit. When he confessed that he believed, the saint said, 'Since you believe in these names, rise up'. When he stood up, he commanded him to carry the tribal leader on his shoulders to his tent. Now the leader was a large man, but he picked him up immediately and was off, while the bystanders broke out into hymns praising God.

17. Simeon commanded this in imitation of the Master who ordered the paralytic to carry his bed.[24] But no one should say

---

[23] Literally 'of the Saracens,' but Saracen in English has the connotation of a follower of Muhammad. The Saracens in Greco-Roman times were one of the tribes of nomadic peoples in the Syro-Arabian desert.

[24] Mt 9:6.

this imitation was an usurpation of power, for this is the word of the Master himself, 'He who believes in me will also do the works that I do, and greater than these will he do'.[25] We have seen the fulfillment of this promise, for while the shadow of the Lord did not work any miracle at all, the shadow of the famous Peter put an end to death, drove out diseases, and put demons to flight.[26] But it was still the Master who effected these miracles through his servants, and now likewise the divine Simeon works these myriad miracles by invoking his name.

[18.[27] Another miracle occurred, in no way inferior to the preceding. Among those who believed in the saving name of Christ the Master was a distinguished Ishmaelite who had made a vow and promise to God with Simeon as witness: he promised to abstain till death from all animal food. Sometime, I do not know how, he broke this promise: killing a bird, he dared to eat it. But since God wanted to lead him to repentance through a trial and to honor his servant who had been a witness of the now broken promise, the bird's flesh was changed into stone so that then he could not eat it even if he wanted to. For how could he eat the body which he had seized for food if it had been turned into stone? Astonished at this extraordinary sight, the barbarian came with great haste to the holy man and made public his hidden sin. He told everyone his transgression, asking God forgiveness of his fault and calling on the saint for help to set him free by his all-powerful prayer from the bonds of sin. There were many eye-witnesses of this miracle who touched the part of the bird near the breast which was a combination of bone and stone.]

19. I have not only seen his miracles with my own eyes, but I have also heard predictions of future events. For example, he foretold two years in advance the drought which took place and the very poor crop of that year with the ensuing famine and pestilence. He said that he saw a rod laid upon people, which indicated beforehand the blows that would be inflicted by it. Another time he announced beforehand the attack of what is

---

[25] Jn 14:12.

[26] Acts 5:15.

[27] The story in this paragraph is missing in numerous manuscripts and, as Canivet suggests, is to be regarded as an interpolation.

called the grasshopper,[28] and that it would not cause great damage as God's love of human-kind would follow hard on the punishment. After thirty days had passed, an enormous swarm of them flew overhead so as to cut off the rays of the sun and form a shadow—we all saw this clearly. But it damaged only the animal fodder, and brought no ruin to human food resources. When I myself was under attack from someone, he intimated to me fifteen days in advance the destruction of my enemy, and I learned by experience the truth of his prediction. [Once two rods appeared to him coming from heaven and falling to earth in both the east and the west. The divine man interpreted this as the revolt of the Persians and the Scythians against Roman rule. He declared the vision to those present and, by his abundant tears and ceaseless entreaties, he stopped the blows which menaced the empire. Certainly the Persian nation, already armed and ready to attack the Romans, was checked in its projected assault by an opposing counter-move and became wholly occupied in internal squabbles.][29]

20. Although I know very many other such phenomena, I will pass over them so as to avoid too long a discourse. Certainly these are enough to indicate the spiritual insight of his intelligence. His renown is great even with the King of the Persians, for, as the ambassadors coming to him related, he would carefully inquire both what kind of life the man led and what kind of miracles he did. It is said that his wife even sought some oil made precious by his blessing and that she received it as a great gift. All the king's court, on the one hand struck by his repute and on the other hearing the calumnies of the Persian priests against him, made a thorough investigation and, properly informed, declared him a divine man. The rest of the crowd, approaching the mule-drivers,

---

[28] For a discussion of this animal, see A. Leroy Molinghen 'A propos du texte de l'"Histoire Philothéé' de Théodoret de Cyr', *Zetesis. Album Amicorum*, Festschrift E. de Strycker (Antwerp/Utrecht: De Nederlandsche Bockhandel, 1973) 734.

[29] This bracketed prediction is found in some manuscripts but Canivet rightly considers it an interpolation. The two rods referred to are the Persians and the Huns. The Persians invaded in 440–441, but were forced to withdraw when they in turn were invaded from the rear by a force from Central Asia; the Huns overran the Balkans in 441.

the domestic servants, and the soldiers, used to offer them money and beg to share in the blessing attached to the oil.

21. The queen of the Ishmaelites was sterile but longed to have children. First she sent some of her highest dignitaries to implore that she become a mother, and when her request was granted and she bore a child as she desired, she took the king she had borne and hastened to the divine elder. Since women are not allowed entrance, she sent the baby to him and implored him to give him his blessing. 'For this sheaf', she said, 'is your doing; for, with tears, I brought the seed, which is prayer, but you made the seed into a sheaf since by your prayer you attracted the shower of divine grace.'[30] But how long shall I strive to measure the depth of the Atlantic ocean? For just as humans cannot measure that, so what he accomplishes day after day cannot be narrated.

22. Above all these prodigies, I myself admire his patient endurance. For night and day he stands in open view. He had the doors taken away and a good part of the enclosing wall destroyed, and so presents to everyone a new and extraordinary spectacle: sometimes he stands for a long time, sometimes he bends over many times and offers worship to God. Many of the bystanders try to count these prostrations. Once one of my attendants counted one thousand, two hundred and forty-four, but then was distracted and lost count. When he bends down he always brings his forehead near his toes, for since his stomach only takes in food once a week, and a small amount at that, this allows his back to bend easily.

23. It is said that, as a result of the standing, his left foot has developed a malignant ulcer[31] from which a great deal of pus continually oozes. None of these calamities, however, have refuted his philosophy, but he nobly bears them, whether voluntary or involuntary, and overcomes both in his zeal. As for his ulcer, he was once obliged to show it to someone; I will tell the reason why.

---

[30] One might compare this with the account of Theodoret's own birth in *HR* 13.16. The same metaphor also occurs in *HR* 14.2. Canivet discusses it at *Le monachisme syrien*, 134.

[31] Literally, 'an ulcer of Cheiron', perhaps named after the incurable and malignant sore that Cheiron received from his wrestle with the Centaurs. See Canivet, *Le monachisme syrien*, 136 n.87.

Someone came from Rabaena,[32] a virtuous man honored with being a deacon of Christ. On reaching the summit he said, 'Tell me, in the name of that truth which has converted the human race to itself, are you human or an incorporeal nature?' The bystanders were annoyed at the question, but he asked them all to be silent and said to him, 'Why in the world did you pose that question?' He replied, 'I hear everyone talking about how you neither eat nor sleep, both of which are characteristic of humans, for no one who has a human nature can live without food or sleep.' At this, [Simeon] ordered a ladder to be placed against the column: he commanded that man to climb up and first examine his hands and then put his hand inside his garment of skins and see not only his feet but also that extremely painful ulcer. The man saw and marvelled at that worst of ulcers, learnt from him that he took food, and then came down and told me all.

24. During the public festivals he exemplifies another kind of patient endurance. For, from the setting of the sun until it rises again on the eastern horizon, he stands all night with his hands stretched out to heaven and is neither cozened by sleep nor conquered by fatigue.

25. Engaged in such labors, with an abundance of virtuous actions and a multitude of miracles, he is so unpretentious in spirit as if he were the last in dignity of all people. Besides his unpretentiousness, he is very approachable, pleasant, and charming and he speaks to each person who addresses him, whether it be someone who works with his hands, or a beggar, or a peasant. From the Master, the great giver of gifts he has also received the gift of teaching. Twice a day he delivers an exhortation, pouring into his listeners' ears an abundant and very charming discourse. He offers them the lessons of the divine Spirit and prompts them to look up to heaven and take wing, to leave the earth, to imagine the longed-for kingdom, to fear the threat of hell, to despise earthly goods, and to wait for those to come.

26. He can be seen sitting in judgement and handing down proper and just sentences. These and similar activities are dealt with after three in the afternoon, for he spends the whole night and

---

[32] A fortified village in the north-west of the province of Euphrates, near modern Marash.

the day up till three PM in prayer. After three PM he first delivers the divine teaching to those present and then, after receiving the request of each and effecting some healings, he resolves the quarrels of the disputants. Around sunset he then begins his conversation with God.

27. Although involved in these activities and doing all these things, he does not overlook the care of the holy churches, now combating pagan impiety, now putting down the audacity of the Jews, at other times scattering the factions of heretics. Sometimes he writes to the Emperor about these things, sometimes he rouses the governors to zeal for God, at other times he encourages the very pastors of the churches to take greater care of their flocks.

28. I have gone through these things and tried from this drop of water to indicate the rain and to give the readers of this work a taste from my fore-finger of the sweetness of honey. The exploits that everyone celebrates are much more numerous than these, but I did not promise to write them all down—I only wanted to indicate through a few examples the type of life-style of each saint. Others will probably write much more than this and, if he lives on, no doubt they will add greater miracles.[33] For my part, I desire and beseech God that, aided by his own prayers, he will persevere in these excellent labors for he beautifies the world and enhances piety, and that my own life may be brought into harmony and directed in line with the gospel way of life.

[He lived for a long time performing many miracles and labors; alone of those who had ever lived he remained unconquered by sun's heat and winter's chill, by violent gusts of the winds and by the weakness of human nature. When at last it was determined that he be with Christ and receive the crown of his countless contests, he demonstrated by his death, to those who did not believe it, that he was human. Even after death he remained upright: his soul had gained heaven, but even so his body could not bear to fall and it remained upright in the place of his contests, like an unbeaten athlete who does not want any of his limbs to touch the ground. So victory remains in attendance on the combatants on Christ's side even when they die. Certainly even today there are performed

---

[33] Compare this with the ending at *HR* 21.35.

healings of all kinds of diseases, miracles and the power of divine activities, just as when he was alive, and this not only where his remains lie buried, but also at the monument to his valor and his continual combat—I mean, the great and famous column of the righteous and praiseworthy Simeon. Through his holy intercession we pray that we ourselves may be saved and be strengthened in the orthodox faith, and that every city and region on which the name of our Lord Jesus Christ is invoked may be protected from experiencing any kind of harm or damage either from heaven or from their enemies. To him be glory for ever and ever.][34]

---

[34] This last paragraph is a later interpolation, found only in one family of manuscripts.

The Life
&
Daily Mode of Living
of the Blessed
Simeon the Stylite

By Antonius

A STRANGE AND INCREDIBLY MYSTERIOUS event took place in our time. I, Antonius, a sinner and least of all, thought to write it down insofar as I understand it, for the treatise is full of usefulness and contrition. So I beseech you: incline your ear and hear exactly what I understand.

2. When Simeon, among the saints and most blessed, was young in years, he cared for his father's sheep, just as the prophet David had done. On the Lord's day, he would enter the church at the time the oracles of God [are read] and joyfully listen to the holy scriptures, although he did not know what it was he heard. When he had come of age, impelled by the word of God he came one day into the holy church. On hearing the [words of the] apostle read aloud, he asked an old man, 'Tell me, father, what is being read?' The old man said to him, 'It is about control of the soul.'[1] Holy Simeon said to him, 'What is control of the soul?' The old man said to him, 'Son, why do you ask me? I see that you are young in years, but possess the understanding of an old man.' Holy Simeon said to him, 'I am not testing you, father, but what was read sounds strange to me.' The old man said to him, 'Self-control is the soul's salvation, for it shows the way to

---

[1] The term is *egkrateia*, but as used here it has nothing to do with the ascetic teaching that all bodily pleasures are evil and must be renounced.

enlightenment and leads to the kingdom of heaven.' Holy Simeon
said to him, 'Teach me about these things that you mention, honored father, for I am uneducated.'

3. The old man said to him, 'Son, if one fasts unceasingly to
God, he will rightfully grant all one's prayers—that is, one prayer
at the third hour, likewise at the sixth, ninth, twelfth, and so on,
just as it is done in the monasteries. So, my son, if you know
what you have heard, reflect on these things in your heart, for
you must hunger and thirst, you must be assaulted and buffeted
and reproached, you must groan and weep and be oppressed and
suffer ups and downs of fortune[2]; you must renounce bodily health
and desires, be humiliated and suffer much from men, for so you
will be comforted by angels. Now that you have heard all these
things, may the Lord of glory grant you good resolve according
to his will.'

4. When he heard this, holy Simeon went out of the church
and came to a deserted area. He lay face down and, taking neither
food nor drink, wept for seven days as he prayed to God. After the
seven days, he got up and ran full-speed to a monastery. Falling
at the feet of the abbot, he cried out and said, 'Have mercy on
me, father, for I am a lowly and wretched man. Save a soul which
is perishing and which yet desires to serve God.' The abbot said,
'Who are you, and what is your background? What is your name
and from where did you come?' Blessed Simeon said, 'I am a free
man named Simeon, but do not ask me, master, I pray, how I
came here or who my parents are! Redeem a soul which perishes.'
When he heard this, the abbot lifted him up from the ground and
said, 'If you come from God, the Lord will protect you from
every evil and deceitful deed; you will serve all, so that all may
love you.'

5. Meanwhile, his parents, with tears, ceaselessly sought him.
The saint, however, stayed in the monastery, serving all and loved
by all and observing the rule of the monastery. One day he went
out from the monastery and came across a bucket in front of the
well from which the water was drawn. It had a rope attached,

---

2 I have read *anōmalēsai* instead of *anomalēsai*, which does not make
sense here.

and he untied the rope, went to a secluded place and wrapped
the rope around his whole body. Over the rope he put a tunic
made of hair. Then he re-entered the monastery and said to the
brethren, 'I went out to draw water and did not find the rope in
the bucket.' The brethren said to him, 'Be quiet, lest someone
tell this to the abbot.' No one perceived that underneath he was
bound with the rope. So he remained a year or more with the
rope wrapped around his flesh, and it ate into his flesh so that
the rope was covered by the rotted flesh of the righteous man.
Because of his stench no one could stand near him, but no one
knew his secret. His bed was covered with worms, but no one
knew what had taken place.

6. He would accept his food, but give it to the poor without
anyone knowing. One day, however, one of the monks went out
and found him giving the poor the bread and pulse he had received. Now everyone would fast till sun-down, but holy Simeon
only ate on Sunday. One of the monks went in and reported
Simeon to the abbot, saying, 'I beseech your holiness: this man
wants to undo the monastery and certainly the rule which you
handed down to us.' The abbot said to him, 'How does he want
to undo the rule?' The monk said, 'We were taught to fast till
sun-down, but he eats only on Sundays, and the bread and pulse
he receives he secretly gives to the poor every day. Not only this,
but the stench from his body is so unbearable that no one can
stand near him; his bed is full of worms, and we simply cannot
bear it. You must choose: either keep him here and we will leave,
or send him back where he came from.'

7. When he heard this, the abbot was astounded. He inspected
his bed and found it full of worms, and because of the stench
he could not stay there. The abbot said, 'Behold, the new Job!'
Taking hold of [Simeon], he said, 'Man, why do you do these
things? Where does this stench come from? Why do you deceive
the brethren? Why do you undo the rule of the monastery? Are
you some kind of spirit? Go somewhere else and die away from
us. Wretch that I am, am I to be tempted by you? For if you
are really a man from real parents, surely you would have told us
who your father and mother and kinsfolk are and from whence
you came?' When he heard these things, the saint, bowing to
the ground, was absolutely silent, but the place where he was

standing was filled with his tears. Quite beside himself, the abbot said to his monks, 'Strip him so we can see where this stench comes from.'

8. Then they wanted to strip him, but they could not do it, for his garment was stuck fast because of the putrefied flesh. So for three days they kept soaking him in warm water mixed with oil and in this way, after a great deal of trouble, they were able to strip him: but with the garment they also took off his putrefied flesh. They found the rope wrapped around his body so that nothing of him could be seen, only the ends of the rope. There was no guessing how many worms were on him. Then all the monks were astounded when they saw that terrible wound and they asked themselves how and by what means they could take the rope off him. But holy Simeon cried out, saying, 'Let me be, my masters and brethren. Let me die as a stinking dog, for so I ought to be judged because of what I have done. For all injustice and covetousness are in me, for I am an ocean of sins.'

The monks and the abbot wept when they saw that terrible wound, and the abbot said to him, 'You are not yet eighteen years old: what kind of sins do you have?' Holy Simeon said to him, 'The prophet David said: "Behold, I was brought forth in iniquities, and in sins did my mother conceive me."[3] I have been clothed the same as everyone else.' The abbot was astonished at his wise answer, that such an uneducated man had been spurred on to the fear of God. However, the abbot called two physicians, and, although the distress and the labor was so great that at one point they gave him up for dead, they finally separated from him the rope with flesh stuck on it. They tended him for fifty days and helped him somewhat, and the abbot said to him, 'Look, son, you are now healthy. Go where you wish.'

9. Then holy Simeon left the monastery. Now there was a well near the monastery which contained no water, but many unclean, evil spirits lived it: not only unclean spirits, but also unimaginable numbers of asps, vipers, serpents and scorpions so that everybody was afraid to pass by that place. Unknown to anyone, holy Simeon

---

[3] Ps 50:7. Note how in the next sentence birth is described in the familiar image of putting on a garment.

went there and, making the sign of the cross, threw himself into that well and hid himself in the side of the well.

10. Seven days after Simeon had left the monastery, the abbot saw in a dream an unimaginable number of men clad in white encircling the monastery. They held torches and said, 'We will burn you up this very moment, unless you hand over to us the servant of God, Simeon. Why did you persecute him? What did he do that you cast him forth from the monastery? What was his fault? Tell us before we burn you. Do you not know what you had in your monastery? For he will be found greater than you in that fearful, terrible day.' When the abbot awoke trembling from his sleep, he said to his monks, 'Truly I see that that man is a true servant of God! For I have suffered much evil this night in a dream because of him.[4] I beseech you, brethren, spread out and find him for me, otherwise none of you can come back here.'

11. They went out and looked for him everywhere, and when they could not find him they went back to the abbot and said, 'Truly, master, there is no place left where we have not looked except that place where no one would dare to travel because of the hordes of wild beasts.' The abbot said to them, 'My sons, praying and bearing torches, go out and look for him there.' After praying above the well for three hours, they, with ropes, let down into the well five monks holding torches. At the sight, the reptiles fled into the corners, but on seeing them holy Simeon called out, saying, 'I beseech you, brothers and servants of God, grant me a little time to die. That I cannot fulfill what I set out to do is too much for me.' But the monks overpowered him with much force and pulled him out of the well, dragging him as if he were a criminal. They brought him to the abbot who, when he saw him, fell at his feet, saying, 'Agree to my request, servant of God: become my teacher, and teach me what patient endurance is and what it offers.'

12. Holy Simeon wept unceasingly and prayed to God; he stayed in the monastery three years[5] and then, without anyone knowing, left and went into a sparsely inhabited area where there

---

[4] At Mt 27:19, Pilate's wife says the same about Jesus.

[5] Delehaye (*Les Saints Stylites*, xvi) suggested reading 'three plus two', but there is no compelling reason to emend the text.

were several villages, the nearest being called Talanis.[6] He built for himself there a small place from unmortared stones[7] and stood in the middle of it for four years through snow, rain and burning sun, and many came to him. He ate soaked lentils and drank water. After this he made a pillar four cubits high and stood on it for seven years, and his fame spread everywhere. After this the crowds built for him two enclosures from unmortared stone and they put up a door to the inner enclosure.[8] They made for him a pillar thirty cubits high, and he stood on it for fifteen years during which time he performed many healings, for many who were possessed went there and were healed.

13. Holy Simeon imitated his teacher, Christ. Calling on him, he made the lame walk, cleansed lepers, made the dumb speak, made paralytics move about with ease, healed the chronically ill. Each one he warned and exhorted, 'If someone asks you who healed you, say, "God healed me". Do not even think of saying, "Simeon healed me", otherwise you will find yourself again in the very same difficulties. I say unto you: never lie or take an oath by God. If you are forced to take an oath, swear by me, your humble servant, either in truth or in deceit. For swearing by God is a great sin and a fearful thing to do.'

14. Hear this awesome and extraordinary wonder. After twenty years the mother of holy Simeon learnt where he was. She came in haste and wanted, after so many years, to see him. She wept much to see him, but she was not allowed to view him. Since she wanted so much to be blessed by his holy hands, she was obliged to climb the wall. While she was climbing the wall of the

---

[6] The manuscripts give widely different renderings of the name of the village. I have given a name closest to the manuscripts F (*thalanis*) and C (*thalanes*), which is the closest to Theodoret's *Telanissos*, *Telanessos*. Lietzmann follows manuscript A and reads *Gelasois*.

[7] Literally, 'dry rock', *xerolithos*. According to this author, Simeon immediately made an open-air enclosure out of available stones. According to Theodoret and the Syriac Life, Simeon first lived in a small hut.

[8] Festugière (*Antioche païenne*, 497, n.1) suggested that there was an enclosure where Simeon stood and a smaller area which served as a vestibule: *ta prothyra* is mentioned in 14, where Simeon's mother lies down at the entrance and immediately dies; in 19, the dragon with the wood in its eye lies down at the entrance vestibule. However, the two enclosures seem to refer to the men's enclosure, and to the women's enclosure as in 25 where the female dragon goes to the women's section.

enclosure, she was thrown to the ground and could not see him.[9] Holy Simeon sent a message to her, 'Leave me alone for now, mother. If we are worthy, we will see one another in the next life.'[10] When she heard this, she only longed more to see him, but holy Simeon sent this message to her, 'Rest, my honored mother, since you have come a long way and grown weary on my humble account. Lie down at least a little while; rest and get your strength back. I will see you soon.' When she heard this, she lay down before the entrance and immediately gave up her spirit to God. The door-keepers came to wake her up, but discovered that she was dead and told the saint what had happened to her. On hearing this, he commanded that she be brought inside and placed before his pillar. When he saw her, he wept and began to say, 'Lord, God of powers, guide of the light and charioteer of the cherubim, who guided Joseph, who made your prophet David prevail over Goliath, who raised Lazarus from the dead after four days, lift up your right hand and receive in peace the soul of your handmaid.' While he was praying, her holy remains moved and she smiled. Everyone who saw it was astonished and praised God. Having performed her funeral, they buried her in front of his pillar so that he kept her in mind as he prayed.

15. Hear another strange and extraordinary mystery. Some people were coming from far away to have him pray [for them] when they came across a pregnant hind grazing. One of them said to the hind, 'I adjure you by the power of the devout Simeon, stand still so that I can catch you.' Immediately the hind stood still; he caught it and slaughtered it and they ate its flesh. The skin was left over. Immediately they could not speak to one another, but began to bleat like dumb animals. They ran and fell down in front of [the saint's] pillar, praying to be healed. The skin of the hind was filled with chaff, and placed on display long enough for many men to know about it. The men spent sufficient time in penance and, when they were healed, returned home.

---

[9] Festugière (*Antioche païenne*, 372) refers to a similar incident in the Life of Pachomius.

[10] I do not see why Festugière (*Antioche païenne*) suggested that Simeon "ne fait pas allusion a l'autre monde, mais au miracle qu'il va accomplir." Simeon is refusing to see his mother and exhorting her with this pious reflection, not holding out hope for quick gratification.

16. Hear another strange and wonderful event. A woman became thirsty during the night and wanted to drink some water. She took hold of the pitcher of water but along with the water drank a small serpent. Nourished in her womb it became large,[11] and her face became like green grass in appearance. Many physicians came to heal her but were unable to. Her kinsmen learnt about the marvels and the healings which the saint of God Simeon was performing, so they took her to the saint and told him everything about her. He commanded them, saying, 'Put in her mouth some of this water and soil'.[12] When they did as he had commanded, the beast stirred in the presence of all; it threw her on the ground, came out, put its head in the middle of the barrier,[13] and perished. Everyone glorified God.

17. They changed his pillar into one forty cubits high, and fame of it spread throughout the whole world. Thus there came to him many Arabs[14] burning with faith, and he spurred them to the fear of God. Then the devil, that hater of men, who habitually tempts the saints and is trampled under foot by them, smote him on his thigh[15] with a pain called a tumour, just as happened to the blessed Job. His thigh grew putrid and accordingly he stood on one foot for two years. Such huge numbers of worms fell from his thigh to the earth that those near him had no other job but to collect them and take them back from where they had fallen, while the saint kept saying, 'Eat from what the Lord has given to you.'

18. By God's will the king of the Arabs came to him to have the saint pray for him. As soon as he came near the pillar to be

---

[11] Conception through eating or drinking is a theme frequent in folklore. See Stith Thompson, *Motif-Index of Folk Literature* (Bloomington: Indiana University, 1955–58) T511–512.

[12] I have read with MSS CDFG *ek tēs gēs tautēs*, whereas Lietzmann, with A, reads *ek tēs pēgēs tautēs* = from this spring. This is the mixture of blessed water and soil that the saint frequently uses in the Syriac life.

[13] The barrier separated the inner enclosure from the outer.

[14] Literally, Saracens. See above, Theodoret, note 23.

[15] D adds to the narrative: '[The devil], transformed into the likeness of the Master, came with the chariot of the cherubim to blessed Simeon and said, "Come, O righteous one, upon this chariot and receive the crown of glory." Since the saint did not think it was a phantasm, he balanced his foot but then checked it. Then, thinking over the command carefully, he withdrew his foot from the perceived phantasm. The blessed one had his thigh struck by the evil one just as . . .'.

blessed by holy Simeon, the saint of God, when he saw him, began to admonish him. While they were talking together, a worm fell from [Simeon's] thigh; it caught the king's attention and, since he did not yet know what it was, he ran and picked it up. He placed it on his eyes and onto his heart and went outside holding it in his hand. The saint sent a message to him, saying, 'Come inside and put away what you have taken up, for you are bringing misery upon me, a sinner. It is a stinking worm from stinking flesh. Why soil your hand, you, a man held in honor?' When the righteous man had said this, the Arab came inside and said to him, 'This will bring blessing and forgiveness of sins to me.' When he opened his hand, a precious pearl was in his hand. When he saw it, he began to glorify God and said to the righteous man, 'Look! What you said was a worm is a pearl—in fact, a priceless one—by means of which the Lord has enlightened me.' On hearing this, the saint said to him, 'As you have believed, so may it be to you all the days of your life—not only to you, but to your children also.' So blessed, the king of the Arabs returned home safe and sound, rejoicing.

19. Hear another mystery. Eastward on the mountain on which he stood, there dwelt a huge dragon, and for this reason no pasture grew in that spot. Now when that dragon went out to cool himself, a piece of wood lodged in his eye and for a long time no one could bear his hissing in pain. Then one day the dragon came, dragging himself out of his cave, and came in open view and lay down at the entrance to [Simeon's] enclosure. All of a sudden his eye opened and the piece of wood came out of his eye. He stayed there three days until he returned to health. So, in open view and without having harmed anybody, he returned to his spot. He had lain before the entrance of the righteous man just like a sheep: everyone was going in and out, and nobody was hurt by him.

20. Hear another extraordinary wonder. There was a robber-chief in Syria named Antiochus, also called Gonatas, whose deeds were recounted throughout the whole world. Soldiers were frequently sent to catch him and lead him to Antioch, but no one could catch him because of his mighty strength. Bears and other beasts were kept ready in Antioch because he would have to fight the beasts, and the whole city of Antioch was in a commotion because of him. Now when they went out to catch him they

found him drinking in an inn in some village and the soldiers surrounded the inn. When he learnt of this, [the robber] began to stage a scene. There was a river in the village and that robber-chief had a mare he used to order about as if it were human. Rising up, he threw his clothes onto the mare and said to it, 'Go to the river and wait for me there'. The mare left the inn biting and kicking, and when it got to the river it waited for him. Then the robber-chief also came out of the inn unsheathing his sword, crying out and saying to the crowd of soldiers, 'Flee lest someone be killed', and none of the soldiers could overpower him. Escaping all those surrounding him, he crossed the river with his mare and, mounting her, reached the enclosure of holy Simeon. He entered and threw himself down in front of his pillar, and the soldiers then gathered together in the saint's enclosure. The saint said to them, 'With our master Jesus Christ were crucified two thieves, one of whom received according to his deeds while the other inherited the kingdom of heaven. If someone can stand against the one who sent him here, let him come and drag him away himself, since I, for my part, neither led him here nor can I send him away. The one who sent him here claims him for himself. So let no one rail at me, your humble servant, one who has suffered much because of my many sins.' When he had said this, he sent them away. After they had gone, the robber-chief said, 'My lord, I too am going away.' The saint said to him, 'Do you return again to your evil ways?' The robber-chief said, 'No, master, the Lord calls me,' and, stretching out his hands towards heaven, he said nothing more except, 'Son of God, receive my spirit in peace'. For two hours he wept so that he made even the righteous [Simeon] and the bystanders shed tears. Then, placing himself in front of the pillar of the righteous one, he immediately gave up his spirit. The crowds wrapped his body and buried him near the enclosure of the righteous one. The next day more than a hundred men came from Antioch with swords to seize [the robber], and they began to cry out to the righteous one, 'Release to us the one you have'. The holy man said to them, 'Brethren, he who sent him here is stronger than you and, since he was useful, he had need of him. He sent to him two terrible soldiers armed to the teeth who could strike your city and its inhabitants with thunderbolts. They took him away and when I, a sinner, saw their terrifying appearance, I was terrified and did not dare stand against them lest they kill me too, your humble servant, as one who resisted God.' When the men heard these things from the saint and learnt how gloriously the robber-chief had died, they glorified God and, trembling, went back again to Antioch.

21. Hear another awesome and glorious miracle. There was no water to be found where the saint lived, and the crowd of animals and people coming to the place of the holy Simeon was on the point of perishing. The saint prayed and did not speak to anyone for seven days, but was praying on bended knee so that everyone thought that he had died. About the fifth hour of the seventh day, water suddenly gushed forth from the eastern side of the enclosure. They dug down and found a sort of cave full of water, and they constructed seven outlets for it. All glorified the God of heaven and earth.[16]

28. So the blessed one stood on different pillars for forty-seven years, and after all these things [the Lord] sought him. It was Friday,[17] and he was confined in prayer and, as was his custom, he spent the whole Friday [this way]; but on the sabbath and on the Lord's day he did not lift up his head, as was his custom, to bless those who knelt. When I saw this, I went up to him and I saw his face and it shone like the sun. Although his custom was to speak to me, he said nothing to me. I said to myself, 'He is dead', but then I was not sure; I feared to approach him, so, taking courage, I said to him, 'My lord, why do you not speak to me and end your prayer? The world has been waiting to be blessed for three whole days.' After standing for an hour, I said to him, 'You have not answered me, my lord.' Stretching out my hand, I touched his beard, and, when I saw that his body was very soft, I knew that he had died. Putting my face in my hands, I wept bitterly. I bent down, kissed his mouth, his eyes and his beard, lifted up his tunic and kissed his feet; taking hold of his hand, I

---

[16] Here in Lietzmann's text are a series of miracles that are found in only a few manuscripts. Festugière (*Antioche païenne*, 370) rightly regarded them as later additions. For a translation of them, see appendix C.

[17] Literally, 'the day of Preparation' which reminds one of Lk 23:54, Jn 19:14,31.

placed it on my eyes. Throughout his body and his garments was a scented perfume which, from its sweet smell, made one's heart merry. I stood attentively for about half-an-hour by his venerable corpse, and behold! his body and the pillar shook and I heard a voice saying, 'Amen! Amen! Amen!' Fearfully I said, 'Bless me, lord, and remember me in your beautiful place of rest.'

29. I came down and did not tell anyone the secret lest an up-roar occur, but, through a trustworthy man, I informed the bishop of Antioch, Martyrius, and the military chief, Ardabur.[18] The next day the bishop of Antioch set out with six other bishops. Ardabur also came with six hundred men so that the assembled villages should not seize the venerable corpse, as they were considering. They formed circles around his pillar, and three bishops went up and kissed his garments, saying three psalms. They brought up a leaden casket; they arranged his holy corpse, and brought it down by means of pullies. Then everyone knew that the holy Simeon was dead. All the Arabs had gathered armed and on camels, for they too wanted to seize the body. Such a crowd was gathering that the mountain could not be seen because of the numbers and the smoke from the incense, the wax tapers, and the innumer-able burning lamps. The sound of the weeping men, women, and children could be heard at a great distance, and the whole moun-tain was shaking from the screeching of the birds which gathered and circled round the enclosure of the saint. So when they had brought him down, they placed him upon the marble altar before his pillar, and, although he was already dead for four days, his holy body looked as if he had died just an hour before. All the bishops gave him the kiss of peace. His face was bright, completely like light, and the hairs of his head and beard were like snow. The bishop of Antioch wished to take a hair from his beard as a relic, but his hand withered [at the attempt.] All the bishops prayed for him, weeping and saying to the holy corpse, 'Nothing is missing from your limbs or clothes, and no one will again take anything from your holy and venerable corpse.' As they spoke thus in tears, the hand of the bishop was restored to health. Then, with psalms and hymns, they placed him in the casket.

---

[18] On this person, see J.R. Martindale, *The Prosopography of the Later Roman Empire*. Vol.II (Cambridge: CUP, 1980) 135–37.

30. Eleven days before his death, I, a sinner, saw a man in frightening raiment which I cannot describe. He was as big as two men, and he spoke to him three times during the day and gave him the kiss of peace. I wanted to tell someone about him, but my mind was seized and I was prevented from speaking until it was over. After the man whom I saw came to him, I saw them apparently[19] eating, but what they ate I do not know. They sang, but what they sang I do not know save only the Amen. Fear gripped me at the sight of the man.

31. The coffin of the saint was placed on the carriage and in this way, with wax tapers and incense and the singing of psalms, he was brought to the city of Antioch. When they were about five miles from the city in a place called Merope, the mules stood still and would not budge. There, an extraordinary mystery happened, for on the right of the road stood a tomb and a certain man stayed in it. Now this is what the man had done: he had loved a married woman twenty years earlier, but could not possess her, and the woman died and was laid in that tomb. Then, so that the hater of good might gain the soul of that man, he went to the tomb, opened up the tombstone, and had intercourse with the dead body. He immediately became deaf and dumb, and was held fast to the tomb and could not leave that place. Travellers-by would notice him sitting on the steps of the tomb, and each, for God's sake, would offer something to him—some water or some food. When, by the will of God, the venerable corpse came by on that day and the carriage and the crowd stood still, the man who neither spoke nor heard came out of the tomb crying out and saying, 'Have pity on me, holy one of God, Simeon!' When he reached the carriage, what had restrained him was immediately taken away and his mind was restored. All who saw what happened glorified God, and that place shook from the shouts of the people. The man cried out, 'Today I have been saved by you, servant of God, for I had perished in sin.'

32. The whole city, clad in white and carrying tapers and lamps, went out to meet the venerable corpse, and it was brought into

---

[19] For this translation of *phēsin*, see Festugière (*Antioche païenne*, 505, n.11).

the church called Cassianus.[20] After thirty days, Ardabur, the military commander, gave a command and had it placed in the great church. There, following a revelation by God, was built an oratory of the holy and revered Simeon, and there, in that oratory, with much glory and hymn singing, his holy body was laid.

33. Many people offered to give gold and silver to receive a relic from his holy limbs, but the bishop took no notice of anyone because of the oaths he had taken. In that place where his venerable remains are laid, many healings are performed through the grace given to him by our Master, Christ. [The saint of God Simeon died on the first of September in the reign of our Lord Jesus Christ,][21] to whom is the glory and the power for ever and ever. Amen.

[34. I, Antonius, least of all and a watchman, have narrated part of his story. For who can worthily describe his wonders and healings, save only partially to represent his undefiled deeds to the praise and glory of God for ever. Amen.][22]

---

[20] Malalas (450.16–18) records that in 529 or 530 C.E. Justinian presented to the people of Antioch one of his own robes, ornamented with precious stones. It was laid out in the church of Cassianus. These are the only two mentions of this church. See G. Downey, *History of Antioch*, 531.

[21] The date for Simeon's death is found only in manuscript A, not in BCDEFG, and is excluded by Festugière. The date is that given for Simeon's feast according to the Greek synaxaries. See Festugière, (*Antioche païenne*, 381–382).

[22] This second epilogue is found only in manuscripts CDG.

The
Syriac Life
of
Saint Simeon
Stylites

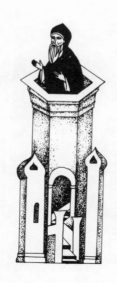

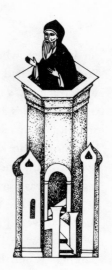

THIS THEN IS THE LINEAGE and native country of the athlete and friend of God, the blessed Mar Simeon:[1] he came from the north,[2] from the region of Nicopolis and the name of his village is Sis. His parents were believers and they had baptized him while he was young. He had a brother whose name was Shemshi—they were the only ones who survived from many that his parents had.

The blessed, holy Mar Simeon loved from his youth to tend his parents' flock and to train himself with blows[3] and buffeting. From the time that he was a boy and became strong and grew up, he had this peculiarity: as the flock grazed, he would very diligently gather storax,[4] kindle a fire and put the storax

---

[1] The V manuscript has part of the first three lines missing. The only words read are: '. . . then . . . native . . . friend [of God]'. I have reconstructed the text following M, which is very close to V in the subsequent lines and which contains the word 'native' in the corresponding position. Both M and B have, previous to this sentence, a more stylized introduction, of which there is no trace in V. For this introduction, see p.46.

[2] On the manuscript can only be read [ ]*by'*. Assemani read *'rby'* = Arabia. M reads *grby'*, a reading Bedjan had already suggested and which agrees with Theodoret.

[3] Both V and M read *bqwph'*. Assemani wrongly read *bswpy'* = in wisdom. B reads: *b'ml' wbl'wt'* = in toil and fatigue.

[4] Storax is a fragrant gum resin which Strabo, in discussing the Taurus mountains of Asia Minor, notes was used 'in large quantities as incense by the worshippers of the gods (*hoi deisidaimones*).' (12.7.3) There was a storax called

on it,[5] even when he did not clearly know why he put it on. For neither had he heard the Scriptures nor was he acquainted with our Lord's religion because from his childhood he had grown up in the fields and on the mountains. Now he was cheery, pleasant, and compassionate, and he had a good character. His intimates and those who knew him from his youth[6] say, 'He kept from his own mouth, and fed others'. He was handsome, could run very fast, and was quite strong although on the short side.[7]

2. When the time came and it was our Lord's will, his parents died and were gathered in peace. As he and his brother were the heirs, he was of necessity forced[8] to return to the house of his parents. When he noticed the villagers going to the church on Sunday, he went along with them. When he heard the epistle being read, he asked those beside him, 'Whose writings are these, and what is in them?' They answered him, 'These are the writings of God who dwells in heaven, and the words of God are in them.' He was greatly astounded and amazed in his mind and on the next Sunday he again went and entered the church and listened

---

the Cilician storax (Dioscorides 1.66.1) and Nicopolis lies in Cilicia. Dioscorides mentions its healing properties and also that its smell is like that of frankincense (1.66.3).

5 I have taken the meaning of M. V simply reads 'and put', without specifying the object. B has a different verb and reads 'and burn the storax as incense'. Here B is explaining what is going on in M and V.

6 At this point in the present folios of V, one finds interpolated Mt 3:1–4:4.

7 In this character sketch of Simon, V and M are identical in their order and word-choice for the description, while B has a different order.

	V and M		*B*
a)	cheery, pleasant, and compassionate	a,d)	cheery, handsome, pleasant, and compassionate
b)	of good character	g)	on the short side
c)	abstains from food to feed others	f)	quite strong
d)	handsome	h)	liked by all
e)	a fast runner	c)	abstains from food to feed others
f)	quite strong		
g)	on the short side		

8 Literally: 'necessity summoned him, and the matter was urgent'. The same phrase is found in M, though not in B.

attentively and diligently with all reverence to the holy Scriptures. From that day he took great pains to gather storax and he also bought what his fellow shepherds collected and, with all reverence, he offered it to our Lord saying, 'Let the sweet smell ascend to God who is in heaven.'

3. After a few days a vision appeared to the blessed man among the sheep: this was the first vision that he saw. He saw a man come and stand above him—he looked like lightning, his outer garments were like the sun and his face like rays of fire. He held a golden rod in his hand, and he prodded Simeon with that rod and called and roused him. When the blessed Simeon lifted up his eyes and saw that amazing sight, he trembled, was terrified and shook; he fell face-down on the ground. The visitor gave his hand and strengthened him and raised him up and said to him, 'Do not fear, but come after me without fear. For I have something I must say to you and show to you. For the Lord wills that his name should be glorified through you. You will become head, overseer, and leader to his people and to the flock of his pasture. By you the laws and ordinances of the holy church will be established, and you will turn many from error to sound knowledge. If you succeed and prosper, your name shall be great and be magnified among the nations from one end of the earth to the other, and kings and judges with everyone else under their authority will obey your word and ordinance. Only gain patience and endurance, and let there be love in you towards everyone. For if you possess endurance and you have perfected love in yourself towards everyone, if you keep pride and boasting far from you, there will not be anyone, either among the ancients or the moderns, greater than you.'

4. After this, the vision led him up the mountain and placed him on top of it and showed him some stones lying there, and said to Simeon, 'Take and build'. But the blessed Mar Simeon said to him, 'My Lord, I do not know how to build, for during my life I have not built for myself any building.' He said to him, 'Stand close by, then, and I will teach you how to build.' He brought forward a huge hewn stone which was finely carved and beautiful, and put it into the saint's hands and said to him, 'Set it up properly at the east, and another at the north and one at the south. Then put one

on top of them, and the building is finished.'⁹ The blessed Mar
Simeon said to him, 'My Lord, what is this?' The man said to him,
'This is the sanctuary of that God whom you worship, to whom
you burn incense, and to whose writings you paid attention.'

5. Then he led him away and again spoke, 'Come after me'. He
brought him and made him enter a nearby martyr shrine in which
lay Mar Timothy, the disciple of Mar Simeon.¹⁰ As he was about to
enter it, he saw before the church's court innumerable people clad
in white and like bridegrooms. At the north were women wear-
ing purple, modest and yet very elegantly adorned. The blessed
man asked, 'My Lord, who are these?' Then he answered and said,
'These are the men and women who, if you succeed, will be converted by you and many more than them, and they will receive
the sign of Christ.' Then over the church entrance before those
men and women flew a flock of many peacocks: it appeared like
a fire, as their faces were blazing rays and from their eyes went
rapid flashes of light. When they saw the saint they spread out their
wings and lifted up their heads and cried out so loudly and strongly
that the earth shook from their cry. Then the man waved the rod
in his hand and gently and easily quieted them down and made
them be still. He led Mar Simeon inside the church and when they
reached the altar and stood to pray, from underneath that very altar
there rose up a good-looking man who was fairer than the sun—
one could not tire of looking at him and his beauty was beyond
compare. His clothes were white as snow, his features were smiling
and his face very cheerful. His head was tinged with white hair
and grew in tresses, and he spoke gently and pleasantly. He wore
a golden inscription on his breast, and he came near and greeted
the blessed Mar Simeon three times with much love and said to
him, 'Blessed are you, Simeon, if you are equal to the portion and
the ministry to which you are called.' The two of them took him

---

⁹ Basilicas of the Constantinian era seem to have had their entrances at the
east and their apses towards the west.

¹⁰ V: Simeon; B and M: Paul the Apostle. There is no tradition linking Paul's
disciple Timothy to a shrine near Nicopolis. All other traditions place his death
near Ephesus, and his relics are said to have been transferred to Constantinople
under Constantius. Perhaps this is the shrine of a disciple of Simeon the Ancient,
mentioned by Theodoret in *HR* 6. The authors of B and M have referred to a
better known Timothy.

and brought him near the altar and opened his mouth. Then the one who had come up from under the altar placed in the saint's mouth something white as snow, round and like a pearl. It tasted sweet as honey so that he said, 'Such a taste and such sweetness is indescribable in this world,' and he felt full and well satisfied. Then the man gave to Simeon the golden rod he held and said to him, 'With this rod you will shepherd the flock of the Christ. Be strong and act bravely.' When they had said these things to him, they disappeared and ascended. This[11] is the first vision that appeared to the blessed man as he shepherded the flock.[12]

6. After this, for twenty-one days the saint did not eat bread or drink water but remained fasting, although he had been brought up from boyhood to eat meat and drink wine. Now, as we narrated the first vision which Mar Simeon saw, so this is the first sign which he wrought.[13] After fasting for twenty days, he longed to eat fish and doubtless this longing came from the Lord so that he might show a marvelous sign through him. For there was a fisherman who had a daughter named Martha.[14] That night the father had caught many fish, as there was a lake near-by. He brought the fish to the house and put them down before his daughter and left. Now the saint came and called her by her name twice and when she answered he said to her, 'On your life, my daughter, if your father has brought fish, give me five pounds, and take the money straightaway.'[15] But she denied there were any and swore by the name of the Lord,[16] 'He brought nothing today'. Turning away, the saint went and stood in the street near some people from his village. There were also present some soldiers, for there had been a raid by the Isaurians[17] and a crowd of soldiers were billeted there. While

---

[11] This sentence is found in M but not in B.

[12] Here in B and M is found a narrative about a raid by Isaurians in which a relative of Simeon is taken captive. In outline it is reminiscent of the narrative in Genesis 14. See Appendix B.1.

[13] This sentence is not found in B and M.

[14] B names her Miriam, M gives no name.

[15] Both B and M have three pounds.

[16] That she swore is not said here in M.

[17] A people dwelling in the mountains of Pisidia in southern Asia Minor, who raided towns and villages in the early fifth century. See A.H.M. Jones, *The Later Roman Empire, 284–602. A Social, Economic and Administrative Survey* (Norman: University of Oklahoma Press, 1964) 1.192.

they were standing around talking, suddenly something[18] got into
that young girl and those fish, and took them and scattered them
outside in the street before all the people. The girl leapt up and
was exposed,[19] she gnashed her teeth, shook her head to and fro
and wept and cried out to the saint to help her. The fish also were
jumping up in front of him on the other side. When all the people,
the soldiers and the villagers, saw that sign they were very scared
and trembled. Many got up and tried either to catch the fish or to
restrain that young girl and keep her still because she was exposed,
but they could not. Finally her father came and he and the bystanders besought the saint and he went and took hold of her. At
once she was still and the fish too stopped jumping up. The saint
said to her,[20] 'Because you lied in the name of the Lord,[21] God
has exposed you publicly.' And from that time he was honored and
accepted over everybody.[22]

7.   Then our Lord did this favor[23] for the saint, and fulfilled his
request because he did not seek it from greed. For when he left the
villagers to go to his flock, as he was wandering on the mountain
he found a huge fish[24] lying in front of him. He made the sign
of the cross and then took it and brought it home[25] with him.
And when those soldiers who were billeted with him in his house
saw it, they marvelled. Then our Lord again performed a marvel
with this. For the soldiers billeted with him, the shepherds and the
household all ate from the fish for three days, and scarcely then was
it consumed because the blessing of the Lord rested on it. Now the
names of the soldiers billeted then with him were Silvanus and Bar
Shabta. They loved him very much. Till he had been standing on
the great pillar for many years they used to come and remind the
saint and they also told it to his disciples. This was the first vision

---

[18] M: a devil.

[19] This is not said here in B and M, but is pre-supposed in the story
later on.

[20] V reads 'to them', but clearly B and M have the right reading.

[21] B has simply 'Because you lied'.

[22] This sentence is found in V and M, but not in B.

[23] B connects this sentence to the previous miracle. M narrates: 'Then our
Lord did this second miracle . . .'.

[24] Both B and M read 'eel'.

[25] Both B and M read *qryt'* = village throughout this passage, not *byt'* =
house, home. The reading of V suggests that Simeon's family was wealthy.

that Mar Simeon saw when he was a youth, and this was the first
sign done through him.[26]

8.   From that time, he began to train himself[27] with fasting and
prayer. He was constantly in the church, day and night, the first
to enter and the last to leave. Most days he spent the night there
till daybreak in prayer. One day he would kneel from evening till
morning, one day he would stand straight in prayer from evening
till morning.[28] After he had been acting in this way for a great
while, his peers began watching him to see if he moved his feet
slightly or changed his position[29] from evening till morning. But
no one could detect any such movement, as they told us.[30]

9.   After that his brother wanted to divide the property with
him and [Simeon] said to him, 'Go, and divide it at your dis-
cretion. Take whatever you want, and there will be no recrimi-
nations.' The brother, however, divided everything correctly, for
he loved him greatly. For he had a paternal aunt who was very
rich and who had just died. Whatever she owned she left to the
saint. But he attacked those possessions like a reaper: the clothing
he gave to the monasteries and to the poor; the other property
and everything that was there he sold and gave to the poor. The
open fields he gave to his brother. To the monastery of Teleda,
the followers of Mar Eusebona, he brought a great deal of clothing and many goods because his first cousin on his father's side
was there.[31] This was a man set for a sign who lived in the

---

[26] This sentence is not found in B and M.

[27] B: he was constant.

[28] B: from morning till evening he would kneel; from evening till morning
he was standing in prayer.

M: till morning he was standing in prayer, and from morning till evening he
was kneeling.

[29] M: if he sat or lay down.

[30] This last clause is not in B and M.

[31] Instead of the preceding three sentences, B and M read:

B	M
Whatever she left to him he ad-ministered in the fear of God and gave to the poor and the needy.	*Whatever she left to him,* at that time he divided *to the poor and the needy* and to monasteries.
Especially he provided the monastery of Mar Eusebona because his first cousin on *his father's side was there.*	*Especially he provided the monastery of the* blessed *Mar Eusebona* with other special provisions. *His first cousin on his father's side was there.*

monastery thirty-five years—from the time he entered he never looked back to see the door through which he entered.[32]

10. This is the reason why [Simeon] went to that monastery after four months: he had sown seed, and he had those other goods to provide to the poor and the monasteries, and even to take with him to the monastery. During Lent while he was in his village, he tasted nothing except the Eucharist which he received midway through the fast. He continued not to taste anything until he received the Eucharist on Easter Sunday and then he ate.

11. Now the Lord also showed a great miracle in the seed he had sown. For he allowed the gleaners and foreigners and the poor[33] to go among the sheaves and said to them, 'Everyone may take as much as he can without fear.' When everyone had gathered as much as he wanted, our Lord sent a blessing on it, and it brought forth sixty-fold.[34] He also brought bread and a pot of mutton and a skin of wine[35] for the reapers to eat. After the reapers had eaten, he made all the gleaners who were there come, both the poor and the foreigners,[36] and he laid the food before them. They ate and drank until they were satisfied. He served them with his own hands, and there was something left over.[37] In God's providence this miracle was wrought because of the excellent works of the righteous one.[38] No one brought any cooked food or other bread but from that small amount of bread and the wineskin and the pot the whole group—the poor, the reapers, and the sowers—were fed till sunset. The saint brought everything and said to them, 'Let everyone take whatever he needs'.[39]

12. The saint told us these things when he was giving thanks

---

[32] Both B and M read: 'The saint made up his mind to enter that monastery, and he remained four months in the village because of the seed he had sown there and because of other pressing matters.'

[33] B: the gleaners and the poor; M: foreigners and the poor.

[34] B: and a hundred-fold; M: thirty-, sixty-, and a hundred-fold.

[35] B: bread and cooked food; M does not specify the food and drink at all.

[36] B: the poor; M: the gleaners and the poor.

[37] B: He served them with his own hands and he refreshed them. Lent translates the last verb, *mrg' hw'*, as 'he mixed wine for them'.

[38] This sentence is not in B and M.

[39] These last two sentences are not found in B and M. M does have: 'When they had eaten and drunk, they carried as much as they were able and went to their homes, giving thanks and praising God.'

to God and praising him for his providence and for the care our Lord had shown to him. He did not tell these as if boasting but to praise our Lord. What the Apostle said applies to this, 'The gift of God is greater than can be spoken.'[40] And this is what our Lord said, 'If you believe in me, the works which I do you will do, and you will do greater than those which I do.' This is what our Lord said in the Gospel, 'Many things Jesus did which, if each one were written down, the world would not be sufficient to contain them.'[41] So also we are relating only a little from many.[42]

13.　　Then, after everything had been set in order, he set out to go to the monastery and took with him considerable goods on camels and beasts of burden[43] in order to leave some of the goods in the monastery and to give some to monasteries in need. After he went and was received and had handed over everything to the abbot, on the third day he was brought to Mar Mara, bishop of Gabula—Mar Mara was a mature ascetic and zealous for Christians because he was a monk[44]—so that he might bless him and be tonsured.[45] He happened to be there then as if actually on account of the saint. When the bishop saw how comely was his face and how fair his features, he was astonished and amazed. For the saint was on the small side but his faith was great. He was ruddy, handsome, and the Lord was with him, as it is written.[46]

14.　　The brother of Mar Simeon also approached to be blessed like the rest of the crowd, because he had come with Simeon to see him admitted and then planned to return. When the bishop saw him, he said to him, 'Look, my son, how your brother who is younger than you has chosen a good and excellent lot for himself.' And the brother agreed that there was nothing like it in the world,[47]

40　This seems to be a reference to 2 Cor 9:15.

41　Jn 14:12, 21:25. These quotations are not found in B and M.

42　This sentence is not found in B and M.

43　This last clause is not in B, but is in M.

44　This description of Mar Mara is not in B and M. Monk: literally, a mourner.

45　This last phrase is not in B. M reads: and enter the novitiate.

46　Compare the description of David in 1 Sam 16:12. These last two sentences are not in B and M.

47　Both B and M connect this last phrase with the previous sentence and read: '. . . has chosen a good lot for himself to which nothing is like. So Mar Shemshi also agreed to become a monk.'

and the bishop blessed and tonsured both of them together. The bishop also reckoned him a chosen vessel which would be suitable for its master's use and that he would finish his life with a good name and with righteous deeds.[48] For after he was blessed and tonsured[49] and they went to the brethren, as if by prophecy and by portent[50] that same bishop Mar Mara said to the abbot and to those there with him, 'If life is granted to that blessed one,[51] he can become a chosen and excellent vessel in whom God is well-pleased and his name will go from end to end of creation. For I know what a crowd I saw following him.'[52]

15.		Then after five months, Mar Shemshi, the saint's brother, went to distribute whatever he had to the poor, the needy, and the monasteries, and returned to his place in the monastery.

16.		After the saint was tonsured, he was not concerned about anything except pleasing the Lord with fasts and standings and prayers and in a sober and excellent manner of life. When his brother came and brought whatever they had, he did not even go out and look at these things but busied himself in the Lord's service. He dug himself a spot in a corner of the garden up to his chest. All summer he stood in it in the hot and sultry weather and it was like a fire.[53]

17.		Even there the Lord manifested great deeds through him. For after he was in [the monastery] for a year or two in toil and hard labor, the devil, the enemy of virtue among monks, stirred them up against him,[54] and they were jealous and envious of him. They caucused together and said to the abbot, 'If he does not stay on the same level as us, he cannot stay here.' The abbot earnestly besought him but he would not agree to lower the excellence of his way of life. So he went away and said to the brethren, 'Since he

---

[48]   B reads the plural here, referring to both Simeon and Shemshi. The sentence is not in M.

[49]   Assemani mistakenly reads the plural here.

[50]   This last phrase is not in B and M.

[51]   Both B and M read: 'If the brethren leave him alone, ...'

[52]   B and M: 'For I know what sign I saw in him.' An alternative translation of V would be: 'what I saw with him that clung to him.'

[53]   B: 'he stood in it two years in the oppressive heat of summer and the severe cold of winter.'

[54]   The devil is not mentioned in B, but is in M.

wants to afflict himself for God's sake, I do not want to be the cause of any loss to him.' Now one of the brethren after terce threatened him out of spite and he came and stood over him to test him. But the justice of the Lord threw him down for five hours and left him sprawling on the ground. The brethren who were standing under the trees praying ran up and carried and placed him before the saint under the trees. He vomited blood. After three days he commanded and they poured water on him and he turned over and fell upon the jar of water and drank; at once he vomited blood and after two days he died.[55]

18.   The saint fasted from Sunday to Sunday, tasting nothing but soaked lentils. There were times that he fasted from two to three weeks.[56] Once he went off and dug in the corner where the wood was placed and confined himself—the brethren thought that he had really left. But after thirty days one of those appointed weekly went to bring the wood and he dug and brought up the warrior:[57] he found him shut up and standing in the corner. He ran and made this known to the abbot. The abbot and many others came and they had to use all their powers of persuasion for him to come back with them and take the Eucharist.

19.   What the brethren made him endure and how roughly they treated him to make him conform to them is more than can be spoken of.[58] For frequently they assembled and said to the abbot, 'If he does not conform to the brethren, let him leave the monastery.' However, the abbot did not act on their demands

---

55   Both B and M have a simpler version of the last four sentences.

B	M
At that very hour *the justice of the Lord threw him down* and he fell and did not move. *The brethren* who happened to be there *ran up; they carried him* and came *and placed him* under one of the trees. He vomited blood and *after three days* died.	At that very hour *the justice of the Lord threw him down* and he fell on the ground and was vomiting blood. When *the brethren* saw him *they ran up; they carried him and placed him* under one of the trees. *After three days* died.

The words underlined are in common between V, B, and M.

56   Both B and M recount here that Simeon, when compelled to sit at table with the brethren, actually ate nothing. See Appendix B.2.

57   The text reads *dnsq drr'* which I take to be a result clause: he dug with the result that he brought up the warrior. Assemani reads *dnsb drr'* and translates *casu delitescentem*.

58   This sentence is not in B but is in M.

because he greatly loved Simeon—he had noted Simeon's toil and worship and he perceived that the brethren spoke out of hatred when they said, 'He should conform to us'.

20.   For at night he made a round piece of wood and he would stand on it so that if perchance he fell asleep[59] that piece of wood would roll around while it was bearing [him].[60]

21.   Once he took a rope harder than wood and fastened it on his body. After a long time, as his body grew it thrust through the bands of that rope. After a further long time the abbot came to know of it, but Simeon would not consent to unfasten it except under duress. He took away that rope and it was full of flesh and covered with blood.

22.   Again, as he was working on a Saturday, one of the brethren out of envy so as to test him heated a poker red-hot and said to him, 'You believe and trust in your Lord, so take this.' Immediately, Simeon simply took it in both his hands. The brethren thought that no skin or flesh would be left on his hand, but he stoked the furnace and oven with it and when he opened his hands, it was as if they had been in cold water. When the abbot heard about it, he wanted to dismiss that monk, but the blessed one would not allow him.[61]

23. Satan also frequently joined battle with him as he tested him incessantly.[62] One day as he was standing and praying Satan came in the form of a thick haze which suddenly struck his eyes and took away his vision. After a long time the abbot asked if he could bring a doctor to him, but he was unwilling and said to his brother, 'Take me down to the sepulchre'.[63] After he had been there thirty days[64]—he had been forty days in this affliction—in the middle of the night suddenly something like a flash of lightning entered the sepulchre and the whole sepulchre was lit up. It passed before

---

[59]   Assemani reads '*m*, instead of *nm*, and adds *npl* to the text after 'roll around'.

[60]   The verb in this last phrase is very hard to read: *š?l*. I have read *šql*. Assemani read *npl*, but the *š* is clearly visible.

[61]   This last sentence is not found in B and M. Several other cruel testings of Simeon by the brethren are found in B and M. See Appendix B.2.

[62]   This sentence is not in B, but is in M.

[63]   Assemani, on no textual basis, reads the plural 'brothers' here, and makes the verb plural.

[64]   B and M have three days and specify the sepulchre as that in which the saints were laid.

his eyes, and at that moment his eyes were opened as though no sickness had affected them. When he went to worship, the brethren saw him and were astonished.[65]

24.   Again, there was a place east[66] of the monastery in the form of a cave, very dark and foreboding. Even if one saw it in daylight one would be scared by the groaning sounds that came from it. At the beginning of Lent, he went out one night and entered into it. He was there throughout Lent and he fought much with Satan. Satan collected and brought against him serpents and vipers which hissed and puffed up. Also beasts like leopards and wolves roared and rushed against him. But the saint did not worry about them, but was completely occupied with heaven—he would make the sign of the cross on his breast and on his forehead and send them scampering for their lives. Suddenly he disappeared and they[67] vanished like smoke before the wind and much light shone inside the cave and a voice was heard saying, 'Behold, your brethren have persecuted you and Satan has harassed you.[68] But do not fear and do not be troubled because your Lord does not let go of you. His grace watches over you, and you are first above your brethren. His right hand sustains you and Satan is trodden under your feet.' When Lent was over, the brethren sought him everywhere but could not find him. So the abbot said to the brethren, 'My sons, take on the charge of God.[69] Take lamps, and go and look for the blessed one, lest he entered that cave and is dying there, and we be smitten in his sin.'[70] Then those of the brethren in whom

---

[65]   M adds: 'and they praised God'.

[66]   M reads: west.

[67]   B: 'he disappeared and vanished....' singular verbs occur throughout this sentence.

M: 'they disappeared and vanished....' Plural verbs throughout.

V has one singular and one plural verb.

[68]   Both B and M have present participles in this sentence.

[69]   This sentence is not found in B. M reads: 'Take upon yourselves the burden for the sake of God.' V may suggest a reference to the parables of the lost sheep and coin at Lk 15:3–10.

[70]   B: 'Let him not die there and be smitten in his sin'.

M: 'See lest the blessed one be there and die there and be smitten in his sin'.

Garritte translates G: '*Videte ne forte ingressus sit ille in antrum et moriatur illic et nos rei fiamus culpae eius.*'

Lent translates B: 'Let him not die there, lest we be punished for sinning against him.' Rather, I suggest that the abbot and monks act out of brotherly

there was love of our Lord and zeal for Christ rose up and took lamps and candles. With much trouble they found him in a corner of the cave, and led him out and he received the Eucharist with the brethren.

25.   After Lent had passed by, all the brethren assembled and said to the abbot, 'You must choose: either take this one brother and we leave, or dismiss him and keep the monastery.' The abbot loved him greatly, and he was dear to him but he did not want his monastery, in which there were one hundred-twenty brothers, to be scattered. So he calmed them cleverly and said, 'If he does not obey and conform to you, I will do what you want.' For a whole year he tried hard to persuade him but he would not neglect his ascetic practices. The brethren too were pressing their demands. As the Lenten fast drew near, the abbot gently called him and said, 'You know, my son, how much I love you, and how I have not annoyed you at all. I did not want you to be sent from here, but the brethren press their demands, and there are laws laid down by our fathers of old and I cannot change their laws. Arise, go wherever the Lord is preparing for you. If our Lord perceives[71] that you seek him with a resolute mind, the Lord will answer your petition and you will be leader to your brethren. You will protect and support this very monastery in which you entered the monastic life. I will hear that our Lord is exalting you, and I will rejoice in you.' This is indeed what came to pass. For while his master lived he was exalted and highly celebrated; news of him went out in the world, even before kings, and his master heard and rejoiced. When that abbot died, he entrusted the monastery to the saint. He also was a perfect man—from childhood till old age he dwelt in the monastic way of life. For he entered the monastery as a boy of five and he died in wondrous deeds at the age of seventy-nine.[72]

26.   Then he gave four dinars to blessed Mar Simeon as he was rising to go and said to him, 'These will be for your food and clothing till men appreciate you.' But the saint said to him, 'Let not Simeon your servant take a dinar in his hand. Do not give me things of no use, but supply me with prayers which do help.' And

---

love and fear Simeon in his stubbornness has brought on his own death.

[71] Assemani omits this phrase from his text through dittography.

[72] M has 42, a clear mistake.

he prayed and blessed him and sent him away as Isaac did to Jacob, and said, 'Go in peace, and may the Lord be with you.' This was the way he left the monastery.

27.   When he had gone a little distance from the gate, the saint turned eastward to pray and this is what he said, 'Lord, mighty God, wherever you want me to do your will, there direct the path before your servant.'[73] After he had passed a little beyond the border of the monastery, he found, as if from the Lord, a path which led north; he turned aside and travelled on it until he entered the borders of Telneshe. Then he turned off the path and stood in prayer under a tree till evening. He asked again in prayer, 'Lord, my holy God, if it is your wish that I perform the lenten fast in this village, at whatever monastery I first knock let whoever comes out say to me directly and with no cross-examination, "Enter."'[74] After he finished his prayer, our Lord guided him to the monastery of Maris bar Barathon of Telneshe who was chief of the village. At that time there was in that monastery an old layman and a youth about seven years old. When the saint knocked, immediately the boy went out very diligently and opened the door. When he saw the saint, he greeted him and said, 'Enter, my lord'. The saint said to him, 'Go, my son, and inform the abbot.' But the boy replied, 'Not until you enter, my lord. I will not leave you here.' And he laid hold of him and forced him to come in. When he had gone and informed the old man, he came out swiftly and diligently received him with affection and love as if he had known him for a long time. For the Lord had prepared the way. Now no brethren dwelt there except

---

[73] This prayer is not in this position in B and M.

[74] B: 'Lord God, who created me in the womb of my mother according to your will, and brought me forth to this light in your kindness, and implanted in my mind fear of you according to your will, and separated me from my father's household in your mercy and I have carried your cross and followed you according to your word and you have protected me from evil and from all their powers in the day of my affliction—be to me a good guide and protector that I may come to the place that pleases your Glory.' When he had finished his prayer, he arose and went along the road until he came to a certain mountain in the village of Telneshe, before the beginning of Lent in the year four hundred and fifty-eight according to the Antiochene calendar. Then he sat down in a valley, pondering in his mind whether he should turn towards the uninhabited region. He stood in prayer a long time and prayed thus, 'Lord, my holy God . . .'.

M is very similar to B.

the old man and the boy; the Lord had arranged for him to come
there and for them to receive him. He spent the night with them
in honor and in the morning the saint said to the old man, 'I
have been looking for a place to seclude myself during this Lent.'
And the old man gladly said, 'Look, here is the whole monastery.
Wherever you want, I myself will set a place for you.' He sent and
summoned his son named Maris, and he prepared for him a small
roof chamber which was just as he wanted.

   28.   Now Mar Bas happened to drop by. He was an itinerant inspector[75] of blessed memory, a wonderful man, a servant of
Christ who rejoiced in virtue and avoided jealousy.[76] By origin
from Edessa in Mesopotamia, he was the son of senators. He came
and spoke with the blessed Mar Simeon in the love of our Lord
those things which are right and proper for the fear of God, for he
was a wise and holy man. Then he blessed him and shut and locked
the door. Now he had overridden the saint and forced him to take
six[77] whole flat round loaves and he had filled a pitcher with water. When the Lenten fast was over, the saintly Mar Bas diligently
came and opened the door. All who happened to be there saw
those six loaves still intact and the pitcher of water still full and the
saint kneeling and praying, and they marvelled and were amazed,
all the more so because as soon as he gave him the Eucharist he was
strengthened and arose and went out with him into the courtyard.
The next day[78] he wanted to go to the desert but they besought
him and built for him an enclosure on the mountain. Now there
also lived in Telneshe a priest named Daniel, a trustworthy man.
He gave Simeon a spot in his field and the enclosure was built.

   29.   The next year[79] at the beginning of Lent Mar Bas again
came and locked the door. After Lent, he took with him as a mark

---

   [75] *Periodeutēs*. On their role in the Church, see Jones, *The Later Roman
Empire*, 2:879, 1365–66 nos 13,14. Canivet, *Le monachisme syrien*, 289 n.148;
Amadou 'Chorévêques et périodeutes', *L'Orient syrien* 4 (1959) 233–240.
   [76] M, in place of this last trait, reads: 'learned in the holy scriptures.'
   [77] B reads seven.
   [78] M: 'after Easter'.
   [79] The text of V should be emended from *lh ptk'* to *lhpkt'* as in B. Assemani
has divided this word, putting a colon after *lh* and connecting it to the previous
clause 'and an enclosure was built for him', but there is no textual basis for this
and it leaves the unknown *ptk'*. Assemani has also read *'tb'yt* instead of *'tbnyt*.

of honor the priests in whose district he was and some of his fellow itinerant inspectors. They came and opened the door and when he had given him Eucharist our lord performed a great miracle. For there was a man from Telneshe, named Maris,[80] one of the chiefs of the village. He was carrying with him a vessel full of oil and, as the blessed Mar Bas and his companions and all the populace were standing around, he brought it to the saint to bless it. At the very moment that he said, 'Let our Lord give a blessing,' it bubbled up and overflowed, like a seething cauldron. The whole place was filled with the overflowing oil. The whole group took some of it—they even brought many vessels to take it away—but it did not give out, but it went away full and overflowing with that man. For many years it stayed in his house full as ever, and there was much healing and help in that oil for everybody. This was the first sign wrought by the blessed Mar Simeon in public after he left the monastery.

30. In secret, he had many battles with the enemy of good. At that time as he was standing and praying at night, Satan brought against him a very fierce black serpent. It swelled up and hissed, it rushed against him and coiled itself between his feet and wound itself in many coils round the saint's leg up to his knee.[81] It bound him tight like a rope to frighten him and make him stop his prayer. The saint, however, was not frightened but continued patiently in prayer. When he had finished praying, the serpent uncoiled itself and went to go away. When it had gone a little way from him, the angel of the Lord smote it and ripped it from top to bottom.

31. Again, ten days later as he was standing and praying at night, he saw the form of a dragon. It was very fierce and frightening, changed its appearance, and blew and hissed violently. It struck the ground with its tail, it snorted, and made a noise so that the ground shook from it. Its open mouth sent out a fiery blaze, its nostrils smoked and its eyes flashed light. It was very long. The heroic saint, however, was not at all frightened but lifted up his eyes and his hands to his Lord. Then he turned and blew on the

---

[80] B: Marenes.
[81] v should be emended from *lbwkrh* to *lbwrkh*, a simple copyist's error.

dragon as he said, 'May our Lord Jesus Christ rebuke you'. At that moment it disappeared[82] and could not be found.

32. After the holy Mar Bas left the saint, in the presence of all the people in the church he said as if inspired, 'Our Lord will perform by the hand of this saint many signs which he did not work by the prophets or by the apostles so that kings of the earth and all their princes will come to greet him and to bow down to him and to ask him to pray for them.'[83] This indeed is what happened.

33. There was a man of Beth Laha, a village about three miles from Telneshe. He was wealthy and chief of his village. He had a daughter who had been paralysed from when she was a young girl. For almost eighteen years she could not even turn over in bed. They carried her and laid her down at the north of the saint's enclosure while her father entered and told the saint about her. He asked the saint to pray for her, and he answered, 'In the name of our Lord Jesus Christ, take some of this dust and go out and apply it to her'. [For there was no oil there to give, nor was it yet the custom to give *ḥnana*[84] for he had been there only fourteen[85] months]. The moment that dust touched her in the name of the Christ, she leapt up and stood healed. All who saw her praised God. On her own feet she walked up the high mountain of her village. Her father built a monastery for her and she lived in it all the days of her life. This was the first paralytic healed there. Her father remained with the saint all the days of his life.

34. After this, two young men who were paralysed came to him. They were the sons of two sisters from the plain of Antioch. One had been born paralysed and six months after the other was born, the evil one smote him and paralysed him too. Now a man from Telneshe happened to pass through their village. When he saw them, he told their parents about the saint. For up till then he had not become famous.[86] When they

---

82 Reading with B *'ttlq*. V has *'tqtl* = it was killed, which does not make good sense here. A simple error reversed the letter order.

83 M: 'signs more than which were not done by former or latter. Even to kings and princes will reach the report of him.'

84 *Ḥnana*: a mixture of water (or oil and water) with dust from a holy place such as a saint's tomb or, as here, the spot where Simeon stood.

85 M has eight months.

86 This sentence is not in M.

brought them, he[87] introduced them and he laid them before him. When he saw them he was very sad because they were handsome youths. They had been afflicted for seven years. When he finished his prayers, he called those who had brought them and said to them, 'Rub on them some of that dust in the name of Christ'. As soon as they rubbed it on them, the boys leapt up and stood. They dashed about in front of the saint. Both of them went away healed and praising our Lord.

35. After this came a soldier who had acted wickedly. As he was travelling along the road he had seen a young maiden and had taken her by force and raped her. Suddenly an evil spirit struck him and threw him off his horse. He shrivelled up and was like dry wood: he could not speak or walk or recognize anyone. They brought him and laid him before the saint a whole day. When he finished his prayer he gave them orders. They rubbed him with some of the dust before the saint and poured water over him. His senses returned and he regained the use of his mind. He sat up and spoke, and the saint said to him, 'Do you promise solemnly never again to do such a wicked deed?' He pledged never again to do anything wicked and shameful. So the saint said to him, 'Rise in the name of our Lord'. Straightaway he sprang up and stood and walked, and he went away healed and praising God.

36. After him came a man tormented[88] by an evil spirit. It would lie with him in bed in the form of a woman, and he was greatly tormented and worn out. When the saint saw him he said, 'Rub some of this dust on yourself in the name of our Lord Jesus Christ. Make with it three crosses[89] in your house, and you will not see her again.' He did as he was told and never again did he see anything hateful until the day he died.

37. Deeds such as these and greater than these our Lord performed by the saint.[90]

---

[87] B has the plural. The singular here must refer to the man from Telneshe.

[88] Assemani reads *sgy* rather than *kd*, that is, a man 'very tormented'.

[89] Lent translates 'signs of the cross'. But here it is a question of power to ward off the entrance of the demon, and one should compare this action to the magical bowls buried in the foundations of houses to ward off evil spirits. See James A. Montgomery, *Aramaic Incantation Texts from Nippur* (Philadelphia: The University Museum, 1913).

[90] This sentence is not in B and M.

38.   After those things[91] they brought to the saint Mar Simeon
a priest from the north who lay in harsh, severe, and bitter affliction.
While he was sitting and reading the scriptures in church, suddenly
he saw something like a mist passing before him. The evil adversary
of humankind struck him on his face and threw him on the ground.
He lost his vision and his reason, and he dried up like wood. All
the parts of his body were weak and he could not speak. When
they entered they found him lying as if dead and they carried
him and put him in bed. He was thus afflicted nine years: he did
not utter a word, he did not recognize anyone, and he could not
turn to one side unless someone did it for him. When they heard
about the saint, they lifted him on a couch to bring him before
the athlete of God. They reached Shih, a village about three miles
from Telneshe, and spent the night there as they were tired from
the trouble and toil of the journey. They hoped to get up early and
come into the presence of blessed Mar Simeon. But God saw both
the faith and the toil of those who carried him and the wretched
affliction of the priest[92] throughout that long period, and God
did not deny him his merciful gift but publicly graced him. For
as the blessed Mar Simeon was standing and praying, God's Spirit
revealed to him the wretched affliction of that priest, just how and
by whom he had been afflicted. So at midnight he summoned one
of his attendants and said to him, 'Take a little water in a vessel
and go down to Shih. In the courtyard of the church you will
find a priest who is paralysed, desiccated, and lying on a couch.
Pour over him some of this water[93] and say to him, "Simeon the
sinner says, 'In the name of Jesus Christ, leave the couch in the
church and rise, walk and come on your feet. You have been
carried about long enough. From now on the grace of your Lord
will strengthen you.' " ' The attendant went down and found him
just as he had said, lying on that couch as if dead in extreme pain.
When they saw the attendant a great crowd gathered. Before them
all he poured that water over him and, as ordered, said to him,
'Mar Simeon says, "Rise in the name of Christ. Leave your couch,

---

[91] For the placement of this story in B and M, see Appendix A.

[92] V reads *twbn'* = the blessed one, but the reference should be, as in B and
M, to the affliction of the priest.

[93] Note the sympathetic power at work: water cures the dried-out man.

walk on your feet and come to me." ' At the moment that the
water touched him together with the blessing of the mouth of the
servant of God Mar Simeon, his pains fled and he was relieved of
his afflictions. His reason and his vision returned, and he recovered
his strength. All the parts of his body grew strong and well, and
he leapt up onto his feet from his couch without pain or injury.
He went in and prayed in the church, praising and giving thanks
to the God of Mar Simeon who had graced him openly. He went
on his own feet while a great crowd followed him, giving thanks
and praising God for this public miracle which their own eyes had
seen. For they had seen him lying on his couch like a useless empty
vessel, but as soon as that water with the blessing of the mouth of
the righteous one touched him, he had leapt up on his feet from
his couch like someone who had never in his life felt injury or
disease. When he had gone up and entered the enclosure he threw
himself down before the blessed Mar Simeon who looked at him
and said, 'Rise up and do not be afraid. Although Satan tried to
trouble you through his servants and the slaves of his will,[94] God's
mercies were moved towards you and He has graced you. As for
those through whom this affliction came upon you, you will find
them in extremely wretched affliction, and they will implore and
beseech you to forgive them. As God has been gracious to you,
so may you forgive the trespasses of those who sinned against you.
Take with you a little *ḥnana*[95] and water and apply it to them, and
God will show mercy to them.' So the priest and his companions
went away, rejoicing and giving thanks and praising God. He found
his enemies in extreme pain and torment, just as the saint had said
to him. But when he poured water over them and applied the
ḥnana to them, our Lord was willing and they were relieved. They
rose up and came to the saint's enclosure and before him in the
sight of everyone they confessed their evil-doing. He charged and
admonished them and they too went away healed and giving thanks
and praising God.

---

[94] Who are these people? No mention has previously been made of them.
One has here the belief that pain can come to a pious man only from the
intervention of wicked people.

[95] Note that here *ḥnana* is present but was not used in healing the priest.
This distinguishes the time frame of this story from that of the previous ones.

39. In those days there came to the saint's enclosure a poor man from Aleppo, and he was weeping, distressed and harassed. He entered and threw himself down before the heroic saint as he wept and said, 'My Lord, I ask your help. I hired a field and planted a cucumber garden so that I and orphaned children who are with me would be provided for and live off it. After it began to appear and come up, a man came in the night and uprooted all the field. There was nothing left except ten beans[96] and even these are spoilt.'[97] He had brought those young gourd and cucumber plants and he put them down before the heroic saint. Then my lord the saint said to that poor man, 'Rise up, do not be distressed. For the stench of death strikes me from this matter. Now take *ḥnana* and go and make three crosses in the field in the name of our Lord Jesus Christ. I have such confidence in the God for whom I toil that if but three young plants remain for you the Lord will bless them and will provide to you from that field three times more than you were expecting. You will see it with your own eyes and you will praise God. As for those who committed that deed, the judgement of God will quickly overtake them. For they have presumptuously despised the patience of God, but quickly it works judgement and vengeance on them. There are three of them: wicked and presumptuous men who have sinned greatly against monasteries and churches and they have troubled many people. Behold, the blow of the Lord is coming on them, and it cannot be healed. Their punishments will be different one from another.' After three days the judgement of God overtook them. Their compact was broken and their association split apart. Their power was brought low and restrained and their stiff necks broken. For their punishments struck them mercilessly. One of them was consumed by elephantiasis, and was all broken up and stank. Another suddenly puffed up like a wineskin. He could not even walk without much pain. They started to bring him to the saint. When he had just gone beyond the village border—he moved very slowly because he could not sit on an ass nor could he be carried by men—he stumbled and fell, his belly burst open and all his innards fell out and immediately

---

[96] M: vines.

[97] This last clause is not in B. M reads: 'these are trampled on and useless'.

he died and they went and buried him. The third was smitten by Satan with an evil spirit—his mouth was distorted, and he was biting and slashing his arms and chewing his tongue. He was even tearing his clothing apart. Bound with chains and bolts, he was brought before the saint and, after he was a long time in that affliction, they persuaded the saint, but only with difficulty, to pray for him. He was a little relieved and his mind restored. He confessed before all their sins, and the saint when he heard this said, 'God has rewarded you according to your deeds so that your punishment is without mercy.'

40. Now about the visions and revelations which were shown to the pious and holy Mar Simeon by God through the Holy Spirit, no one can describe or narrate them. He was very circumspect and was afraid to recount them before men lest either someone would think he spoke boastfully and so suffer loss, or someone might strongly give credence to them and think him more than what he was. For this reason he restrained himself from recounting visions and revelations.[98] To those who served him, however, he sometimes spoke openly and informed them. But he commanded them that they were not to divulge or tell anyone while he lived, lest it were to be thought that the only ones who praised him were those who served him. Furthermore he did not tell everyone who served him but only those whom he loved and trusted.[99]

41. Once he saw a ladder placed on the earth with its top reaching heaven. There were three men standing on it, one at the top, one at the middle, and one at the foot. A magnificent throne was set up and our Lord Jesus Christ sat on it and the hosts of heaven stood to right and left.[100] A voice was heard calling the one in the middle by his name and saying, 'Come, ascend to your brother'.[101] He ascended until he was at the same level. Then the voice was heard again, saying, 'This is Moses, the great prophet who received the law from God on Mount Sinai. Mighty signs and works were done by him, he became great before God and was glorified before all humanity. No prophet equal to him arose after him in Israel.

---

[98] This sentence is in M, but not B.

[99] This sentence is in M, but not in B.

[100] This last sentence is is in B, but not in M.

[101] V and M agree. B reads: 'Come, ascend to me and I will show you.'

You too if you succeed will be exalted above all the men of your generation. As I was with my servant Moses so I will be with you and I will do whatever you wish.'[102] Then he gave him three keys. The saint turned and saw the one standing at the bottom of the ladder and said, 'Lord, who is this?' A voice was heard by him which said, 'Call him and let him come and stand where you are standing. For he shall fill your place after you.' My holy master called him three times and he went up and stood where he had been standing in the middle of the ladder.

42. After this as he was standing and praying in the middle of the day, he saw a wondrous and fearsome vision. When he saw it he was afraid, trembled and was terror-struck. He hid his face in his garment from fear. For he saw a fiery chariot with flaming horses and blazing wheels, its deck aflame and flashes of blazing rays.[103] On it rode a man who came and stood before the victorious Mar Simeon on that chariot and said to him, 'Do not fear or be afraid, but be strong and act bravely, play the man and succeed. Do not fear mortal man, but more than anything be concerned about the poor and the oppressed. Rebuke the oppressors and the rich because of their possessions and their injustices. For the Lord is your helper and there is no one who can humble or harm you. Your name is written in the book of life, and a crown and a glorious garment are prepared for you among the patriarchs and your brothers the Apostles. For I am Elijah the prophet who in my zeal shut up the heavens and gave Ahab and Jezebel as food to the dogs and killed the priests of Baal.' After saying this Mar Elijah disappeared and ascended with the chariot. The saintly servant of God Mar Simeon greatly marvelled at the vision as he reflected and pondered about who really are the poor whom he had been ordered to be concerned about. The crippled and poor who beg? or the oppressed? or those of whom the blessed Apostle speaks, the holy ones who live in monasteries who for the sake of God left their possessions and dwell in hope. For the Mar Apostle was set over the saints by his brother apostles.[104]

---

[102] V and M agree. B does not have this last clause.

[103] As in V and M, while B reads for the last clause: 'and reins of blazing rays'.

[104] Gal 2:10.

43. After the blessed Mar Simeon had been so reflecting for many days and pondering and anxiously thinking about this fearsome vision and the command given to him, Mar Elijah appeared to him openly a second time as he was standing and praying. Mar Elijah was again in that fiery chariot and in burning flames. His own looks matched [the chariot], for his form was like lightning, his face like rays of the sun, his garments like white snow, and he was radiant. He greeted him and drew near, and he stood before blessed Mar Simeon and said in answer to him, 'Why is your mind anxious about these poor upon whom you were put in charge? You should be equally concerned about all humankind: the crippled, the poor who beg, your brother monks who dwell in the hope of their Lord. You should be concerned about God's priests and that the laws of the church be observed. You should make sure that no one despises or scorns the priesthood. You should order everyone to obey the priests and their superiors.[105] Moreover you should care about the oppressed and those who suffer violence cruelly at the hands of their fellow men. Rescue the afflicted from those who afflict them. Represent orphans and widows. Do not fear or be afraid of kings or judges. Do not show favoritism to the rich, but publicly and even-handedly rebuke all men, whether they be rich or poor. For if all the kings and judges together with their courtiers conspire together they will not be able to harm you at all. For once the Lord is someone's helper, how can anyone trouble or hurt him? For Ahab and Jezebel could not hurt or trouble me when I decreed their death and destruction. I gave their corpses as food to animals and I killed their priests and burnt their courtiers. So likewise no one can harm you as long as the Lord helps you. Be strong and brave and play the man. Do not grieve or let your mind be disturbed but gain patience and long-suffering and do not neglect to afflict your body.' After Mar Elijah had said this to Mar Simeon, he again disappeared and ascended in that same fearful, glorious chariot.

44. After these visions and commands the holy Mar Simeon was much strengthened and fortified, heartened and encouraged in his reverence and service of our Lord. He increased his ascetic

---

[105] This sentence is in M, but not in B.

practice tenfold over what he had done before. He pulled down the enclosure[106] and stood openly day and night while everyone looked at him and did not leave him. Secretly he intensified his fast so that after these visions he consented to take what he did[107] from time to time only because of their persuasion. He was constantly meditating and marvelling on those two men set for a sign, Mar Moses and Mar Elijah, saying, 'Who truly will tell me and teach and show me how and by what means these two men pleased God their Lord and deserved all this excellent portion? Was it by fasting that they truly pleased God? or by prayer and faith? or by love? or by humility? or by bodily chastity? or by zeal for their Lord?'[108] For he was greatly amazed by their wonderful appearance and the dignity given to them by God their Creator. He was always quizzing experts in the scriptures to learn from them about the life-styles of these two powerful athletes, Moses and Elijah. Now one said by humility, another by love, another by zeal for God— everyone had his own opinion. So he asked everyone in order to learn from everyone; it was not demeaning to that importance and that spiritual wisdom that it humble itself and ask even the least what manner of life was suitable to the service of his master. When he had learnt all these things from everybody and he had been instructed in the holy scriptures which were read before him, the saint began to fix them all in his own self: fasting without limit; standing day and night (a thing whose very narration is beyond mortal man without God's help); continual, uninterrupted prayer at all times; formidable supplication whose like had not been seen

---

106 B:'he made himself an enclosure'. B reads *'bd* instead of *'qr*. The phrase is missing in M. That Simeon could be seen by all agrees with Theodoret, *HR* 26.22.

107 M: the Eucharist.

108 The virtues are given differently in the three recensions:

V	M	B
fasting	fasting	faith
prayer	love	love
faith	faith	humility
love	humility	chastity
humility	chastity	zeal
chastity	zeal	

among men; zeal for God in the service of his Lord burning like a fire; chastity of body with pure limbs.

45. For what mouth or tongue could possibly say or relate anything without awe and fear about a man who, while clothed in the body, showed among humans works and deeds of spiritual beings? For he stood like a valiant man and was brave like a combatant and trained like an athlete and armed like a warrior in the army of the Lord. He endured all afflictions and despised all diseases. He held the evil one in contempt, and trampled sin under foot. He defeated Satan and routed his forces. He conquered his enemy with the weapons of his Lord and destroyed the whole army of the devil through his confidence in Christ, and he received the crown of victory from the right hand of his creator. For he outwardly bound his feet upon a stone,[109] while clothed inwardly with the true faith. In open view the flesh of his feet ruptured from much standing, but his steadfast mind was on fire for his Lord, a contest in secret. The vertebrae of his spine were dislocated through constant supplication, but he was fastened[110] and held[111] together by the love of Christ. He did not become negligent from the severe bodily pains because his mind was on fire at all times for his Lord. He was not disheartened in the afflictions and perils and the waves which were buffeting him all the time, for his trust was placed in God. He did not fear his bodily wounds nor did holy Mar Simeon give relief to his body. His eyes wasted away from lack of sleep,[112] but his mind was enlightened with the vision of his Lord. His feet stood on the stone, but his firm footing was with the Lord. His body was with human beings, but his mind with spiritual beings. What can we say about these things or tell how of his own accord he chose to be a vessel of honor and how freely he purified his limbs to be a priest of the holy spirit?[113] For he chose affliction

---

[109] B: a pillar.

[110] V has a play on words between 'tprq = to be dislocated, and 'tdbq = to fasten; B plays on ḥṣ = vertebrae and ḥwṣ = to bind.

[111] The text reads 'ttpys = be instructed, but from the parallelism I emend to 'ttpy from tp' = to cleave. A copyist may have added the s as pys is a more common verb. M reads 'tgmr = to be perfected or destroyed.

[112] The text reads 'from sleep', which is clearly wrong. Both B and M read 'from vigils'.

[113] This sentence is not in B. M reads: 'dwelling place of the Holy Spirit'.

over relief, exhaustion over rest, and hunger over fullness. He loved and desired to be in affliction in this world on account of Christ that he might luxuriate with him in the city of the saints. For he chose such afflictions that were not seen either among the ancients or in middle or modern times.

46. For what kind of body or what limbs were there that could endure the affliction the saint's body endured? For during forty years[114] he stood on a pillar forty cubits high and a cubit wide. His feet were fastened and bound as if in the stocks so that he could not move them either to the right or to the left, with the result that their flesh was worn away from the frequent affliction and bone and sinew could be seen. His belly was ruptured from standing so long, so that his attendants even said, 'The affliction of his belly is even more severe than that of his feet'. Three joints of his spine were dislocated: because of his constant supplication, bending and standing up straight and then bowing down before his Lord, one used to separate from the other and not attach itself to the others until he had finished his discipline. He lost his eyesight three times for periods of forty days as he stood on the pillar because of his vigils and frequent fasting without limit. No one knew this except those who served him, and not even all those. For his eyes were open and he spoke with everyone, but he could not see anyone. When our Lord wished and he had finished forty days, suddenly his eyesight was restored by the providence of Christ. Strangers did not know either that he had lost his sight or that it had been restored, because he commanded those disciples who served him not to speak or relate before anyone his toil and afflictions. 'For it is sufficient for me that God knows, the God whom I worship and whom only I serve.'

47. These afflictions, and many more, the athlete of God endured both openly and in secret. For he withstood bravely and valiantly the heat of the sun in summer and the force of the intense cold in winter. For the sun was like a fire and the skin which clothed him like a crucible, and the righteous one was like gold in the midst of it. But the fire abated and the crucible of testing cooled and the athlete of God was victorious. Then winter came with a

---

[114] Assemani wrongly reads thirty years.

blast, a winter to marvel at as does scripture when it says, 'Who can stand before its cold?'[115] A powerful wind came with it: the north wind came with snow, and the east wind with violence,[116] and the south wind with its sultry heat. All of them combined forces together with a battering rain, they joined battle with a wise builder who had built his building upon rock.[117] So the wind ceased and became calm,[118] the ice and snow changed and melted, and the rain was absorbed, while Mar Simeon grew strong.

48. Who then would see this and not marvel, who hear and not be amazed at the man whose feet were worn away and yet stood day and night, whose belly was ruptured and yet he was not moved, whose eyes were wasted away from vigils yet persevered against sleep, the joints of whose back were dislocated yet offered supplication, like a man dead in body like Job yet raised spiritually like him.[119] As Job sat upon a dung-heap of afflictions yet the prayers of his mouth rose on high, so his brother and companion holy Mar Simeon had his feet tied and fastened on the pillar, yet his prayers were free and pleasing to God on high. The victorious Mar Simeon, like Job, was slandered by Satan before God saying, 'You have not given me power over him to engage in a struggle with him as I like'. We will narrate what was decided and pass over what the dialogue was and simply relate the afflictions of the saint.[120] So Satan, that enemy of harmony, received power from God over the saint. While he was standing and praying at the ninth hour,[121] suddenly a sharp pain struck him on his left foot.[122] Towards evening it was full of boils and towards morning it burst open and stank; it swarmed with worms and putrid matter was oozing from the saint's foot—it and the worms mixed together and were falling from the pillar to the ground. The stench was so

---

115 Ps 147:17.
116 The text should be emended from the unknown *b'ḥph* to *bḥ'ph* as in B and M. B also adds that the west wind came with its ice, perhaps rounding out the four corners.
117 Mt 7:24–25.
118 Emending *'štnq* = be punished to *'šttq* with M.
119 Reading *bdmwth* with B and M rather than *byd mwth* = by his death.
120 This sentence is also in M, but not in B.
121 This statement of time is also in M but not in B. Is Simeon's passion being likened to Jesus' as, for example, at Mk 15:33–34?
122 The left is always the devil's side.

strong and foul that no one could go even half-way up the ladder without great affliction from the severe rankness of the smell. Even those who served the saint could not go up to him until they had put cedar resin and perfume on their noses. The saint was thus afflicted for nine months until all he could do was breathe.

49. The news of that wound spread everywhere, even to kings. People assembled, both bishops with itinerant inspectors and priests and a great multitude and they came to the saint frequently to persuade him either to take away from the pillar even one section or to come down for a little while till he was relieved of his affliction. For that affliction was more severe than the one which was chronic in his feet and which was with him for forty-five years.[123] The victorious kings, worthy of good remembrance, Theodosius and his sisters[124] wrote letters magnificently as befits the wisdom of their royal majesty, and sent them by distinguished men along with three bishops to petition and beseech him either to descend and rest a little while till he was relieved of that severe affliction or to take away a little of that pillar so that it would be easier to climb up to him and they could send a skilled[125] physician to look at that affliction and apply healing herbs to it.[126]

50. But the blessed servant of God, Mar Simeon, as became our Lord who dwelt in him,[127] lovingly and pleasantly dismissed everyone—the holy bishops, the clergy, and everyone according to his rank, even the Christian emperors and lovers of Christ, Mar Theodosius and his sisters. To them he wrote what was suitable, honorable, correct and fitting to the reverence of the God whom they served and which would edify and be of use to their rule.[128] Then he answered everyone and with this explanation dismissed

---

[123] This sentence is also in M, but not in B.

[124] In V, the sentence starts off in the plural 'those kings' but then refers only to Theodosius, although the third person plural suffix is attached to 'royal majesty' and the verb 'send' in the third person plural. I have read as in B and M, inserting 'and his sisters' and making the verb plural. Later in this section, mention is made of both Theodosius and his sisters.

[125] The text reads *kym'* which should be emended to *ḥkym'* as in B and M.

[126] This last phrase is also in M, but not in B.

[127] This last clause is not in B. M reads: 'who dwelt in his holiness'. Assemani misread the text as *'mh* rather than *'mr.*

[128] This last clause is in M, but not in B.

them, the bishops, the clergy of God, and the entire people. What he said to all of them he wrote with thanks to the emperors, 'Please pray for me, and I have confidence in our Lord Jesus Christ that he will not loosen his hold on his servant so that it should come to pass that he would come down from his station. For he knows that I have handed my life over to him. I have no need of herbs and medicines nor the help of mortals. Sufficient for me is the healing that comes from him. For he has authority like[129] a good master over the creation of his hands to rule and to possess.'

51. After eight months less ten days were completed, the disease had not ended but had grown stronger and the suffering increased and the wound had become worse. Now the first day of Lent approached, the feast-day when he used to shut the door. Many priests and a large crowd gathered to beseech him not to shut the door because of that severe and bitter affliction which he had.[130] 'Let us be entering and receiving blessing by you lest you die from this great affliction that you have while the door of your cell is closed and we should be deprived of seeing you and of the blessing of your mouth.' The saint replied, 'Far be it from me[131] all the days of my life that I should break the covenant I have made to my God. I will do what I have to do, and let my Lord do what he will. For if I die, I am his. But if he wishes to leave me in this life, let his pleasure and will be done.' The door of his enclosure was shut, and, after thirty[132] days in that violent affliction with that severe wound, those disciples who served him were sure that the time of his death was near. For he was wasting away and all that remained was his skeleton. He could not speak, and he looked as if dead. They were greatly troubled and began to weep and to ask him to pray for them, to bless them and to commend them to our Lord. The saint, when he saw that those who served him were troubled and weeping, forced himself and in great pain spoke to them, and encouraged and comforted them saying, 'Do not be troubled. For

---

[129] Assemani has left out *'yk* = like.

[130] There is an awkward transition here, as in M, to the first person plural, and so I have placed this section in direct speech. Sebastian Brock, in a private communication, suggested that perhaps *'pn* should be emended to *'psn*, 'Permit us to enter. . . .'.

[131] Emending with B and M from *dsḥ* to *dḥs*. Assemani read *dḥs*.

[132] B: three. M agrees with V.

I trust in the God whom I have served from my youth that he will quickly and swiftly work deliverance.'

52. When he had been shut up in Lent for thirty-eight days, in the week in which the door of the monastery was to be opened, between Tuesday and Wednesday at the middle of the night, suddenly something like lightning appeared and lit up all the enclosure. Then appeared to him one like a handsome youth clothed in white. He stood in front of the saint, twixt heaven and earth and answering said to him, 'Do not fear or tremble, but be strong and of good courage. Lo, your struggle is over, your slanderer has been shamed, and a crown is fashioned for you in heaven.' As he spoke, he stretched out his hand and touched and held the foot in pain. At that moment the disease vanished and his affliction ceased; his body grew strong, his face was radiant and shone. His speech was restored and that foul stench disappeared.

53. When those who served him arose early at daybreak to go to him, they found him radiant and cheerful, praying and giving thanks to God. He had sent them down away from his presence the evening before as if grace had shown him what our Lord was about to do for him. For one of those whom he loved used not to leave him but would stand beside him on the step of the ladder from evening to morning—there were two of them that served him.[133] When they saw him so completely cheerful, his mind calm and cheerful, and when they observed how quickly his foot had recovered from that violent disease and how that severe wound had gone away, how suddenly that unbearably foul stench had disappeared and been replaced by a fragrant odor, his disciples asked him [about this]. The one whom the blessed man loved[134] and who stood constantly by him day and night especially asked and besought him to reveal how our Lord had healed him. He demanded of them and ordered them to tell no one during his lifetime. Then he revealed to them what had been said to him in that vision, fearful and amazing words about something that was about to happen in the world. However he did not exactly

---

133   This sentence is not in B. M has added after 'to morning': 'he who placed his hand on his eyes when he gave up his spirit to his creator'. M also notes that their names were Marcellus and Antonius.

134   B states that his name was John.

reveal this to anyone, but with groans and prayers he beseeched and requested in prayer that he might leave the world before something that had been shown to him should occur in the creation.

54. After one day an innumerable crowd gathered with priests and bishops and, God willing, the door of the monastery was opened. They entered and found his body restored, and they marvelled and were astonished. For they had left him almost dead thinking that they would never see him alive again. But, our Lord willing, here he was restored, glad and merry and asking mercy from God. Bishop Domnus of Antioch went up with his disciple and gave him Eucharist; with his companions he praised and gave thanks to God for what they had seen with their own eyes. Then everyone returned in peace, and God's athlete remained in the arena.

55. These[135] then are the sufferings and bitter afflictions, and many more than these, that the saint endured. The grace of his Lord at all times strengthened and encouraged him, and never during his lifetime was he down-hearted in his afflictions. Because of this, God, who saw his endurance, exalted him and magnified his victory from one end of creation to the other. He multiplied heroic deeds by his hands and mighty signs, and he graciously bestowed [on him] before all men that his word was acceptable to both the great and small; as if from the mouth of God, they obeyed and accepted his command in fear and reverence. For our Lord said, 'Whoever hears you hears me, and whoever rejects you rejects God.'[136] So our Lord graced those who received the saint's word, but there were many signs on those who withstood his command and opposed his will. For the Lord's blessing rested on the houses of those who received the saint's word and did his will, in numbers so great they cannot be counted. But many of those who opposed his command received punishment and sentence as their presumption deserved.

56. One of these was a counsellor of the large city of Antioch. He was an evil and wicked man, and in the year that he administered the city he harassed many. Upon the poor who dyed skins red he tripled their yearly tax. About three hundred fled the city and came

---

135 This paragraph is in M, but not in B.
136 Lk 10:16.

to the saint; they cast themselves down before him and told him
what had happened. When the saint learnt how they had been
oppressed, he sent to the counsellor saying, 'My son, do not by
your hand bring this hardship upon these poor people, and do not
let this cruel burden be laid on them for ever (for this is what they
feared he would do). Rather be merciful to them, and require of
them the customary amount.' But he in his proud anger said to
the messenger, 'Go and tell Simeon who sent you that if he likes
he can give in their stead some of the gold that he has hoarded
for himself. For if I catch them, I will kill[137] them in prison and
I will not remit to them one coin[138] because of what you said.'
When the saint learnt of this from the messenger, he lifted his eyes
to heaven and said, 'If God knows that his servant owns anything
more than these skins which clothe me or if I have appropriated
for myself any coin[139] since I embraced the monastic life, I will
give account before the judgement-seat of his righteousness. As
for those who think or say these things about me, our Lord will
dismiss[140] them on the day of judgement; but as for the oppressed,
as his lordship knows, he will be a saviour to them.' After three days,
a fearful judgement overtook that wicked man—a bitter, incurable
disease. Suddenly his belly swelled and was puffed up like an inflated
wineskin. While those poor people were still at the enclosure, he
was cast down and worn out with great affliction. He wrote to
persuade the saint and he sent to all his villages and to the priests
in them that they might try to persuade the saint to pray for him.
He gave great sums of money to doctors: they applied herbs and
soothing ointments; they even covered him with sand and placed
him in the sun till he was baked and shed the skin of his body.
They added to his afflictions and no one was any help. When
those clients from the villages and the priests had importuned him
greatly, the saint placed the affair in the hands of God. He ordered
water to be brought and said to those petitioners, 'Take this water

---

[137] Perhaps the reading of B and M is to be preferred: 'lock them in
prison'.

[138] Assemani reads 'one day *ywm*', but *nwm'* = nummus, a small silver coin,
should be read as the trace of a *n* can clearly be seen.

[139] Literally: 'the image of a mortal king'.

[140] Lent translates: 'Lord, forgive them', but this meaning of *šbq* seems out
of keeping with the context.

and go. If God knows that he will turn from his evil deeds if he recovers from his affliction, then as soon as this water touches him Christ's mercy will be upon him. But if our Lord knows that he will not turn aside from his wickedness, he will never see this water.' As the one carrying the water was about to enter the counsellor's house, the counsellor suddenly turned around in bed from pain. His belly ripped open, his innards fell out and he died. He did not even catch a glimpse of that water, as the saint had said. And there was great fear, and the oppressed were delivered and praised God.

57. Again there was a tribune of the empress in the north[141] in the region of Nicopolis. He lived unjustly, harassed many, and robbed and oppressed and plundered with violence what did not belong to him. He persecuted orphans and widows and did not heed God's judgement. Many collected together and came and informed the saint about him. When the saint heard about the evil deeds he had done, he sent to him, 'Turn away from the wicked deeds that I have heard you are committing. Do not take by force what does not belong to you, lest you lose even what is your own.' Then that evil and wicked man in his mad rage and pride not only did not obey the word of the righteous one but he even increased his evil. He seized the messenger, treated him shamefully, and said to him, 'Go and show the one who sent you'. Towards dawn,[142] the Lord's judgement overtook the wicked man: a ravaging disease struck and he withered up like wood even while the messenger was present. No word left his mouth except only this, 'I beseech you, Mar Simeon, have pity on me'. In that hour he died and they carried him out and buried him while the saint's messenger was there.

58. Again God's saint Mar Simeon once heard that people were murmuring because he had sent to them, concerning the oppressed poor and the orphans and widows who were very badly off because of unjust violence from evil and wicked men, men who did not heed God's judgement. At this the saint was grieved in his conscience and said, 'Sufficient for me is God who charged me in soul

---

[141] Assemani reads 'Arabia', not 'north'.

[142] Assemani reads *tdgh*, which does not mean anything, instead of *dtgh* from *ngh* = to dawn.

and mind both to advise them for their own lives and for the good
of their souls and to persuade them to benefit and be merciful to
the poor. As for the poor I was to exhort them to live uprightly
and to fear God. But since this annoys them I place the affair in
God's hands that he should deal with it as his grace knows.' To the
disciples who served him he commanded, 'Do not send a word to
anyone, and do not accept anything from anyone until I see what
God's will and desire is'. After about thirty[143] days had passed by,
the oppressed had come, but no one had answered them and no
word concerning them had been sent. Also the people had come
bringing gifts for our Lord but no one had accepted them. So both
sides went away distressed.

59. Then an amazing and frightful vision appeared to the blessed
one of God Mar Simeon as he stood and prayed in the middle of
the night. He was afraid, he trembled, and he was deeply troubled.
For he saw two men of majestic and splendid appearance standing
before him—mortal man could not describe their splendid and
majestic form. A great crowd in splendid, majestic, and excellent
clothing had gone out to them. Now one of those two men found
fault a great deal with the saint and angrily spoke menacing words
to him, 'These are the orders you received: to possess self-control,
and to be patient towards everyone - then you would succeed and
prosper. But you have changed these: you have become impatient.
In the short time that people whom I sent[144] pressed around you,
you have become tired of them and you refused to send a word for
the oppressed, the afflicted, the distressed, and the persecuted. You
have wanted to stop the service of God that you desired since you
ordered that no one should accept gifts from those who brought
them. Since this is what you want, I will take away those keys you
received and another will carry them. You will remain silent, and
take care only of your own affairs.' But the other, when he saw
how deeply distressed the saint was, intervened for him and said,
'I will be sponsor for him that whatever he was ordered he will
assuredly do.' He approached the saint and said, 'Your task is to

---

[143] B: three months; M: three days.

[144] Assemani reads *dšrr'*. The last letter is mostly missing, but it is impossible
that it be an '. I have read *dšdrt*, which fits what is left of the missing letter; one
should clearly read *d* as the third letter.

speak out, and your Lord knows how to arrange the affairs. You do what is yours, and your Lord will do his part.'

60. In the days after that vision two youths came to the saint. They were the sons of a friend of the saint, and they informed him that a commander, an evil man who governed the East, was harassing them a great deal and causing them trouble. He wanted to make them enter the council. He had previously had a grievance against their grandfather[145] and he was trying to exact vengeance. Now they had been born in Antioch. When the saint learnt about this, he sent to the wicked man, 'Do not harass or distress these youths, for they are mine'. Then that unclean one, clothed like a lamb but inside like a ravenous wolf, covered his deceit in truth and sent a message as if in mockery to the saint, 'If you command me, I will carry baskets after them and wait on them like a slave'. Lent was at hand and he learnt that the saint used to close the door of the enclosure. When the youths entered the city, he seized them and put pressure on them and finally got promises from them to enter and serve on the council. But they sent their own guardians with a servant who was attached to them to make known to the saint [what had happened]. When he learnt of it, he sent to him, 'Twice I have said to you, "Leave these youths alone and do not harass them lest you come to harm and you yourself be accused and there be no one to aid you."' But that wicked and evil man, a second Pharaoh in the pride and arrogance of his mind, could not cover the deceit buried in his mind but showed his evil character plainly. Before all his attendants he said to the saint's messenger, 'Go, tell Simeon who sent you, "I have heard that you go into seclusion for Lent, and no one can enter and bother you during that time. But you may take the trouble to curse me thoroughly throughout the period, for I do not need any of your prayer."' This is what happened to him. The fool did not know that the Lord's judgement hung over him, and that his sword was unsheathed. When the saint heard the report of his messenger he shook his head and laughed softly under his breath and said, 'That idiot! He wanted us to worry about him all during Lent, and to abandon petitioning God for our own sins and those of the whole world!

---

[145] B and M: their father.

For who can stand before one puff of the judgement of our Lord? We gave him advice that we knew would help him. But since he chose a curse instead of blessings, what he asked for from the Lord will swiftly be granted to him.' So the saint shut the door of his enclosure on Sunday, and that unclean one had only one day of respite. The fearful judgement overtook him as his deed deserved. For accusations were laid against him unawares before the emperor and the provincial governor because of his evil deeds and because he oppressed many. Five courtiers were sent after him, and their bent was crueler than his. On the Tuesday of the first week of Lent, two days after the saint shut the door of his enclosure, they seized him publicly in the forum as he was being borne in state. They pulled him out of his chariot to his great shame; they unbelted him and took away his mantle. They tied his feet with a rope and hung him up head downward and pulled him along most mercilessly, for his ruin was from the Lord. They caused him great harm, and cast him in irons as they had been ordered. Then he sent and had those youths with whom he had clashed brought to him and asked them, 'Go and ask the saint to write to the emperor on my behalf, for I know that all this affliction happened to me because I despised his word.' But they answered him saying, 'Mar Simeon has shut the door of his enclosure and speaks to no one but to his Lord in prayer. If the door of his enclosure were open and he were to hear about this, he would write to the emperor and to the governor, for Mar Simeon is as merciful as his Lord.' Then they led him away and he went in disgrace through all the towns along the way. When he came to the royal city he suffered great disgrace as well. All his property was confiscated, and he was exiled. As he was on his way to exile, he died a cruel death. That curse that he asked for accompanied him to the day of this death.

61. Again, after the door of the saint's enclosure was opened, a great crowd came from the region of Aphshon. They informed his holiness about huge mice and rats who were biting live sheep and eating their insides so that they died. They even began[146] on oxen and beasts so that the animals there, either sheep or asses, would

---

[146] Lent suggests emending to *šwnw* = to leap instead of *šryw* = to begin, but B, V, and M all read *šryw*.

flee, and the rats, fifty or a hundred of them, would run after one [of them] until the animal was exhausted and fell. Then they would eat it. They used to grunt[147] like swine and not run away when men appeared. They even ventured up to small children and would run after them like dogs. When the saint heard this, he was astonished and marvelled, and groaned saying, 'Before loathsome vermin, if it is given power, no one can stand. Before the justice of the Lord who can bear to stand?' When they fervently besought him with tears and groans he said to them, 'Take some of this *ḥnana* in the name of our Lord Jesus Christ. Make three crosses in every house. On the four sides of the villages make crosses, and keep vigil and perform the eucharist there three days and pray to our Lord. I have hope in the God whom I serve that on that third day one will not be found even if it were sought.' They went and did as he had said. On that third day, no one knew what had happened to them but it was as if the earth had opened its mouth and swallowed them. The people returned, giving thanks and praising our Lord who had done this favor for them by the saint's prayer.

62. After this a great crowd came to the saint from Lebanon. They told him about evil animals who roamed over all the mountain of Lebanon ravaging and attacking and devouring men. Wailing and mourning were raised throughout the whole region, for there was not one village of the whole mountainous region in which two or three people were not being devoured every day at least.[148]

63. As they told it, sometimes [the creatures] looked like women with shorn hair, wandering and lamenting; sometimes like wild beasts. They would even enter into houses and seize people and snatch children from their nursing mothers' arms and eat them right in front of their eyes and [the mothers] could not lift a finger to help their little ones, so that there was mourning and lamentation. No one could go out into the open country alone but only in groups armed with swords and clubs. Even then the animals did not turn aside out of people's way except for a little distance—then

---

[147] The verb *n's* is given the meaning 'to grunt' by Brockelmann and Payne Smith, but have only this one case as an example. The meaning in Hebrew, 'to wedge in', might be more appropriate as the context seems to suggest what happens when the rats are eating.

[148] Assemani reads *n'wr*, but the text, as B, reads *z'wr*.

[the animals] would follow in their footsteps. When the saint heard these things from them he said, 'God has repaid you according to your deeds. For you forsook the one who in his benevolence made you and provides for you and nourishes you in his mercy, and you fled for help to dumb, useless idols who can neither help nor harm you. Because of this God handed you over to wicked beasts who wreaked vengeance on you as your deeds deserved. Go now and call on those idols whom you worship. Let them help you and rid you of this wrath sent upon you from God.' [The people from Lebanon] kept imploring him greatly and they entered and cast themselves down before his pillar with a loud cry. Besides them a great crowd of those who were present to pray also petitioned on their behalf. When the saint saw how they had cast themselves down and were crying out and how the crowd also was weeping and petitioning—for their story brought tears to the eyes, as their scourge was merciless, parents seeing their children devoured before their eyes, their limbs torn apart and their bodies dragged off, and they could not help them,—he answered them, 'If you leave the error which was committed by you, and you turn to God your Maker, and you make a covenant to become Christians and receive baptism, I also will petition the God whom I serve. You will see with your own eyes the mercies he will perform for you, and that he will put far away from you this rod of wrath that came upon you.' With heartfelt sorrow they all answered as if with one voice and said, 'If you pray for us and this rod of wrath passes from us, we will make a covenant in writing before your holiness that we will become Christians and receive baptism, that we will renounce idols, uproot their shrines and break their images. Only let this affliction pass from us.'

When the saint saw them promise to turn to God, he said to them, 'In the name of our Lord Jesus Christ take some of this *ḥnana*. Go and set up four stones on all the borders of the villages. If any priests are there, summon them, and make on the stone three crosses. Keep a vigil for three days, and you will see what God works there. For I have hope in my Lord Jesus Christ that from that day on they will not destroy the image of humans there.' This is indeed what God worked. For they went away and found that from the moment the blessed Mar Simeon prayed and said 'I have hope in God that they would not destroy the likeness of man', not one beast would enter the villages or be able to hurt or ravage people. They came and went in the open country but did not enter the villages or oppress anybody. They acted as if a heavenly command was upon them. After they had gone and done as the righteous one had said to them, a great sign and an amazing portent was performed. For from all that region came a great crowd without number—men, women, youths and children. They received baptism and became Christians, they turned to God from their worthless error as they had promised. Before all the people they related, 'We went and set up those stones and made crosses on them as your holiness commanded, and kept vigil for three days. After that we saw those animals going to and fro, marching around where the crosses had been made and howling so loud it carried over the mountain. Some of them fell down and burst open on the spot beside those stones, some went away howling. At night they sounded like women lamenting and crying out, "Alas for you, Simeon! what have you done to us?" ' The people brought with them the skins of three which had died there. They hung on the door of the enclosure for a long time. They told us they were ten days wailing and lamenting;[149] some died and the rest were sought and not one of them could be found in all that region.[150] Now their skins were not like those of leopards or bears, but the colors varied and were different from anything seen in these times. After the people of that region had received baptism and become Christians, had renounced idols and graven images and believed in our Lord Jesus Christ, they remained at the saint's enclosure about a week. Then they returned home rejoicing and giving thanks and praising God who had worked this double kindness among them. From that time on they did not cease to visit the saint frequently. Those who had not received baptism did so, as did their children. This was for their advantage and salvation.

64. Again in a little village near Gindaris there was a large spring which watered many fields. Suddenly it failed and dried up, and the trees withered and whatever had been sown among their irrigation

---

[149] I have followed M in this sentence. Literally, V reads: 'And as I/he said, they were thus in this wailing and lamenting'. Both B and V seem to have left something out. M's reading makes sense, and incorporates elements of both B and V. Assemani wrongly transcribed *'mry* for *'mr*.

[150] This sentence has been transposed with the next in B.

system died completely. They brought in workmen who dug and toiled and were of no help. At last they were forced to go and tell the saint. Now, at first they were ashamed to tell him because of what they had done. For the saint had commanded that on Sundays no one should work until evening. But they had violated the command, since one of them dared to go and water on a Sunday morning and, when they noticed it, they did not blame or fine him. Rather, as if what pleased him was their own idea, all of them scattered and left the church and each went to his own plot. They returned that evening and left the spring full and spouting. They arose early in the morning but they could not find in it even one drop of water. Whatever had been watered on Sunday was as if on fire. It faded and dried up. When they saw what had happened to them because of their rashness, they beat their faces with their hands. After they had toiled and tried every means and help from all sides,[151] finally they were forced to go and tell the saint. As soon as he heard their confused story, he perceived and said, 'Herein there seems to me to be a transgression of law'. When they saw their guilt uncovered, they told him what had really happened. When the blessed Mar Simeon learnt it all, he was very annoyed with them and abused them roundly. He cast them out from his presence with insults and blows. For he was burning like a fire with the zeal of his Lord. When they had left him, in grief they threw themselves down at the outside door of the enclosure and lay there prostrate for three days. They beseeched and implored whoever went in or out to ask the saint on their behalf. Their priest went and summoned other village priests and itinerant inspectors to try to persuade his holiness. When he learnt that they had really been at the door for three days, he had pity on them and ordered that they come before him. He said, 'I give you advice for your salvation. I do not want your gold and silver; what I want are your souls that I may present them before God with confidence.' When they had gained their senses and made a covenant in writing never again to act like this, he said to them, 'In the name of our Lord Jesus Christ, take three small pebbles, make on them crosses and throw them down in the middle of that spring where it gushes forth. Take *ḥnana* and

---

[151] B and M: 'and there was no help from any side'.

make on it crosses and throw it in the spring. Place three crosses on this and that side and keep a vigil in the church. At dawn go out early and see what our Lord does.' They went and did as he said. When they went out early in the morning they found all the fields inundated, the spring full and pouring forth three times as much as previously. Then they all came back together and praised God who had done this favor for them, and they departed in peace.

65. These, and greater and more amazing and many times more than these, our Lord performed through his saint. For what mouth can speak or relate the heroic deeds and signs that our divine Lord would do by his athlete not only nearby but even far-off, on the sea and among the Gentiles and the Persians who worship water and fire? I really think that the blessed Mar Simeon fulfilled what our Lord said in his life-giving Gospel, 'Those who believe in me and love me will also do the works which I do and greater works than those that I do they will do in my name.'[152] For it is written about blessed Mar Simeon Cephas that as he was passing by, his shadow fell upon the sick and they were healed;[153] about the apostle Paul that they used to take his belt or his turban and go and place them on those injured by the enemy and they would recover and on those sick with persistent and odious diseases and they would be healed of their affliction. So concerning the blessed Mar Simeon. He was very much in spirit their brother and their disciple; he rejoiced greatly in their labors and followed in their footsteps.[154] His soul eagerly awaited whenever he might hear of their heroic deeds. Yet his measure was exalted more than anyone. For he did not walk upon the ground so that his shadow would fall on anyone nor did he send any of his clothing anywhere to the sick, but only the word of prayer issued from his mouth and went to far-off regions and his Lord worked healing and relief.

66. Now we will speak a little from much about what I said that our Lord did by his hand and by his prayer and for his sake in far-off places, on the sea, and among the pagans. For they are numerous and who would venture to tell or narrate them? For

---

[152] Jn 14:12.

[153] Acts 5:15.

[154] M: 'he was their brother in spirit and their disciple in their labors. He taught like them and he followed in their footsteps.'

the treasure-trove of the faithful is a great ocean whose breadth is without limit and whose depth is bottomless. Just as someone who fills a bottle from the ocean or takes a spoonful from the Euphrates or lifts a grain from the sand does not decrease their amount nor lessen their number, so also whoever draws and takes and delights in the gift of the Spirit which the servants of God receive from their Lord gains, and they lose nothing.[155] So this tiny bit of the heroic acts of the faithful is written as a help to mankind and as the ear can receive. For those who follow in the steps of their master are like him also in their deeds. About the master the evangelist said in wondrous astonishment when he saw the merciful works and deeds which cannot be quantified or numbered, 'If each one which our Lord Jesus Christ did were written down, the world would not be sufficient for the books that would be written.'[156] As for the excellent man of God Mar Simeon, since you love to hear about his heroic acts and since the noble deeds that our Lord wrought by his athlete are even more delectable to you than honey is to those who eat it, we will narrate a little from much before your love[157] from the huge treasure-trove of the heroic acts of the saint, both what we saw with our eyes and touched with our hands[158] and what were worked far away and written by truthful men to the saint.

67. For Antiochus, son of Sabinus,[159] came to him when he was made prefect in Damascus and said to his holiness before everyone, 'Naaman came up to the desert near Damascus and made a feast to which he invited me. At that time there was no hostility between him and the Romans. While we were dining he brought up the affair of the saint and said to me, "This person whom you call Mar Simeon, is he a god?" I replied, "He is not a god, but a servant of God." So Naaman again said to me, "When reports of the saint reached us, some of our Arabs began to go up to him. Then the

---

[155]   M: 'for they are rich, and he loses nothing'. Lent refers this sentence to God, but the context in V and B demands that it refer to the reader who delights in the gifts of the Spirit to the servants of God.

[156]   Jn 21:25.

[157]   Lent translates 'dear Sir', but in 78.112.113 the phrase refers to the brethren. M simply has: 'to you (plural)'.

[158]   Cf. 1 Jn 1:1.

[159]   See Martindale, *Prosopography*, 104.

chiefs of our camp came and said to me, 'If you allow them to go up to him, they will become Christians and follow the Romans. They will defy you and desert you.' So I sent to summon and gather all the camp and said to them, 'If anyone dares to go up to Simeon, I will take off with the sword his head and the heads of all his family.' After I had given the command and dismissed them, at midnight as I was sleeping in the tent I saw a splendid man whose like I have never seen. There were five others with him. When I saw him my heart fell, my knees shook and I fell down and worshipped him. Angrily and severely he said to me, 'Who are you to prohibit the people of God?'[160] He commanded four of them and they stretched him[161] out by his hands and feet while one gave him a severe and cruel beating. There was no one to deliver him from his hands until he wished to have mercy on me and he ordered to release me. Then he unsheathed a sword which he was carrying and showed it to me and solemnly swore, 'If you again dare to prevent even one man from praying at the house of Mar Simeon, with this sword I will cut off your limbs and those of all your family.' So I rose up in the morning and gathered all the camp and said to them, 'Whoever wishes to go up to the house of Mar Simeon to pray and to become a Christian,[162] let him go without fear or fright."' He also said to me, "Were it not that I am a servant of the Persian king, I also would go up and become a Christian. For from that frightful beating it was more than a month before I could stand up and go outside. I ordered churches and bishops and priests to be in my camp, and I said, 'Whoever wants to become a Christian, let him do so without fear; and whoever wants to be a heathen, that is his own business."' Whoever heard him relating the story gave praise to God who so expanded the exploits of his worshippers everywhere.[163]

---

[160] B and M add: 'from the presence of God's servant'.

[161] Note the change of person here. Both B and M retain the first person singular.

[162] The term actually used here and later is 'Nazarene'. However, Sebastian Brock has shown that 'Nazarene' is a standard term for Christian in Persian martyr acts. Sebastian Brock, *Syriac Perspectives on Late Antiquity* (London: Variorum reprints, 1984) ch. 4, 91–95.

[163] The manuscript at this point is illegible. I have reconstructed it following M: *dkm' mwrb nshn' dsgwdwhy bkwl pnyn*. This is the same as B except for the

68. Again a Magus in the land of the Persians, head of all the Magi, that is to say, leader of all evil, came before him who is called King of Kings and asked that he be given power over the Christians, whom they called Nazarenes, to afflict and strike, to beat and imprison them as he wished to make them renounce their religion. Over those who stuck by their opinions and would not renounce their religion he would have the power to kill after cruel tortures and ill-treatment. When this wicked and unclean man received power over the flocks of Christ, he was like a brazen wolf without mercy. The devil's whelp[164] seized and bound and struck[165] and beat many people both men, women, priests and *bnay Qyāmā*,[166] not a few laymen with their wives and sons. He inflicted much harm on them and passed on them all kinds of sentences and tortures like a man who does not have the judgement of God before his eyes. The wicked man did not know that swiftly the sentence of the Lord's justice would come upon him. After he had tormented them as he wished with all tortures and punishments, he seized and bound about three hundred fifty people, men and women, monks and laymen, and had placed on them fetters and chains and shackles. He imprisoned them all together in a house without light. He placed guards so that no one could give them either bread to eat or water to drink so that they might die of hunger and thirst. After they had been so afflicted for about ten days and no one had mercy on them or relieved them, they prayed, 'O God, to whom all these hardships are easy, as it pleases your lordship, by the prayer of Mar Simeon your worshipper refresh the souls of those who take refuge in you. Let not these unclean persons say that the Christians have no God.' While they all together implored and made supplication, in the middle of the night our Lord wrought a great miracle on their behalf. The blessed one of God Mar Simeon appeared to them standing on the pillar. He came and stood in their midst. A great light was with him, and many blazing torches. He was clothed in

---

last word. Assemani's reconstruction would not fit the lines and should not be followed.

[164] Literally: the son of the left hand.

[165] The v text is illegible. I have followed B and M. Assemani read *sgy'* ' = 'seized many'.

[166] On this group in the Syriac church, see the Introduction, pp. 24–25.

white skins and his face was like lightning and he said to them, 'Peace be with you, my brothers.[167] I am Simeon, your brother, he who lives westward in the land of the Romans.' He descended and gave them the greeting of peace and said to them, 'Be strong and valiant. Do not let your mind be disheartened, or your spirit despair. For your trial is at an end, your crown is prepared and kept in heaven before your Lord. You will be here for two more days. On the third day you will be released and you will go out in honor and glory. The persecution of the people of God and of the church of Christ will cease and come to an end. As for your enemy, today a fearful judgement will overtake him and a merciless affliction strike him. As he was exalted so shall he be humbled, and all the East shall know of his affliction.' When he had spoken to them he was again standing beside the pillar the same way in which he entered, and he flew away and disappeared from view. Their affliction was so greatly relieved at the sight of the saint that they did not even think themselves in prison.

69. Meanwhile the hero went into that wicked man in frightening aspect. His face was angry as he stood on his pillar with torches blazing like lightning. When the wicked man saw him, his heart trembled, his knees shook, the vertebrae of his spine were loosened, his color changed to yellow and he looked as if dead. The saint spoke angrily and frighteningly, 'Unclean and abominable of all men, who do you think you are that you tried to oppose the name of our Lord Jesus Christ? You asked for power over his servants to afflict and scourge them so as to force them to deny their religion. Well, quickly the weighty justice of God will overtake you. Who can save you or deliver you from its hands?' As the saint spoke these angry words to him, suddenly something like an awesome bolt of lightning struck that wicked man and threw him on his face. A fierce fire burned on him, all his body caught fire, and the stench of his burning went a great distance. The saint said to him, 'Send back those documents which you received from the king, and deliver this message to him, "Thus says Simeon, he who stands on a pillar in the land of the West: unless you send and free all those servants of God who are imprisoned, and unless you stop

---

[167] Cf. Jn 20:19.

completely the persecution of the churches of Christ either giving
the order in person or by written documents, I will bring upon
you[168] after three more days an affliction and a sentence far crueler
than that of your servant." ' When he had said this to him, the saint
was taken away and removed to his proper place. But the wicked
man was prostrate, crying out loud and screaming because of the
bitterly cruel judgement which had gripped him. At the sound of
his screech a large crowd gathered, and when they saw him in that
merciless torment they trembled and feared and were terrified as
they asked him what had happened to him. He said to me, 'Simeon
the Christian who stands on a pillar among the Romans, he did
this to me because I afflicted the members of his religion. He also
said to me, "You worship fire, so I will burn you with fire. We will
see if it comes to help you." He also commanded me that I should
send back those documents about the Christians that I received
from the King of Kings, and that I should deliver a message to him
that he should order that all the Christians who are bound and in
prison be released. Thus he said to me, "Tell him that unless he
commands them to be freed and there is peace for the churches
of the Nazarenes within two days, I will bring a crueler and more
severe sentence than your own on him." ' When he who is called
the King of Kings received the letters and learnt from many people about the affliction and the bitter and cruel torment of that
wicked man, he immediately commanded all the Christians who
had been imprisoned to be set free. Also the churches which had
been closed were opened. A written decree was posted in villages
and towns that no one should say a harmful word to the Nazarenes
but they should perform their rites as formerly without worry or
fear. The bishops and priests who dwelt far away were unaware
of what had happened. When they saw him suddenly issuing this
decree, they were astonished and amazed. But when those blessed
ones who had been imprisoned went forth with great honor, the
bishops and priests learnt from them how the saint had appeared to
them and spoken with them, and how all that he had said to them

---

[168] There has been a transposition of pronouns in the text: the threat is
against the king, not against the Magus. That is how the king understands it,
and how I have translated. See later in the story when the king receives word
of the punishments of his courtier.

was proven true and had been realized. They also heard about the scourge and the cruel sentence passed on that unclean one, and they gave thanks and praised God. Assembling together, they put down everything just as it happened in writing and sent it to the saint by three priests from that region. It was read before everyone often, and they remained with the saint two weeks before returning home giving thanks and rejoicing and praising God. As for the wicked one, he remained in that affliction for about twenty days as if broiled by fire and consumed by worms. Then he died an odious and tormented death which frightened and terrified all who witnessed it. Because of this many turned to the fear of God, and became Christians and received baptism.

70. Now, on the sea the saint appeared publicly very many times to many sailors. He helped them in their afflictions in times of distress, when storms and tempests rose against them. They came and related before him how they had clearly seen him in time of peril. As soon as he appeared to them the storm had calmed. For the saint was much concerned about those who travel by sea.

71. Once a ship was travelling down from Arabia from the upper region carrying a great crowd of men and women going down to their homes in Syria. They had gone half the distance. All of a sudden a storm arose; the sea became rough and the waves rose up, the wind blew violently and darkness fell upon them. The ship was near to capsizing, for they were rising skyward and then plummeting to the abyss, as it is written.[169] They cried out, were distressed, and wept with tears and groans. There was no help or rescue from any quarter. Everyone covered himself and fell on his face so as not to see his own death. They were convinced that they would never see earth or dry land again, especially since they saw a black man like an Indian who came and stood on top of the mast in the middle of the ship. For it was said that whenever he was seen in a ship he sank it. So everyone had despaired of life and decided that he would die. They all lay down lamenting and covering their faces. Now there was a man there from Atma, a village near Ami.[170] He had on him a little of the saint's *ḥnana*. Our Lord determined to show a mighty deed through his worshipper

---

[169] Ps 107:2.3.6.
[170] B: Ames; M: Ames of Gazira. Assemani reads Amid, an error.

and rescue those anguished souls through his believer. The man remembered the *ḥnana* and he rose up and went and made a cross with it on the great mast in the middle of the ship. He rubbed handfuls of that *ḥnana* on all sides of the ship while everyone as they lay down cried out, 'Mar Simeon, ask your Lord, help us by your prayer'. Immediately the saint was seen holding a whip in his hand. He went and stood on the top sail and grabbed hold of that Indian by his hair. He strung him up and scourged him with that whip, and his wailing could be heard all over the sea. When the saint had whipped him severely, he let him go. He fled away crying out as if many were chasing him. As he fled he said, 'Woe to you, Simeon! Are you not satisfied to banish me from dry land? Must you also expel me from the sea? Where can I go?' From the time the saint appeared the waves quieted down and the storm ceased, the air was clear and the sea ceased from tossing. The saint said to them, 'Do not fear, for nothing bad will happen to you'. He was then lifted away from them. From then on gentle breezes blew, and they journeyed calmly without fear until, our Lord willing, they entered the harbour. Many of them went with the man from Atma to the saint's enclosure. They told him the whole story in the sight of everyone. Everyone who heard it gave thanks and praised God who had so graced them and helped them through the prayer of his believer.

72. Again, another large ship was standing in port in Cyprus, laden with much cargo and ready to sail to the West. There was a large crowd of passengers on board going up to trade. Suddenly a hurricane closed in on them, darkness fell, and violent winds blew. It attacked that ship like a whirlwind[171] and tossed it up from among the other ships. It went up twisting around out of sight like a stone hurled from an engine. Those in it were wailing, those outside were crying out and appealing for help. It was indeed a time for groans and tears. For either the ship would be sunk in the sea below and never be seen again or it would be smashed on the dry land and all the people on board would die. When they saw that it was all over for them and there was no help from anyone but God's mercy, they began to cry out and to pray, 'Mar Simeon, help

---

[171] A copyist's error in v should be emended from *qrḥrh'* to *qrḥ'*.

us with your prayer!' At that moment the saint suddenly appeared to them, standing alongside the ship. He heartened those on board. Stretching out his right hand he grasped the ship. Ever so calmly and gently he set it down and, towing it along, brought it to stand in the sea inside the harbour, a little like someone who grabs something light. No harm or injury was done to the ship or to anything in it. At the moment the ship touched down and stood in its place, the tossing waves ceased, and many saw the saint. Those who were on the ship told everyone how he had heartened them as he stood by them. Everyone who saw and heard these things narrated gave praise to God. The ship's captain, since he had seen this great miracle worked, led five of the sailors who had been on board to the saint and they told the story before everyone. The captain said, 'If your holiness orders me to sail on the sea, I will; otherwise I will not set sail but will go and sell the ship and no longer seek profit in sea-trade.' The saint said to him, 'Take some of this *ḥnana* in the name of our Lord Jesus Christ and go make three crosses on the ship and then set sail. I have confidence in our Lord that he will accompany you. You will depart tranquilly and return safely.' All who heard the story marvelled and were astonished and praised God who effects the desire of those who fear him.

73. Again, among the Persians there was a maiden who was the daughter of a Christian. She was very beautiful to see and fair of face. But more than her outer appearance, her inner mind was beautiful and comely, fair and acceptable before God. Then one of those fire-worshippers saw her—a snake called a Marzban. He lusted after her to marry her. Although young she was virtuous.[172] Although he had sent to her father many times, she did not even glance at those sent or give them answer. For she said, 'Let me not go to the bed of an unclean man, a fire and water worshipper.' When he saw that he could not persuade her,[173] he took her by

---

[172] B: a believing lay-person.

[173] M has here a longer text which V could have left out through haplography: 'When he saw that he could not persuade (*mttpys'*) her, he went and sought her by an edict of the king. When he again tried to persuade her and she did not wish to obey (*ttpys*), he took her by force with a great crowd as if at the king's command.' B has basically the same text, although the haplography is not so clear.

force with a great crowd as if at the King's command. But she stood by her former resolve and said, 'Even if I die, I will not go to bed with you for I am the handmaid of the Lord.' He beat her severely, and confined her and inflicted cruel tortures and harsh treatment. When he saw that she in no way changed her mind and he could not accomplish his desire—the more he tormented her, the more she despised him—he ordered his servants to put on the neck of Christ's handmaid a great stone with a hole in it and to throw her into the river where the Euphrates and the Tigris join. When they were taking her out to throw her in, she raised her eyes to heaven and said, 'God of Mar Simeon, you are righteous. Help your maid-servant. Note that I die for your name's sake, because I would have no part in the bed of that unclean and abominable one, for he denies your name and worships dead idols.' After they had lifted onto her the heavy weight and threw her into the river, at the very moment that she fell into it blessed Mar Simeon was there in the midst of the river. He stretched out his hand and grabbed her to stop her from drowning. He pulled her out of the river and placed her on dry land. He lifted that weight off her and said, 'Do not fear, my daughter. The God in whom you believe is your saviour. As for that infidel, the right hand of the Lord will smite him an incurable blow.' He led her to the boundary of her village, holding her right hand and encouraging her not to fear. When she arrived at the village, he said to her, 'Go in peace, my daughter, and the Lord be with you'. When she entered and her parents saw her, they were astounded, agitated, and amazed. For they had been sitting in mourning and in great sorrow over her. When they asked her how she had come there, she told everything exactly as it happened: how the blessed Mar Simeon drew her up and brought her out of the river and led her to the village boundary. She told them everything he said to her and also how he had suddenly been taken up from before her eyes when she reached the village boundary. As she was telling this to her parents, a large crowd gathered to look at her. Suddenly, the sound of violent lament reverberated from the house of that wicked man who had abducted her. For as he reclined and dined, surrounded by his servants, he was scheming how to harm the girl's parents. As he hatched those plots, a frightful judgement overtook him. For as he reclined he saw a frightening man enter with his sword unsheathed. As he saw him he became agitated and trembled. He leapt up to rise from his position, but that man struck him on his head with his sword. At that moment his whole right side shriveled from his head down to his toes. He cried out violently with raised voice and said, 'This has happened to me because I persecuted the handmaid of the God of the Christians. Woe to whoever fights or opposes him!' He never uttered another word. He was thus afflicted a long time—tormented, suffering and tortured, paralysed like a dry stick. Fear and terror struck those who saw him, and because of this many infidels trembled and feared and stopped persecuting or harassing the Christians. The father of that young girl took the trouble to go up with many people of his region to the saint's enclosure. He recounted everything before the saint in the presence of all the people. Everyone who heard this account gave praise to God. The father and his villagers stayed a week with the saint. They were blessed and returned in peace, rejoicing and giving thanks and praising God.

74. These and many more than these our Lord did by the hand of this athlete.[174] Many times, for example, rain was late in coming. The people would assemble and come and beseech him. He then would ask his Lord, who would do what he wanted and rain would fall. Wearied souls would be relieved and rejoice and praise God and go down happy from his enclosure.

75. Once there was a long drought—the whole winter passed by and it was nearly Lent and not a drop of rain had fallen. Everyone was crying out and making supplication. Beth Gubbe[175] was parched with thirst, and also the enclosure of the saint.[176] Every day priests came, covered with sackcloth and sprinkling their heads with ashes, and they were accompanied by their flocks weeping and groaning. As the drought continued, every day the whole creation was prostrating in the saint's enclosure. There was no relief in sight. Winter was almost over, Lent almost at hand, and soon the blessed Mar [Simeon] would close the door of his enclosure. Now a certain procurator happened to be there. He was frequently

---

174 Assemani reads 'Simeon'.
175 From the name of the town, Place of Wells, the extent of the drought is evident.
176 Both B and M connect this last phrase to the following sentence: 'Also to the saint's enclosure every day priests were coming. . . .'

at the enclosure and he was also friendly with the saint's disciples and could speak openly with them. As they stood and talked he said to them boldly,[177] 'Elijah prayed and his Lord did as he wished and there was rain; Samuel too prayed at the harvest and our Lord answered him and rain fell at the harvest. Perhaps today there is no one for whom his Lord does as he wishes as he did for those earlier men. For see how long the whole creation is exhausted and there is no help from any side.' When prayer was completed and everyone went to his work, the saint's disciples drew near and said to him, 'Kyriakos the procurator spoke to us in this way'. The saint was greatly astonished when he heard this from his disciples and said to them, 'On oath I tell you truly: I have not prayed before my Lord for rain to fall on earth because I saw their rebellious deeds. But since the evil one has planted this in their minds, send men everywhere and summon the priests and their flocks from all over the place to come here on Friday.' The disciples of the saint approached him and entreated him, 'Look! Every day crowds fill the enclosure. Be careful lest someone be scandalized and say, "Look how he is sending to gather the world to show off." Whether your holiness knows that something will happen or not, leave them alone to their own devices. They come and go every day of their own accord.' Then the saint said to his disciples, 'You just go ahead and gather them. Whatever our Lord does is not for you to worry about. You just carry out whatever is commanded to you. Our Lord knows what to do for the glory of his name.' So they sent and summoned them for Friday. An innumerable crowd collected; the mountains were covered and the land filled with men and women. The enclosure was filled inside and out from one end to the other. They brought in small boys who were learning the alphabet and placed them before him as their teachers sang antiphonally in Greek, 'Kyrie eleison'. When the saint saw all this—the priests with their heads covered in dust standing in sorrow and distress, men and women within and without raising their voices on high, those children like innocent lambs, the sun as hot as in summer—he was deeply distressed and his merciful heart opened. After he had prayed and made supplication before his Lord

---

[177] B reads: 'jokingly'.

for a long time, he raised his eyes to heaven and groaned. He beat his breast three times inside his cloak, he clasped his hands behind him and placed his face on his knees. He remained bowed a long time. All the people were praying that our Lord might do the will of his worshipper. While he was bowed in prayer and everyone in sorrow and tears was looking to see what our Lord would do, all of a sudden a misty white cloud appeared. Deep thunder growled behind it and echoed everywhere and the sky was filled with it. The wind blew violently and rain began to fall heavily and it got very cold. All the crowd who a little before were running to shade away from the burning heat now tried to find shelter from the wind and cold, fierce rain. The saint as he bowed heard the sound of water flowing into the wells and the sound of people praising God for what they saw. He straightened himself up from his prayerful bow, and his face was like rays of the sun. His mind rejoiced because our Lord had done what he wanted. When he spied the people huddling together under shelter from the cold and the rain, he called out to them and said, 'A little while ago you wanted the rain, and now you are running away from it'. He buoyed them up by saying, 'Look at the rain which the Lord in whom I trust gave you. If you walk in your religion, fearing God and keeping his law and his commandments, the Lord will bless this year whose crop you thought was lost now that winter has passed. He will double your harvest, and your bellies will be full and you will praise the Lord God.' So he dismissed them, happy and giving God thanks. It rained again and there were frequent showers and, as the saint had said, the year was blessed. The granaries were filled to double their normal rate.[178] They ate and were satisfied and gave thanks to God their provider.

76. After everyone had been dismissed in peace and evening came, the saint remained alone with the two disciples who served him (for the enclosure had not yet been pulled down[179]). They

---

[178] M has a longer text: 'they ate (*'klw*) and were filled and they gathered in large crops and filled their houses with the fruits of the earth and they ate (*'klw*) and gave thanks to God their preserver.' M seems here a conflation of B and V.

[179] Unfortunately this phrase is not in B. The same difference in verbs occurs here as at ¶44 fn.103: M reads *'t'bdt* = was made, whereas V reads *'t'qrt* = was uprooted, pulled down. The difference in the Syriac script between the

both drew near and threw themselves down before the saint. They implored and besought him to reveal and make known to them how he had interceded or what he had said in his prayer as he prayed and supplicated and besought his Lord. The saint, however, hesitated and made excuses rather than reveal or tell either anything he said or anything that he saw and heard. But they increased their entreaties and kept asking him diligently and imploringly. So he demanded of them that they tell no one during his life-time. When they had pledged this, he revealed it to them saying, 'When I saw the priests distressed and covering their heads with ashes and all the people crying out and the children calling for help, I was saddened and wearied unto death and I said in prayer to my Lord, "Lord God, gracious and compassionate, either work mercy and relief to those distressed souls who cry out to you and are gathered together because of your name, or take the life of your servant and so I will not witness the distress of your people." Then I bowed down and my tears fell. And I saw a handsome youth who came passing in front of me, and he said to me, "Behold, your prayer is heard, your petition accepted. What you wish will happen, what you request be granted." The moment he spoke to me and passed on, I heard the rumbling sound of thunder and the sound of the blowing wind and the falling rain. I gave thanks and praised God who had not turned down his servant's request.'

77. Those kings[180] and the nobles under their authority joyfully received the saint's written answers. They immediately did all that he wished them to do. They praised God for the excellent and fine reports of Simeon that they heard. What our Lord said in his gospel was fulfilled in the saint: 'Blessed is that servant on whose account the name of his Lord is praised'.[181] For by his diligence and industry he profited himself and many others, and the name of God was praised on his account and because of him from the rising of the sun to its setting.[182] Thousands, countless, limitless

---

two verbs is very small, but I have decided to follow v in both cases. It suggests that originally a small enclosure or cell was built on the mountain, ¶28, which later was torn down before a larger one was constructed.

180 This is located at a different place in B. See Appendix A. M does not contain a reference to letters received by kings.

181 The reference is unknown.

182 This sentence is not found in V, as it has fallen out through haplography of *mtlth*. It is found in both B and M.

multitudes, who were not aware that there is a God were converted because of the saint; they came to know God their Creator and worshipped him and sang his praises. For how many unclean persons were sanctified, how many debauched became chaste at sight of him. How many who were not convinced about our Lord's religion came from many regions to hear him. When they saw his wondrous stance[183] and his struggle and continual toil, they truly despised and left this passing world with all that is in it and became disciples of the word of truth and vessels of honor. Again how many prostitutes came there. They saw the saint from afar off, and then abandoned and left their districts and the towns in which they lived; they delivered themselves over to Christ and went to dwell in convents. They became vessels of honor and by their tears appeased their Lord and he blotted out their debts. How many distant Arabs, who did not know what bread is but ate animal flesh, when they came and saw the saint were instructed and became Christians, they renounced the idols of their ancestors and worshipped God. How many barbarians, Armenians, Urtaye and infidels of every language came streaming in. Every day crowds received baptism and acknowledged the living God. There was no limit to the Arabs, their kings and chiefs as to how many received baptism there, believed in God and confessed Christ. At the word of the saint they even built churches among their tents. How many oppressed were delivered from their oppressors at his word. How many bonds were torn up through the efforts of the saint. How many afflicted were relieved from their coercers. How many slaves were freed and their documents torn up before the saint. How many orphans and widows, by our Lord's design, were brought up and nourished through the saint's stance only his Lord knows. He used to extol diligently God's priests, and the rules and laws of the church according to our Lord were strengthened with diligence. He gave orders that the usury that might be collected on everything be halved.[184] Everyone accepted his order joyfully so that many remitted all of it and did not exact usury after the saint's order.

---

[183] B: 'his wondrous person'; M: 'his wondrous person and marvelous stance'.

[184] The grammar here is difficult. V: 'upon usury that half might be collected upon everything'. M: 'upon usury that half might be collected upon everything that was collected'. See the letter of Cosmas at the end of the Syriac life.

78. It is beyond the capability of mortals to talk about the healings our Lord worked by his hands, or of how much deliverance and aid came to men through his prayer, or of how many wearied lives, afflicted and suffering from different kinds of scourges effected by the slanderer, God was pleased to relieve and to free from slavery to the adversary through the blessed Mar Simeon. How many thousands and tens of thousands there were for whom our Lord worked healing and relief and they left the presence of the saint rejoicing and praising God. What our Lord said was fulfilled about the saint: 'Those who believe in me will do more works than those that I do'.[185] What mouth would dare to say that it could number or count the healings which occurred at the saint's monastery during one year, let alone for the span of fifty years. For how many lepers were cleansed there, how many blind came led along and our Lord granted them to see the light and they walked away giving thanks to God. How many hunchbacks were straightened as a result of his prayers. Numberless paralytics came there carried like baggage, some of them on couches, who could not even turn around. Our Lord gave them healing and relief by his prayer, and they left him healthy and active, joyfully carrying their beds and praising God who had been so exceedingly gracious to them. But because your mind longs to hear the glorious deeds of the saints, and your hearing desires to learn both what God did through his servants and how he magnifies and honors those who love him, we will narrate, as far as our intelligence is capable, a little from much. For who, except God their creator, can measure the great abyss or number the grains of sand on the sea-shore? So also no one knows the treasure-trove of the faithful and the glorious deeds of the blessed, except God their bestower.

79. Now there came a rich man from Sheba who had a grievous and cruel affliction. For a severe disease had attacked his brain for many years. He had paid a great deal in doctors' expenses, but no one helped him at all. The more often he went [to the doctors], the stronger the affliction became. He had pegs driven into the wall and he would sit between them, knocking and thwacking his head against this side and that. When he learned about the saint

---

[185] A shortened version of Jn 14:12.

from merchants travelling to that region, he gave up and left all that he possessed just so he might find relief. He took with him five servants and five concubines[186] and set out for the saint. The God who saw his faith worked a great miracle for him. For they did not know the way and it was harsh desert country. But he said it was as if someone was guiding their camels, for they did not lose their way nor were they even troubled or confused. No one from the Arab robbers harmed them, no wild beast annoyed them even though there were plenty of lions in that whole area. After he started out, the pain eased day by day. What was more marvelous than all this, so they said, was that their provisions did not diminish at all. They remained as they were when they started out, although they were living off them for a full year until they reached the saint's enclosure. When he entered, he cast himself down before the saint and told him the whole business just as it had happened and how many pains and afflictions he had endured now so many years. The saint ordered water to be brought. He prayed and blessed it. He ordered him in the name of Christ, and the man drank and even poured some over his head. The moment the water touched him his affliction fled and he never noticed it again. All his body was light and free from pain. He confessed and praised God, he received baptism and became a Christian. Finally he died with a great confession.[187]

80. Then from the Persian territory there came a chorepiscopus, sent by one of the Persian rulers. For this ruler had an only son whom Satan had smitten. He was paralysed and had been lying in bed fifteen years. Unless someone turned him to one side, he could not move. The ruler had spent a great deal of money on Magi and sorcerers, but they did not help at all. When he learned about the saint, he persuaded the chorepiscopus and sent him to ask the saint to pray for his son. He sent by his hand two precious silken shawls—on them were golden crosses and golden bells all around the edges. When he had arrived and informed the saint about the

---

[186] Both B and M read *rkwbn* = mounts, horses. This appears to be a toning down of V.

[187] I have restored the text following B and M: *wlḥrt' twb npq mn 'lm' hn' bshdwt' rbt'*. V has left out this clause through haplography. The scribe, however, has marked in the text that the previous narrative ended here.

boy's affliction and had shown him those shawls, the saint said to him, 'Take these with you, in the name of our Lord Christ, all tied up, and go in peace. When you reach the city boundary, dismount from your ass and take them in your arms. Do not speak to anyone, but carefully enter and place them on the boy's chest and say to him, "Simeon the sinner says, 'In the name of our Lord Jesus Christ, rise up!' " ' He went and did as ordered. The moment he placed them on his heart and said what he had been told to say, the affliction fled. He jumped up, healed and without pain. He gave thanks and praised God, and he, his mother, and his sister became Christians and received baptism. After a short while he came and was blessed by the saint as he affirmed in the presence of all the favor our Lord had done for him.

81. Again, a governor from Armenia came to the saint. He was the son of the ruler of all Armenia who was highly esteemed by the emperors (the emperors had even allowed him sometimes to wear purple garments). The boy unexpectedly was apoplectic: his entire right side shrivelled, his mouth was twisted and his eye was fixed, dull. He lay for many years on a couch in great affliction. He could not turn over on either side, nor could he eat anything except what could be poured in a spoon, and that in great distress. When news of the saint reached them, they placed him on a litter and carried him along. There accompanied him many armed cavalry, a huge crowd[188] and much baggage. Three priests and five deacons also came with a letter from the bishop of that whole region urging the saint to pray for the youth. For he was much loved as he was a compassionate youth, and his father was a believer and one who honored the Christians. When they had brought him in and laid him before the saint and the bishop's letters were read to him, he groaned and lifted up his eyes to heaven, and ordered all the people to pray for him. When they had finished the prayer, he ordered them to bring water. He blessed it, and at his word they poured some over him and he cried out, 'In the name of our Lord Jesus, be healed, sit up.' At that moment he turned around and sat up. He was conscious and he even understood where he was. The saint said to him, 'In the name of our Lord, take some of the water in

---

[188] B and M: 'servants'.

your hands and wash[189] yourself with it. Pour it over your face and your whole body.' He carefully took it and drank it and poured it all over his body. Then the saint said, 'In the name of our Lord Jesus Christ, stand up.' He jumped up healed. He ran about all the enclosure rejoicing and praising God. This was a man who had not been able even to turn around in bed. He was there about a week standing in prayer. He freed thirty slaves. He went to Antioch, he came and prayed and was blessed. He returned to his region in peace, giving thanks and praising God.

82. Again some Easteners came from a land so distant that they took thirteen months to reach the enclosure, as they told the saint. Four were full of leprosy and three seized by evil spirits. When they entered they threw themselves down before him and told him of their afflictions and the remoteness of the region. They even opened their pouches and declared before all the people, 'These are the provisions we took from our homes. We were not provisioned at any other spot, yet the provisions are the same as what we set out with. We have been travelling thirteen months and we never got lost.' When the saint heard what they said, he replied, 'The God who directed your way will restore that for which you have worn yourselves out.' He ordered them to bring water, he blessed it and said, 'Take this in the name of our Lord Jesus Christ in hope of whom you came. All of you drink from it, and also pour it over all your body.' The moment they did as ordered, their afflictions fled and they were cleansed and healed from their injuries. They gave thanks and praised God, they renounced their superstition, received baptism, and became Christians. They left rejoicing and giving thanks to our Lord.

83. Again, in the days of Dionysius the commander[190] there came a youth from inner Anazit on the border of Armenia and Persia. He had a grievous and obstinate affliction. The disease had seized him suddenly in the head. His face was swollen up, his eyesight taken away and his whole body became weak and feeble. Mucus which had an extremely offensive smell was coming from his nose and eyes. When his father heard reports of the saint, he

---

[189] B and M: 'drink some of it'.
[190] Dionysius 13 in Martindale, *Prosopography*, 365–366.

sent his son to Dionysius the commander, and wrote him to ask the saint on his account. He also sent many gifts to Simeon through him. Dionysius sent along with him Dalmatius,[191] his sister's son. When they had arrived and entered, they laid him down before the saint and told him where he came from and how cruel his affliction was. He ordered them to loosen the bandages with which his face and head were wrapped, and cried out, 'Rise up in the name of our Lord Jesus Christ'. At that moment he jumped up, and the saint said to him, 'Go in the name of Christ, and take some of that water in your hands. Pour it on your face and over all your body.' The instant the water touched him in the name of our Lord, his affliction fled and he was healed. He was fully restored and could walk around. He stayed three days in prayer and then returned to his region, healed and praising God. On hearing the news, Dionysius also wondered greatly, was amazed and gave thanks to God.[192]

84. No small favor was also worked by God, by means of the saint, towards Dionysius himself. When he was in Antioch, Dionysius received instructions from the Emperors to go on an embassy to the Persians. Suddenly Satan smote him on his face; his mouth was distorted and his whole face after it. Doctors came and applied medicinal herbs and ointments to him but they did no good at all. He was brought to the saint in distress and said to him, 'I received instructions from the Emperor to go to the Persians but look what happened to me all of a sudden. I beseech you, pray for me.' He ordered water to be brought; he prayed and blessed it and said to him, 'In the name of our Lord, take this in your hands and pour it over your face and head.' When he had washed as ordered, his face and mouth were restored as though no damage had ever in his life affected him. He rejoiced and gave thanks and praised God. Then the saint again spoke to him, 'Go and the Lord will grant you success on your journey and you will accomplish all you desire. You will go in peace, and return in peace.' And the Lord prospered his journey. He negotiated[193] brilliantly and accomplished all that he wanted. He returned in honor and great pomp. And coming [back], he bowed down to the saint and was blessed by him. As long

---

191   Dalmatius 2 in Martindale, *Prosopography,* 341.
192   B:'was edified in the faith'. M:'was edified and profited'.
193   Both B and M have the Ethpael form of *qbl* = was received.

as he lived he gladly received anything that the saint commanded him on behalf of the poor or about any matter. He would bow down and do his command.

85. Again, a priest from the region of Samosata came a great distance[194] to him. He told him about a spring in his village which irrigated all their fields and from which by the Lord's design their lives were sustained. All of a sudden it failed and dried up, and they were exhausted from thirst and hunger. They had brought workmen. They had dug and labored and spent a good deal of money and they did not find one drop of water in it. When the priest came and told the whole matter just as it was, the saint said, 'I trust in our Lord Jesus that when you start to leave this enclosure our Lord will make it return to normal. But go, keep vigil and celebrate the Eucharist and give thanks to our Lord.' The priest noted the time the saint spoke to him and our Lord did a favor. The priest went and found that the spring had gushed forth and overflowed and irrigated all the fields of the village. When he asked the villagers they told him that on such and such a day it suddenly gave a violent sound and gushed forth and watered all the fields of the village double what it used to. He took out the note he had written and saw that the spring had gushed forth into its canal at the very moment the saint blessed him. Then the priest led all his congregation and they came and ministered before the saint for three days. Then they returned rejoicing and praising God.

86. Again, another priest from Dalok. There was a mountain about two miles away from their village. It kept crawling nearer little by little until it had reached the village limits. From beneath it was heard the sound of many waters like the abyss. From fear all the inhabitants had deserted and fled the village. For that a mountain should creep and come to bury[195] them was cause for terror and wonder. When they saw that evil was aimed at them and there was no help for them from any quarter, the priest rose up and led all the village from the greatest to the least to the saint. When they had all entered and cast themselves down before him and told him the whole affair he said to them, 'In the name of our Lord

---

[194] B and M: 'about seven days' journey'.
[195] Assemani wrongly reads *dḥnp'* instead of *dnḥp'*.

Jesus Christ, take three stones and make three crosses on them. Then go and fix them on it: one on its top, one at the bottom, and one in the middle. Keep vigil there three days and celebrate the Eucharist. I trust in my Lord that it will not again come any closer.' Our Lord wrought a great sign. They went and did as ordered and, on the third day, all of a sudden the sound of a violent crash like thunder was heard under that mountain, and it sank down. From underneath it rose up a great deal of water which watered the whole area. By our Lord's will all that water was swallowed up after three days, causing no damage. The mountain was levelled to the earth and was like a plain. That year they planted small peas on it and harvested two hundred cors.[196] They loaded up and brought some of them on camels and many beasts of burden. They shared them out among the monasteries and the poor, as they affirmed before everyone the favor done among them.

87. Again, another priest from the region of Mar'ash. He had to go to the neighboring village. While astride his ass journeying on the mountain with two brothers,[197] he saw eleven goats, the kind called mountain-goats. They were going to pass by him, when from a distance he cried out for a test[198] and said to them, 'By the prayer of Mar Simeon, be held in check. Do not pass by till I come'. All of them gathered together and stood still until he came to them. He got down from his ass and took two or three of them and put his hand on their back and stroked them. They stood still by him as if previously accustomed to it. He was amazed and astounded. After a little while he said to them, 'By the prayer of that saint, pass by and go on your way'. And they left him. But he was terrified and distressed over what he had done. Something seized him in his heart and was suffocating him. He did not re-enter his village, but turned towards the saint, for he looked like death. He entered and fell down before him and said with tears in front of everyone just what had happened. When the saint heard, he said, 'See how

---

[196] In place of this last clause and the rest of the story, M reads: 'they brought some of them and showed them to blessed Mar Simeon while they rejoiced and praised God for the marvel performed.' The cor has been estimated to be five to six bushels, the load a donkey could bear.

[197] I.e., monks.

[198] Assemani reads *m'q* = as distressed, but the text clearly reads *mns*. B and M read *mns'*.

beasts obey the word of God and men resist his will!' To the priest he said, 'Take some of this water and pour it over your face and your heart in the name of Christ. Then go and fast for three days and offer the Eucharist to God. Do not tempt the Lord's spirit lest the Lord's anger come upon you.' And he went away healed from his affliction.

88. Again, at another time a fierce lion was seen on Mount Ukkama (Black Mountain). A lion had never been seen there before. It devoured and cruelly ravaged people. It ate and mangled an innumerable crowd. Travel was disrupted, for no one dared for fear to pass beyond the door of his house, either to go to work or to travel. In one day it could appear in many places. News of it reached the cities, the prefects also heard about it and sent hunters and soldiers and Isaurians[199] armed with spears and swords. But no one did him any harm at all. He was not scared by a crowd, but many people trembled and were afraid when he roared. After he had so ravaged for a long time, a great crowd from the north gathered and came and told the saint, 'He enters sheepfolds and houses;[200] he leaves the wild animals alone and eats people.' When the saint learnt how he had ravaged and how many people he had destroyed he said, 'I trust my Lord Jesus Christ that he will never again destroy the form of man. In the name of Christ take some of this *ḥnana* and oil. Wherever you see him—whether he is lying down or standing up—make crosses on all sides. Behold, the angel of the Lord will smite and paralyse him.' Then our divine Lord worked this favor for him publicly. For as they went along they spotted him crouching before them on the road. When he saw them, he leapt up in his usual manner and they on seeing it trembled and were afraid. He was about to attack them when he trembled, shuddered, and fell. They recognized that his wound was from the Lord and one of them drew his spear, went up close and struck him in the heart and killed him. They skinned him and

---

[199] Assemani left this word out; it is also found in M. Isaurians were highlanders of Asia Minor who frequently raided their settled neighbors. For their incursions in the Later Roman Empire, see A.H.M. Jones, *The Later Roman Empire* 1:25, 116, 192.

[200] B reads *bqr'* = herds, instead of *bt'* = houses, but this misses the contrast in the next sentence. M reads *bbny'* = in buildings.

brought the skin to the enclosure. While there they all gave thanks exceedingly and praised our Lord, for the devastation had been evil and cruel.

89. In those days[201] there came to him a man from Aleppo. He brought with him his son, bound in chains because an evil spirit possessed him. He would throw stones at his father,[202] and his reason had left him completely. He wore no clothes, and would chew his tongue and bite his shoulders. When his father entered he threw himself down before the saint (because the saint was standing on the ground[203]) and he wept with sighs and bitter tears. The saint answered the father saying, 'Do not weep, but take these chains off him'. When he had unchained him, the saint called the youth. At once the boy joyfully responded, and the saint said to him, 'In the name of our Lord Jesus Christ, take some of the dust in front of you and rub it over all your body'. The boy took it in his hands and rubbed it over all his body. The saint ordered water to be brought, and blessed it. The boy took it, drank some of it and poured it over his face. At that moment his reason returned and he recognized his father. He ran and kissed the saint's garments and was blessed by him. He stayed there that night. In the morning he went away with his father, healed and giving thanks and praising God who had cured him through the saint.

90. After this a deacon who lived about three miles from the enclosure went out to the harvest accompanied by a young boy. While the deacon was reaping and the child playing, a fierce black snake came out and coiled itself around the boy's feet. It began to squeeze his feet and the boy began to cry out and lament bitterly. When the deacon saw the snake he said, 'By the prayer of Mar Simeon who stands at Telneshe, do not harm him'. The snake left him at once and wound itself up like a ball of thread and did him no harm. It was like this for three days, and all the village went to see it. They came and told the saint and he said to the deacon, 'Go and say to it, "In the name of our Lord Jesus Christ, go away and do not hurt anyone."' After that the snake uncoiled and went away.

---

201 B and M place this story elsewhere. See Appendix A.

202 B reads 'parents'. M has been corrected from 'father' to 'parents'.

203 In M, this clause is not placed here but later in the story when the healed youth kisses the saint's garments.

91. Again, a youth came to him from the low-lying country. He had a stone in his bladder and was greatly afflicted and tormented. His father spent a great deal on doctors but no one helped him. When he came to the righteous one, he looked at him and ordered water to be brought and said to the father, 'Pour some of this dust into the water in the name of our Lord Jesus Christ, and give it to him to drink.' The moment he drank that water he found relief. A round bead like a stone came out of his bowels and all at once his limbs were restored and he went away praising and rejoicing in God.

92. Now the priest of Telneshe greatly loved the saint and was always with him. It was in his field that the saint stood and whatever he wore—he was clothed in skins[204]—he bought at his own expense. One day the priest and all his congregation came to the saint on business.[205] One of the deacons, who was the church steward, said jokingly to the saint, 'Untie that purse you have and make a gift to my master's household.' But the saint said to him, 'Did someone tell you I have money, or have you yourself noticed this?' At once his innards changed and were loose as water and he destroyed his garments and became a laughing-stock.[206] They carried him down and he was two days in great affliction, tormented and gnashing his teeth. Then he died.

93. After this, the saint decided to shut himself up for three years. He would see no one and no one would see him. He made a chain twenty[207] cubits long. He placed it on his foot and fastened it in a rock. Now the holy friend of God Mar Bas happened to drop by with the priest of the village and the elders and they forcefully persuaded him to halve those three years. Mar Bas prevailed upon him and left for him a peck and a half of dry pulse[208]—a peck per year—and a large vessel of water which held three half-pints. After the saint closed the door and was alone, the enemy suddenly appeared to him. He fought mightily with the saint and began from then on to fight with him outwardly. For he came against him in the form of soldiers mounted on horses with swords unsheathed

---

204 This information is not in B. M does not have these first two sentences.
205 M has, instead of this last phrase, 'to greet him and be blessed by him'.
206 The last clause is not in B; the last two clauses are not in M.
207 M:ten cubits.
208 M:lentils.

and bows drawn. They let loose their uproar[209] as they rushed towards the saint. But the saint did not cease from the service of his lord. Again they came up and stood on the enclosure wall. They would roll stones down on him to make him move from where he was. One day there appeared the shape of a camel, lustful, foaming at the mouth and out for mischief. As it came, it was turning its head onto its back. When it reached the saint, someone in the likeness of an old man stood in front of the saint and took some dust and threw it in the mouth of the camel. At once it was sought but could not be found, it vanished like smoke before fire.[210] The old man said to him, 'Do not fear, but be strong and valiant.'

94. Again, Satan often came with his host carrying lighted torches and appearing like flashes of fire going skyward. Again they would come and stand over him, crying out and shrieking for a long time to make the saint stop his service. But he did not fear nor was he scared by their outburst but busied himself in the service of his Lord. Sometimes they appeared as if smashing rocky stones, sometimes they sounded like thunder or like weeping, sometimes like men fighting each other with swords and spears. There were some who pronounced their own doom, saying 'You have slain me'.

95. Again, Satan appeared to him in the form of a lion who came from the door with its mouth open like a blazing fire. It roared and lifted up its voice, it pawed with its feet and sent gravel up to the sky, then rushed violently at him. As it kept up its usual senseless rage, and the saint was not distracted from his service, it also like its fellows was sought and not found.

96. Then, as the saint stood praying at midday, there appeared to him that unclean doer of evil deeds and that lover of hateful things like a beautiful woman clothed in golden garments and adorned with precious ornaments. She was merry and frolicsome as she came towards him. When the saint saw her he crossed himself and turned and breathed on her in the name of our Lord Jesus Christ. All at once she looked like an old Indian[211] whose hands and feet were mutilated, writhing and going away and howling as if many

---

[209]   Assemani reads *g'ryhwn* = their arrows, but the text clearly reads *rgšyhwn*.

[210]   B: wind. The image is not in M.

[211]   B and M: an animal.

were chasing and beating her until she reached a corner of the enclosure and she disappeared and vanished like smoke.

97. For five months the saint was cloistered and the enemy attacked him in all disguises and appeared to him in all sorts of ways and yet the saint never stopped serving his lord or neglected his heavenly exercises. After this, Satan went and collected snakes and scorpions and rats and mice and all loathsome creeping and crawling things. He brought them and filled that urn of water with them until he made it foul, and the stench reached outside the enclosure. When the saint noticed that the place stank, he was troubled by the reeking smell and filled it up with earth and stones. Many days passed, and the heat was fierce in the month of Tammuz. There was not a drop of water for him and the day the door would be opened was still thirteen months away. He knelt[212] before the Lord and stretched out his hands to heaven in prayer and said, 'Mighty Lord, owner of heaven and earth, care for your servant as your divinity knows'. He continued praying to God a long time. When he finished his prayer, he turned to his right and saw a small round urn[213] full of water—limpid, chilled, and sweet. When he saw it he thought to himself that it was an illusion, so he came and prayed by it for a good while. When it did not budge, he knew that God had done this for him and he used it up to the day the enclosure was opened.[214]

98. For our Lord—may he be worshipped—did not desert his athlete in this contest, but swiftly sent encouragement and comfort. For after that commotion and uproar and strife from the evil one, a handsome man clothed in a white robe appeared to him. He came and stood before the Eucharist niche[215] and joined his hands

---

[212] B reads: 'Since he was very thirsty, he dug in the ground where he was standing. He knelt *and put his mouth in it, breathing* in the coolness of the clay.'

M reads: 'Since he was very thirsty, he dug in the ground where he was standing. He knelt in the coolness of the clay.'

The italics indicates the difference between B and M.

[213] B and M use the term *pṣyd'* = a brook, a lake, a tank. In the context of M, which says that it was filled with water up to the rim, the meaning 'tank' is to be preferred to 'brook', which Lent chose. Even this is rather incongruous.

[214] B adds here Appendix B.3. M immediately begins with the arrival of Mar Bas, ¶101.

[215] A niche in the wall where a vessel containing consecrated Eucharistic hosts were kept.

behind his back. He bowed down and straightened himself up many times. After he had finished his prayer, he went to the eastern wall and stretched out his hands to heaven and prayed a good long time. Thus it was from him that the saint learnt the way he used to bow and straighten up. For he knew and perceived that this was how he was to attend to our Lord.

99. Again, after this handsome youth clothed in white appeared to him. They carried blazing wax-candles and golden crosses, and stood on the enclosure just above and in front of the Eucharist niche as they sang praises, saying, 'Blessed be the Lord who has chosen for himself the elect in a fortified city.'[216] The sound of the service, of the hallelujah and canticles, was heard frequently, and the youths were bearing crosses and standing on the wall. Even many villagers who used to remain during the night in the fields and rise early to go to work heard the sounds and saw the sights.

100. No one had begun to lodge there yet so Satan even provoked three robbers to come against him. They came down the wall in the middle of the night. One of them drew his sword and threatened him with violence while the other two raised their iron-bound spears against him. As the first ran on violently, our Lord suddenly struck him on his face and darkened his eyes. He swayed like a reed and became paralysed, his sword fell from his hand, his mouth was stopped up, and he stood in position and could not move to one side or the other. His companions also, dumbfounded at what had happened, remained with their spears raised and their mouths closed. From dawn on they were standing all day in great affliction, bowed down before him. As evening drew near the saint spoke with them and said, 'Where do you come from and what do you want?' Two of them in great pain said to him, 'We are robbers, and we came to kill you.' One could not open his mouth but remained with his mouth closed. Then the saint cried out three times and they could pull their feet off the ground. He said to them, 'Go away, but do not ever harm anyone again lest you suffer a worse evil than this.'

101. After the days of his confinement were complete and the year and a half was up, the blessed Mar Bas came and a large

---

[216] Ps 31:21.

crowd gathered. [Mar Simeon] opened the door and received the Eucharist.[217] On that day God worked his favor and performed a marvelous sign. He opened that urn and looked at where the lentils which Mar Bas had left for him had been placed. He found it as full as when he had left it. They were astonished and amazed. The priests and deacons got up and gave presents from it to all the crowd who had come. They did this from 9 in the morning to 3 in the afternoon and it was not exhausted because the blessing of our Lord rested on it.[218]

102. After this he set up a stone and stood on it. It was two cubits high.[219]

103. Mar Bas excused himself from the matter, and entered and dwelt in a monastery. The Lord prospered his handwork and he made an excellent monastery in which God was pleased. For he[220] was faithful and greatly loved the blessed Mar Simeon. All the days of his life he recounted his victorious deeds before the brethren. As if revealed to him by the Spirit of God he said, 'Truly he will be a vessel of honor, and his name will go out from one end of the earth to the other.'

104. After this, news about Mar Simeon began to be reported in the world and people began to visit him from every region. For he stood on [that stone] five years. News began to spread to all corners and people visited from every place. After he had stood on the stone five years, his brother Mar Shemshi died well-respected and with works of righteousness.

105. Our Lord also revealed to him and did not hide from him his brother's death. For three months[221] earlier he summoned three elders of the village[222] and said to them, 'During the time of

---

[217] For the rest of the paragraph, M reads only: 'he was astonished and amazed and offered praise to God'.

[218] Instead of this last clause, B reads: 'Widows of the village also went up and filled their skirts and went down and still it remained just as it was. Mar Bas also greatly wondered at this as did everyone else, for it was a marvel.'

[219] B adds: 'it had four bases'. M places this paragraph after Mar Bas enters his monastery. Assemani inserts 'sryn and makes the stone twenty-two cubits high.

[220] The rest of this description of Mar Bas is not in B and M.

[221] B: days; M does not give the date.

[222] B gives the names Marenes, Demetrianus and Maris. M gives the names Alis, Maris, and Martinus.

confinement, before the door opens, Mar Shemshi will die. Make
a coffin and place him in it. Watch over it lest someone take him
from you.' For he had this vision: there was a tree bearing many
fruits, it was beautiful to look at and its top-branches were adorned
and loaded with fruit. Its leaves delighted the eye. Now there was a
branch sprouting up from it. Along came a splendid-looking man
leading four men carrying axes in their hands. He said to them,
'Cut that branch off that tree, for it is getting big and preventing a
lot of fruit'. Now there was another man standing beside him and
he also was beautifully dressed and good to look at. He said to the
first man, 'Let us make it another companion'. But he answered
and said to him, 'It does not need a companion. It alone is sufficient
both for insiders and outsiders.' When the branch had been cut off
from the tree, the man ordered the four men saying, 'Now dig
down deep and put the root of that tree on a rock. Then fill in
the sides,[223] and shore it up strongly so that it will not be shaken.
For it will bear much fruit, and strong winds and tempests and
powerful storms will beat on it.' Once they had gone deep and
set and shored its root, at that moment it put forth new buds and
luxurious growth. Its vines grew[224] strong on all sides, and it bore a
hundred times more than before. From under the root of that tree a
strong, heavy flow of water spouted forth: it covered the mountains
and the hills and gushed forth and spread out on all sides. Suddenly
much animal life appeared and innumerable birds of all species and
types both large and small. They were arriving and coming from
all quarters, eating from the fruit of that tree and drinking from
the spring. As many as ate and drank from it, so much more the
fruits of the tree increased in bounds and the spring was strong and
vigorous. Now the tree was the saint, the branch cut off his brother
Mar Shemshi who died as he had said during that Lent.

106. When the day arrived that the door of the saint's enclosure opened, God aroused all humankind. It was as if a heavenly
command from on high was over all the world and moved all humankind to come to him. There was no limit to those who came;
the mountains were covered and the roads filled. No one could see

---

[223] B reads *'npwhy* = to its upper branches; M reads *'wpwhy* = to its branches
or its vine-shoots; V reads *knpwhy* = to its edges.
[224] Both B and M read as in the previous note.

anything except that throng. One could not decide whether it was at rest or in motion. His fame spread to the four corners of the world, he was extolled and became known even to the Emperor of the West. Again, his fame was heard even by the King of the East. Our Lord began to do and by his hand to perform wonderful powers and mighty signs. The gift of healing was given to him by God in a way greater than mortal man can recount. The word of the apostle was fulfilled which says, 'The gift of God is greater than can be told'.[225] For what mortal's mouth could dare to tell or what writers could write or what wise mind could number or count how many benefits came to the whole world from God by the saint? How many afar off were brought near? How many lost were at his word turned from error to the knowledge of the truth? How many thousands and tens of thousands of strangers heard his word and became members of the family and harnessed themselves in the yoke of Christ? Who can count or reckon the thousands without number of wild people who, on seeing him and hearing him and his divine teaching, gladly surrendered themselves to Christ's religion and became worshippers and servants of the truth? For the report of the benefit which his Lord did by his hand travelled from one end of the world to the other, and there was fulfilled what was written: 'Their good tidings have gone out through all the earth, and their words to the ends of the world'.[226] For letters of kings poured in, and they sent hand-delivered documents accompanied by commanders to his holiness, asking him to bless them and to pray for their rule and for the rulers under their authority and to instruct them as to what was agreeable behavior. For they gladly accepted his instructions. In the address of their letters they named him 'Abba, God-given teacher,' and they instructed him to give orders to them on any matter with full confidence. So he counselled and advised them about everything: what would please and glorify God, what would profit the life of their soul, what would help the poor, and what would consolidate their rule.

107. These[227] then and ten times more than these are the glorious deeds and signs which our Lord worked by the hand of the

---

225 A reference to 2 Cor 9:15?
226 Ps 19:4; Rom 10:18.
227 This section is found elsewhere in B and M. See Appendix A.

saint. For we said earlier that no mortal human could reckon or count all the benefit and relief that God did for people by him and that no mouth could tell or relate the glorious deeds wrought in far-off places through his prayer. Again our Lord revealed and explained to him many visions. Many of them he concealed and told to no one for he was careful that no one should think that he repeated them out of pride. On this point he had a revelation and information. For he saw two men, splendidly dressed and excellently outfitted, standing in front of him and discussing the matter between them. One of them said to the other, 'Look at how many visions and revelations are shown to him, but he conceals and hides them and does not reveal a one of them to anyone.' The other replied and said to his companion, 'He does quite correctly. In this point is his goodness commended: that he does not reveal or tell or make known anything revealed to him by God. By this it is clear that he does not seek his own glory, nor is there room for others to say what they want.' They discussed these things and much more about the matter with each other while walking to and fro in the enclosure. Then they departed. They said nothing to the saint about the matter.[228] Then the saint knew, although they had not spoken to him at all, that they had spoken so as to caution him. Because of this he was extremely careful and refrained from repeating or telling people anything that he saw or that was revealed to him by God.

108. Now concerning the monastic customs and practices and exercises which he followed and practiced and wore himself out with before God both inwardly and outwardly: it was clearly obvious to everyone that neither among the ancients nor among more recent people could be found a body clothed in flesh that could endure, sustain, and withstand the afflictions which the saint's body endured and withstood. For we all know and are convinced that the Holy Spirit had the victorious acts of the believers in the Holy Scriptures written with miracles and wonders for the consolation, encouragement, help, and admonition of humankind. For Moses— the great prophet, the clear-seeing eye of all Israel, the victorious

---

[228] This sentence is not in Assemani who has left out two lines of text through haplography.

athlete, the wise master-builder, the diligent servant, the watchful sailor, the famous pilot, the trained scribe, the faithful steward— fasted twice only for forty days and forty nights. He did not eat bread or drink water while he was on the mountain with his Lord. Clouds circled him and darkness surrounded him, there were fiery flames and smoke ascending, horns blowing and trumpets sounding. Angels were alarmed, and the watchers of heaven troubled; seraphim cried out 'Holy! Holy! Holy!' and the cherubim were making a joyful noise.[229] Moses spoke, and God answered with a voice.[230] Moses was refreshed: his food was the divine vision, his drink the heavenly glory. He grew fat during his fast, and he glowed during his prayers. Again, Elijah the zealot, a burning fire, walked for forty days and nights in the desert on the strength of the food which he received from the angel at the visitation of his Lord, food which men had not sown and which mortals do not prepare.[231] Far from food, with no drink nearby, he climbed the mountain and entered the cave. By his fast of forty days he was deemed worthy to hear the voice of God and to see that awesome and stupendous vision at which heavenly beings tremble and earthly beings are terrified. He was sent to anoint kings and prophets. He received there a pledge from his fast that he would be lifted up from this sorrowful world and ascend to Eden full of all delights. Again, Daniel, a man all one could ask for, a faithful steward, fasted for twenty-one days: he did not eat bread or drink water, he did not wash or anoint himself with oil. A watcher of heaven, a captain of angels, was sent to him and in his fast and prayers revealed secret things to him and explained to him what would happen.[232] By his prayers he brought back the captivity from Babylon, and by his fast the seed of Abraham, the friend of God, was delivered from slavery to their enemies.

109. We worship our Lord for his grace because he was merciful towards the creation of his hands and he was compassionate: he came down and formed and put on a body[233] which he in his

---

[229] This last clause is missing in Assemani.
[230] Ex 19:19. The two times mentioned are at Ex 24:18; 34:28.
[231] 1 Kings 19.
[232] Daniel 10–12.
[233] M: 'put on in the womb the garment of a body'.

grace fashioned with his holy hands as seemed good to him. When he led it to the desert to be tempted (that is, to be tried and proved[234]), it is written that he remained forty days and nights in fast and prayer without eating bread or drinking water.[235] As much therefore as his divinity knew the body could endure, so much it allowed the holy body it clothed to endure. After he had remained forty days in fast and prayer, it pleased his divinity to give the nod to hunger and it came, he commanded and it approached that he might show forth and prove that truly it pleased his high divinity to be clothed in the body of Adam, subject to hunger and thirst, to weariness and sleep. That body conquered his enemy, put Satan to shame and scattered his hosts; it trampled sin under foot, killed death, laid waste Sheol and received the crown of victory.

110. If then, as we said before, our Lord performed these glorious acts and signs by the hands of these warriors, men of renown, by their fasts of forty days, what can we say about the blessed Mar Simeon? No one knows how to describe fully the practices of his ascetic life. God alone knows and is aware of his exercises and his labors—how he wore himself out and labored and toiled before God with severe unspeakable fasting and with rigorous, countless prayers, in hunger and thirst, in heat and cold, so that continually, unceasingly, he offered perpetual intercession and he was standing at all times so that he would not give sleep to his eyes. There was no rest for his body, day or night, for fifty-six years. He was in the monastery nine years in amazing ascetic practices and harsh works of discipline—we wrote and noted them down above. And he was in the enclosure at Telneshe for forty-seven[236] years. He stood in a corner of the enclosure for ten years, some of the time locked up in confinement while he struggled mightily and waged war and fought against the enemy. After this he stood on those smaller columns, seven years on the ones eleven and seventeen and twenty-two cubits high. He stood for thirty years on the column forty cubits high. Our Lord gave him strength and endurance and he finished his days on this column in peace and tranquility and

---

[234] This explanatory gloss is not in B, but is in M. The author cannot simply say that Jesus was tempted. See Introduction, n. 82.

[235] Mt 4:2; Lk 4:2.

[236] M: forty-six.

in works of righteousness. He had, as it is written, a good end with men of peace.[237] His end was magnified ten times more than his beginning. His Lord worked for him his will and pleasure, and answered his request: he asked and he received, he sought and he found, he knocked at the door of his Lord in truth, and it was opened for him.[238] He honored God with a perfect heart, and he was honored by God with all good things. He loved his Lord with all his heart, more than himself and his life, for he surrendered and placed himself in the hands of his Lord. So it was that the Lord, who saw his diligence, gave him favor in the eyes of all humans and extolled the fame of his glorious deeds from one end of creation to the other, and he granted whatever his soul desired. For often he asked and petitioned his Lord in prayer, speaking in this way, 'Lord, almighty God, do not force me into the power of mortals, that I should dismount from my place here and people see me on the ground. But grant me that on this stone, on which I stood at your command and order, I may complete the days of my life. From it receive the soul of your servant according to your Lordship's will.'

111. Perhaps someone will say, 'What made it necessary or required that he mount on a pillar? Could he not please our Lord on the ground or at most in that corner?' Truly, we all know and are convinced that God is everywhere—in heaven and on earth, on high and in the deep, in the sea and in the abyss, below the earth and above the heavens. There is no place where his divinity is absent, except in humans who do not do his will. Wherever a human calls on him in truth, there he finds him. For Jonah called to him in the deep abyss and he heard his prayer and received his request. From the inner depth of Sheol he lifted him up. Again, Daniel and the followers of Hananiah called on him from the pit and the furnace, and he sent an angel with his grace as he asked, and he delivered and rescued them.[239] Everyone of his servants found him wherever they sought him—Elijah on Carmel, Abraham on the top of the mountain. Immediately he heard their prayer, did their will, and answered their request. It also seemed

---

[237] Ps 37:27.
[238] Mt 7:7.
[239] Jonah 2; Daniel 2.

good to his lordship to send each one of his servants to preach
and to teach at the time that seemed fitting and right to him.
Again as he desired he gave them laws and commandments: to the
household of Adam, not to eat of the tree; to the sons of Seth to
have nothing to do with the household of Cain;[240] to Noah the
rainbow and the indissoluble covenant; to Abraham the sign and
seal of circumcision; to Moses, the Sabbath and the keeping of the
law. He clothed Elijah with zeal glowing like a flaming fire. He
had Isaiah walk before him naked and barefoot. He commanded
Jeremiah to put on his neck the yoke and its collar. He said to
Ezechiel, 'Shave your beard and your head with a razor, and put
your baggage on your shoulder. Breach the wall and go out as
though one departing.' To Hosea a holy prophet he commanded,
'Take a harlot as your wife'.[241] Thus to each and every one of his
servants at the right time he commanded how to behave, because
he has authority as master in his creation and as God in his hand-
iwork and there is no one who can fault the will of his lordship.
Whoever obeys and keeps and does his will is kept and magnified and becomes famous. For Abraham was counted worthy to
be called 'friend of God',[242] Moses shone out and became head
and ruler,[243] and our Lord worked great and astounding exploits
through him. Again Elijah flew and was taken up and did not taste
death.[244] So therefore it pleased his Lord that Mar Simeon stand
on a pillar in these days because he saw creation as if asleep. He
sought by his affliction to awaken the world from the heavy torpor
of its inhabitants[245] and to have the name of his divinity praised
through his believers.[246]

---

[240] B: 'with the daughters of Cain'. This prohibition is not found in the
Hebrew Scriptures, but is part of the early tradition which interpreted 'the sons
of God' of Gen 6:2 as 'the sons of Seth'. See A.F.J. Klijn, *Seth in Jewish, Christian
and Gnostic Literature*, Supplements to Novum Testamentum, 46. (Leiden: Brill,
1977), as well as the discussion in Gedaliahu A.G. Stroumsa, *Another Seed: Studies
in Gnostic Mythology* (Leiden: Brill, 1984) 125–134.

[241] Gen 2:17; Gen 9:12–16; Ex 20–31; 1 Kgs 18:20–40; Is 20:2; Jer 27:2;
Ezech 5:1;12:3; Hos 1:2.

[242] James 2:23.

[243] Ex 3:10.

[244] 2 Kgs 2:11.

[245] B and M: its sleep.

[246] B and M have the singular.

112. To convince you that this was truly the work of the Lord:[247] the saint had a recess for storing the holy vessels.[248] Before it a stone about three cubits high was placed, with incense and a censer on it. After about three weeks into the lenten confinement, there appeared to blessed Mar Simeon a splendid man whose face glowed like a fire and who was girded for battle. He saw him come and pray before that recess. After he finished his prayer he went up and stood on that stone. He joined his hands behind him and was bending and straightening up and praying earnestly. He turned around and looked at the saint and then again raised his hands heavenward and lifted his eyes upward. He turned again as he prayed and supplicated and looked at the saint. For three nights he acted this way from evening till morning. Thus the saint perceived and understood that he was acting this way on his account and had been sent by the Lord to show and teach him how to be diligent in prayer. When he stopped after those three days and went away, the blessed Mar went and stood on that stone. He was happy and content so to stand, especially as he realized this was from God, and after Lent and the door of his enclosure was opened he had that stone brought to him and he set it up and stood on it[249] three months. After that he began to make those columns until he had made that one of twenty cubits.[250]

113. And to convince you truly that this was God's doing that he should so stand on a pillar, I will again tell you what really in truth happened. After he had stood on those smaller ones, up to that one of twenty cubits, for seven years, he had a mind to change the one of twenty cubits to one of thirty cubits. As Lent approached he called his disciple—the one who was with him and had served him for many years and who placed his hands upon his eyes and upon whose shoulder the saint laid his head when he yielded his spirit to his Lord—and ordered him, 'Till

---

[247] B and M add: 'I will tell you the affair as it really happened'.

[248] On the V manuscript two words are missing, seemingly rubbed out. The only words that M has in addition to those legible on the V manuscript is 'in the enclosure'. Perhaps a copyist rubbed out his mistake on V, while M conflated the readings of V and B.

[249] The section 'He was happy . . . on it' is not in B, left out by haplography.

[250] Assemani adds *trtyn* and makes it twenty-two cubits.

182   *The Lives of Simeon Stylites*

our Lord wills and the door of the enclosure is opened, make and
construct for me a pillar thirty cubits long of two sections.' He
also summoned craftsmen and ordered them, 'Before the door
is opened, let it be made and constructed and placed by the
door.' When the door of the enclosure was closed, the workmen began to hew, but it was as if some force opposed them.
Whenever they hewed a section and set it up, something struck it
and broke it in pieces. They were hewing and the sections were
getting broken till four weeks of Lent had passed by. Only two
weeks were left before the door would be opened. Both the disciple and the workmen were upset that Lent was passing by and
they had done nothing at all yet. His disciple came to him at
night and called out and said in distress to the saint, 'My Lord,
I beseech your holiness. Ask your Lord about this matter. If it
is his will, let him open the door and reveal it to your righteousness because the adversary has opposed us in this way. If
it is not his will, why do we labor in vain and the workmen
achieve nothing?' The saint refused to speak with his disciple
and said to him, 'Go away and come back tomorrow'. When
he came again on the next night as ordered, he called out and
said to him, 'My Lord, what does your holiness command me:
to work or to stop?' Then blessed Mar Simeon spoke encour-
agingly to him and said, 'Do not be distressed. See, God prepared it as he desired. He revealed and explained it to me a sinner
as I asked him. For during the night a splendid man as handsome as could be came and said to me, "Do not be distressed
by what your disciple told you. For your Lord wants you to make a
pillar of forty cubits, but as you are a believer make it out of three
sections for the sake of the Trinity." He gave me three gifts, pure
and white, very beautiful and desireable. He also mentioned you
by name, "Sacristan so-and-so, behold, this is your gift: call out
and proclaim and say, 'Sing to God a new song, all the earth'."[251]
But now go and do as I told you. I trust the Lord God that he
will help you.'[252] When the disciple of my lord rose early in the
morning and led the craftsmen with him to go out and hew a
suitable stone, the Lord helped them. Close to the enclosure itself

----

251 Ps 96:1.
252 Literally: 'open a door for you'.

they found a suitably good and strong stone. Every day they had been going back and forth over it. They set their hand to begin work on it and the Lord too stretched out his right hand. In a single week they had hewn, carved, and constructed it and had brought it and placed it by the door of the enclosure. When the saint opened the door they brought it in and erected and set up that , column.[253] He went up and stood on it for thirty years as though it were one day.

114. Our Lord allowed him to finish his days on it as he had requested God in high repute for works of righteousness, for acts of justice, and for deeds of perfection. He profited himself and many others. The name of his Lord was praised because of him and for his sake from one end of creation to the other.[254] And by his death his glory grew stronger and spread wider and he became more famous than by his life. The holy church was exalted by him and the horn of Christianity lifted up. His end was much more exalted than his beginning. If anyone doubted, his mind was put right and he was strengthened in the faith. For his Lord did not simply allow his death to occur in an ordinary way, nor did he fully hide from him the day of his crowning. For he revealed it to him in the way I am about to tell. After he had been in the enclosure seven years, two men appeared standing before him, dressed in glorious light. One of them held a measuring rod in his right hand and with it he measured off forty rods. Then he turned and said to his companion, 'When this number forty is filled, he has reached his end and he will be taken away. But I will do such a sign as has not been seen in these times, and then I will take him away.' The saint did not understand him completely.[255] He turned again and measured twice, and spoke in this way to his companion. They spoke not a word to the saint about the matter, but talked to each other quite a time and then were taken away. The saint then was certain that it had been spoken on his account, and he

---

[253] These last two words, except for traces of the first and last letters, have been wiped out on the manuscript. I have supplied them from B and M. Assemani makes no notice of an omission.

[254] Here M inserts the narrative which begins at ¶121 through ¶123 and adds a story not found in B and V. See Appendix B.6.

[255] This sentence is in the positive in V, but I have followed B and M and made it negative, as it makes more sense in the context.

reflected very much on it at all times. When he saw the number drawing closer, he was on the alert to notice that sign spoken of, 'I will do it and then I will take him'. He reflected on what that sign might be. Then when he saw that sign of anger in the city and region of Antioch, when he saw all creation gathered there, thousands and tens of thousands without number or limit, when he saw priests leading their flocks, earnestly and diligently taking pains with censers and lighted torches and crosses, when he saw all the people running from all quarters with shouts and tears and bitter groans, when finally he saw that he had completed the number, his mind made him anxious and he called his first disciple and said to him privately, 'As I consider that the number is complete and that there is a very serious sign, I do not know for sure whether the definite time has come and I am about to be taken away. But look, I am telling you ahead of time because you know that you have been with me many years and you know that clothing of any other kind except these skins has never touched my body. Now, let God be witness against you if you allow any kind of clothing except skins to touch my limbs!' And so it was. For no other kind of clothing except skins did touch his holy body.

115. Then his Lord made a departure for him such as I think never existed before in these times to those born of woman. For no one could describe or reckon that concourse of people and creation for fifty-one days after the last sign that occurred in the region. No one dared even to enter his house except in terror and no one went out to the field except in fear. No one did absolutely any work at all but everyone was numbed: the hands of all people hung slack, and the minds of everyone were distracted and wandering. They stood waiting for what the saint would order them to do: as from the mouth of his Lord so they looked to receive the command from his holiness. After fifty-one days had passed, as we said, there was that major commemoration in the month of Tammuz. The saint did not make another commemoration after it and no-one can describe its assembly. For since time began its like was not heard of in creation. For God aroused the whole world to greet and worship his friend and manifest his glory in his life-time, as he did to holy Mar Moses when he brought him up the mountain and showed him the land of promise and then led

him away.[256] The blessed Mar Simeon summoned all humankind, priests and their flocks, the great and the small. He encouraged and comforted them, he commanded and admonished them to keep the laws and commandments of our Lord. As a good and compassionate father charges his beloved[257] sons he said to them, 'Go in the name of our Lord Jesus Christ and keep a vigil for three days in your districts. Then go out in the name of our Lord and set to work. Let everyone do his job and I am confident that the Lord God will preserve you.'

116. After he had sent[258] everyone to his work in peace, thirty days[259] elapsed. On the twenty-ninth of Ab,[260] at the eleventh[261] hour of Saturday as Sunday was about to begin, as some of his disciples stood around him, he suddenly felt weary. Pain struck him and he suffered. His whole body felt feverish. He continued in this lassitude from Sunday till Tuesday. Then God did such a favor for him that was so great it might be hard to believe. To believers everything is possible because they know that everything is easy for their Lord. Now this was the sign: the heat was severe and so intense that the land was scorched from its heat in those days at the end of Ab and the beginning of Elul. Then occurred that favor to the saint of which we shall speak. Perhaps even that heat was as intense as a crucible on account of this favor. For his lord, for the sake of the sign, decreed to give him during his life-time a pledge of his achievement. A cool, refreshing, and very fragrant wind blew as though a heavenly dew were falling on the saint and were sending forth a fragrant scent from him such as has not been spoken of in the world. There was not just one smell exuding from it, but wave upon wave kept coming. There were multiple scents, each different from the other. To those billowing fragrances none of the sweet spices or excellent and pleasurable herbs of this world can be compared, for they were dispensed by the providence of

---

256 Dt 34:1–8.

257 Reading *ḥbyb'* = beloved, with B and M, not *ḥykm'* = wise, as in the V manuscript.

258 Assemani reads *šn'* = depart, instead of *šr'*.

259 This is not in M.

260 July/August.

261 Around 5 PM in the afternoon. Note how time is reckoned from the evening.

God. Nor did they exude their perfume in every place, not even the whole length of the ladder but from the middle up. Wave upon wave went out into all the enclosure,[262] but no one perceived it because of the burning incense. When that first disciple noticed it—the one who loved him and was with him constantly day and night and never left his side at all especially in those days when he was dying[263]—he comforted and encouraged him and said, 'Look my lord, see how much your Lord loves you. For he effects ease and delight for you in two ways: all creation and the whole world comes to greet and worship you, and he has shown you your glory with your own eyes; and behold, he does for your holiness what does not belong to humankind: in this world he has given you a pledge of your reward of your labors. For as this scent which pours forth has never been heard of or perceived in this world, so it follows God has honored you as your labors deserve. However, my Lord, I beseech you: from your God whom you have loved from your childhood fill this holy mouth and bless your servant whom your perfection knows how I have served your holiness.'[264] He blessed him and warned and commanded him, 'Speak to no one about this fragrance for the moment'. For the saint knew how this was by the providence of God.

117. On the Wednesday of the week, on the second of the month Elul, at the ninth hour,[265] as all his disciples were standing around him, he set those two over their colleagues and entrusted all of them to our Lord. He stood upright, he bent three times all at once. He looked to heaven and then turned and looked at the whole world. All the people present cried out, 'Bless, my lord!' He looked east and west and all around, he lifted up his hand from inside his cloak and blessed them and entrusted them to our Lord three times. As his disciples stood around holding fast to him as sons to a good and gentle father, they again said, 'My lord, bless your servants, we beseech you, by your Lord who does what you want and is now taking you to himself as you asked him'. He grasped those two by their hands and gave charge to them about

---

262　B: 'not in the enclosure'.
263　B and M read *m'nt* = weary, not *m't* = dying.
264　B has a first person plural subject for this sentence.
265　I.e., 3 PM.

each other, that they love one another. He also set them over their companions. He lifted up his hand to heaven and entrusted them to our Lord. He lifted up his eyes to heaven and beat his breast three times with his right hand. He bent and placed his head upon the shoulder of that first disciple. His two disciples placed their hands upon his eyes and he yielded his spirit to his Lord. He slept and ceased from labor, toil, and trouble as he placed his head on the shoulder of that disciple and they placed their hands on his eyes and all the people stood around and gave heed to him.

118. Then his disciples, since they were afraid of the populace lest the villages gather and come to snatch him away and there might be stranglings[266] and murder, made a coffin for him and placed him in it on the column until they could arrange a place of honor for him. Suddenly this became known and the news spread throughout all the world. Everyone was astonished and wonder-struck, and all flesh amazed because it was as if suddenly they heard something they could not believe. The minds of all people were troubled and their thinking disturbed, their hands failed and many mourned. Some were in mourning and grief, while others gave thanks and praise—gladness was thus mixed with grief, comfort with mourning, rejoicing with sadness. Some mourned and lamented, some raised their hands to heaven and gave thanks and blessing to God, Lord of all, that this report and the good news of the crowning of the genuine servant of our Lord had reached their ears. So the affair was one of grief and joy, of sadness and comfort.[267] Of grief, that such a wise pilot and helmsman of the ship of the world with God's wisdom was taken from the world; of gladness, that the ship of the body of the vigilant sailor had entered and arrived at a haven of gladness carrying a profitable cargo. He was delivered from the cares[268] which beat on him continually. The storms with winds and sudden gusts which had battled and opposed him were stilled. He had kept possession of his cargo and made his Lord glad at his profit. Of sadness, my brethren, that such a reliable master-builder, who by his intercession carried the weight of creation, was taken away from the world. For his prayers—just

---

[266] Both B and M have *šhq'* = strife, rather than *ḥnq'* = stranglings.
[267] Assemani leaves out this last word.
[268] Both B and M read 'tempests'.

like the beams in buildings—held up creation. Of rejoicing, that his Lord had stretched out to him his right hand to help him and had given him power and endurance. He began in his name, and finished in his grace. His building was completed: it was not shaken by the winds and rain and floods of sin that for forty-seven years buffeted him with all conflicts. Of tears and groans, that such a spiritual father who had fed and brought up his sons with heavenly nourishment had departed from among them. Of rejoicing, that, even though he left behind his sons orphans in the flesh, he flew around and about like an eagle in the sky and mounted to a high precipice far from all fears and out of the reach of all harm.

119. The orphans and widows mourned for him with heavy tears as they said, 'Where shall we seek or where find you, our preserver and our nourisher according to his Lord?' The oppressed remembered and trembled, the despoiled were alarmed, they groaned and were agitated and said, 'Woe to us because now the mouth of greedy and voracious wolves is opened against us. Whom shall we ask to awaken the powerful lion, who lies in the deep sleep of death? At his roaring, they trembled like cowards and were terrified; at his powerful voice they fled like foxes to their holes and thrust themselves in to hide.' They were grieving for him with all kinds of dirges and wailing for him with chants and saying, 'Where shall we go or where shall we seek and find a healer like you, either your equal or comparable to you? When disease saw you it fled, pain at your presence vanished. They benefited more by your word and command than by all the herbs and medicines.'

120. The church also mourned[269] for him with her children, the priests and their flocks, the shepherds and their sheep-folds, in grief and in joy, with tears and litanies, with groans and prayers. For they prayed in grief to one who had been to them a calm haven and restful resort. For whenever some thing from the Evil One sprang up to trouble and disturb [them] or when there were winds of sin or the billows of deceit, he was at hand. He stood ready like a wise master-builder, a hard-working husbandman, like a skillful pilot and watchful sailor, like a winning athlete and a practiced scribe, like a stout-hearted warrior with the breast-plate of righteousness. He

---

269 Both B and M read *bky'* = mourn, not *b'y'* = pray.

was strenuously valiant in the orthodox faith, and spiritually strong in reliance on his Lord. He took refuge in prayer, and found help in supplication.[270] He lifted his eyes and looked upwards, he asked mercy from his Lord and sought compassion and aid from his God. He rebuked the winds of sin and they were quelled, the whirlwinds of deceit and they became still. He roared like a lion, and smote all who belong to the wrong side. So they[271] were consoled and were glad. With their gladness was mingled thanksgiving and blessing. For they gave thanks and blessed God their Lord who had endowed his servant to do battle and to conquer. He fought and won, he asked and received, he sought and found, he knocked and it was opened to him.[272] He began in truth and ended in righteousness. The horn of the holy church was exalted and all rejoiced, all her children[273] with their priests and their high-priests, and their folds with their flocks. All heresies, which look for one thing rather than another, were disgraced and put to shame. But they were distressed and grieved lest ever at any time an evil root might bring forth a bitter plant like it and harm or choke many by its bitter taste. Where would they be able to seek a healer and burden-bearer like or equal to him? As the ulcer burst he healed it, as the disease or pain arrived unexpectedly he stamped it out by his prayer.

121. For once a tempest of sin arose and a storm of evil opposed the church of Christ by means of a wicked and evil man named Ascepliades. He was uncle to the empress and chief procurator in the time when Theodosius was emperor and John bishop of Antioch.[274] That evil and wicked man was of the same mind as pagans and Jews. He hated Christians very much and issued an

---

[270] B: 'he soared (*ts*) in prayer, and found help in courage'.

M: 'he soared (*ts*) in prayer, and found help in supplication.'

The second stich of B sounds strange, and the reading of V and M is to be preferred. If that is so, the first stich should be as in V, *tps* = take refuge, on grounds of parallelism.

[271] M specifies: 'all the poor.'

[272] Mt 7:7.

[273] V reads *'ly'* = superior beings. It should be emended to read, with B and M, *yldyh* = her children. The phrase is found later at V 75.1,21; 75.4,14; 76.1,12–14. For an explanation of these numbers, see Appendix A, n.1.

[274] Actually, the 'evil man' was Asclepiodotus (Martindale, *Prosopography*, 160). This event occurred in 423 (Codex Theodosianus, 616.8.25–27). John was patriarch of Antioch from 428–441.

edict that all the knessets and synagogues of the Jews which the Christians had taken away from them should be returned to them and that the Christians should pay out of their own funds for those that they wanted.[275] The edict of the King and the mandate of the procurator on this affair was promulgated in many towns and publicly proclaimed. All Christians were greatly distressed and grieved, especially when they saw Jews and pagans clothed in white, rejoicing and merry. The fools did not know or perceive that grief and remorse would suddenly overtake them. The affair would end for them the same way it had in the time of our Lord—their leaders and priests both lost their money and did not conceal the truth.[276] The same thing happened to them: they lost the bribe they gave, and they became a laughing-stock in the world as their sabbaths and synagogues remained deserted and empty.

122. For bishops came to the blessed Mar Simeon in great distress and grief and informed him about the affair. They had with them copies of those letters of the king and the procurator and when they read them before the saint he was greatly perturbed and amazed. He burnt like a blazing fire with zeal for his Lord, and he stood powerfully. He boldly wrote strong words filled with threats. He did not name Theodosius Emperor in his letters, but wrote thus to him:

> 'Now that your heart is exalted and you have disregarded the Lord your God who gave you the glorious diadem and the royal throne, now that you have become a friend and companion and protector to unbelieving Jews, behold suddenly the righteous judgement of God will overtake you and all who are of the same mind as you in this matter. You will lift up your hands to heaven and say in your affliction, 'Truly this anger has come on me because I broke faith with the Lord God.'

123. When the emperor read this, his heart trembled and he was mortally afraid, he was distressed and deeply repentant. He immediately ordered letters written to all the towns to abrogate those earlier ones and to honor Christians and the priests of God.

---

275 Both B and M read *nbnwn* = should build. V reads *nb'wn* = seek, desire.
276 Mt 28:11–15.

As for that procurator, the Emperor dismissed him from his position in disgrace. The Emperor sent letters to the saint through princes, entreating him to pray for him and to bless him and be reconciled with him. So the trouble passed away: the holy church and all her children rejoiced, while the evil one with all his servants was put to shame. Truth conquered, and God was glorified through his believer.

124. On account of these things and many more like them they were distressed and sad that he departed from them. All the priests of God were like sons to the blessed father, and he embraced them under the arms of his prayers like a mother her children. On the other hand they were glad, and their souls exulted and rejoiced. For they saw that the athlete was crowned; that the spiritual warrior who stood bravely in the battle and strove valiantly had conquered his enemy, trampled sin underfoot, and was inscribed in the roll of victors; the hard-working husbandman whose seed brought forth a hundredfold; the wise master-builder whose house was complete and not shaken by the violent winds or the powerful storms and the on-rush of rivers which beat against it for a long time; the skillful sailor and watchful pilot whose ship arrived at a safe harbour and was not harmed by the many tempests and violent storms which raged and beat against it for years—the ship overcame and got the better of them all[277] with help from his Lord, and made its sailor happy by its huge profits; the faithful steward who managed his fellow-servants honestly and received the promise from his Lord that he should be in charge of his treasury; the practiced scribe who both did and taught—the teaching of his mouth was obeyed and all meditated day and night on the word of his tongue—men and women, old and young, unmarried youths and virgins. All regions rejoiced in the teaching of the just man. The Evil One was put to shame, and God was glorified in his good and diligent servant whose talent was doubled in profits and his master rejoiced in his gains. The horn of the holy church was exalted at the term of his toil and the consummation of his struggle. She opened her mouth in glad praise and spiritual songs. As her face beamed and

---

[277] Literally: 'trod their necks under foot'—not an appropriate mixture of metaphors.

her heart exulted and her mind rejoiced, she began to say in her
joy, 'Now my head is exalted over my enemies who surround
me.'[278] For with her children she saw how her Lord had meted
out so much glory to her friend, to one who honored her priests
and upheld her laws. She forgot the fear and pain which always
plagued her, and lifted up her voice in praise and began to say,
'Now I give thanks to you because you answered me and became
to me a saviour.'[279]

125. For his Lord did not devise a simple exit for his believer,
but glorified his heroic deeds both in life and death more than all
the people of his day and age. During his life came peoples from
far-off and of barbarian tongues from the ends of the earth for his
greeting, for sight of his beloved face, and for his divine doctrine.
Kings revered him in their letters. At his death came priests and
high-priests and their folds and flocks, along with commanders of
the emperor with many attendants under their authority. For at the
time the saint of God Mar Simeon died, Ardabur the general, the
son of Aspar,[280] was the commander who ruled over all the East.
Both [father and son] were honored like kings in the areas under
their authority. He brought along with him twenty-one prefects,
many tribunes and a numberless host of soldiers. He came to the
saint's funeral because the city[281] had petitioned and besought him
with many groans and tears to transport him there so that he might
be its fortified wall and it might be defended by his prayer. This
was devised by the Lord to show how much glory he meted out
to one who glorified him with good works and righteous deeds.
For he led him down in great pomp and circumstance. Priests
and high-priests and all the children of the holy church carried
him on their shoulders until he reached Shih, a village four[282]
miles distance from the saint's enclosure. There he was placed on
a chariot, surrounded by commanders, princes, city prefects. many
soldiers and a crowd no-one could number or estimate. Villages
came out with great diligence—men and women, old and young,

---

[278] Ps 27:6.
[279] Ps 118:21.
[280] See Martindale, *Prosopography*, 135–137.
[281] Antioch.
[282] B and M: three.

unmarried youths and virgins, slaves and free-born—to greet him and be blessed by him as they burnt incense and lit candles.

126. The saint's body was travelling in state for five days. He left his enclosure on the Monday, and on the Friday entered the great city Antioch in great pomp and such honor as cannot be described. They burnt incense and lit candles, they strewed precious spices before him upon all the people who had accompanied him. They chanted psalms and spiritual hymns before him until he entered and was placed in the holy and great church which Constantine—the victorious Emperor whose memory be blessed—had built. This had not happened to any of the saints, either ancient or contemporary. For no one had previously been laid in the great church, neither one of the prophets nor one of the apostles nor one of the martyrs. The blessed Mar Simeon was the first to be buried in the great church. The bishop of Antioch, head of the bishops, and all his clergy each day as a mark of distinction sing and chant spiritual songs before him. Great silver censers of incense are placed before him continually, while every minute excellent perfumes and chosen spices rise up just as they rose up during his life-time so that God might make known how he honored him both in life and in death.

127. During his funeral procession also his Lord manifested a great exploit through him so that all who saw it were astonished, and he made known the gift of healing given to him by God as his labors deserved. For a man in whom dwelt an evil spirit had lived among the tombs for many years. The cemetery was close by the road near a town named Maru. Everyone who travelled to and fro along that road saw him. His ability to speak intelligently had been taken away, and his understanding removed. He roared all the time and paced back and forth at the entrance of the cemetery. He did not recognize anyone, and no one dared approach him for fear and because of the sound of his roaring. When he saw the saint's body passing by on the chariot—as if heaven's mercies shone on him, as if it were for this that he had been reserved—he left the cemetery where he dwelt and ran at full speed and threw himself on the coffin in which the saint's body lay. The moment he reached the coffin, the demon fled and the evil spirit which had consumed him left him. His reason returned and he understood and recognized everyone. The bond of his tongue was loosened and he opened his

mouth and gave thanks and praise to God. Wonder seized everyone and this scripture was fulfilled, 'He has shown his people the power of his works.'[283] He followed the saint and entered the city with him. He spent many days in the church rejoicing and giving thanks and praise to God.

128. The victorious and Christian Emperor Leo, a believer,[284] sent letters by ambassadors with great assiduousness. He wrote to the commander-in-chief and to the bishop to send for the body of holy Mar Simeon so that he might honor it there with him as his exertions deserved and that his kingdom might be guarded by his prayer. At this all Antioch and its inhabitants arose and with tears and groans wrote and petitioned him, 'Because our city has no wall as it fell in anger, we brought him to be for us a fortified wall that we might be protected by his prayer.' With difficulty he was persuaded to leave the saint with them. To such a high degree God magnified him. He who gave glory to God was glorified by God and worshipped by men.

129. Here ends the book of the narrative of the victorious deeds of the blessed Mar Simeon.[285]

LETTER OF COSMAS OF PANIR

130. TO OUR FATHER AND OUR CHOSEN, true, faithful and victorious Lord who deserves the peace which is from heaven, glorious in his fasting and constant in the service of his Lord, the fortified wall of our region and the promoter of our people, glorious in his appearance and splendid in his customs, the promoter of the churches of Christ, the herald of life who stood between God and his creation and proclaims relief to his audience who receive from the holy altar, to him who watches over his affairs and whose victory was proclaimed openly in the world, who commands the nations that they also should keep the commandments of God and follow in his footsteps, to him who loves the three things that

---

[283] Ps 111:16.

[284] Two lines have been rubbed out on manuscript V. I have reconstructed following M. B reads: 'The victorious and Christian Emperor Leo, worthy of blessed memory . . . .'

[285] This sentence is written in red on the manuscript. For the ending of B and M, see Appendix B.5. Assemani supplies a title to the following section: The Letter of Cosmas the Priest to Mar Simeon the Stylite.

endure, love, hope, and faith as the great Apostle Paul[286] taught him, and who spoke familiarly with his Lord, to him who set his heart upon his Lord in truth and loved his God in justice, a fine model which appeared to the creation and a beautiful example fixed in the world, a firm pillar which arose in our generation and his truthfulness carried the weight of our consciences, to the praiseworthy ploughman whose tongue sowed life for us to hear, to the anointed priest given to us by God who effected reconciliation between God and his creation, to him who placed his treasure above in a place far from fear, to him who placed his building on rock and it is not shaken by winds and waves, to him who pleased his master in his person and petitioned his God by the pain of his limbs and rejoiced his maker by ascetic practices, to him who was a stranger to the world and fulfilled the commands of our Saviour, to him who hated his family and relations and became brother and companion to spiritual beings, to him who despised those things which pass away and perish and who loves those which abide and are still to come, to him who was a believer like Abraham, humble and holy like Moses, a companion of Joshua bar Nun and of Elijah, to him who exhibited signs and miracles like Elisha, to him whose victory is proclaimed publicly as his own, to him who triumphed and conquered in his struggle like Job in his trials, to the companion of prophets and colleague of apostles, who fulfilled the accounts of their actions in his own person, to Mar Simeon who resembled in name and in deed Simon Cephas, the foundation of the church of Christ, to the servant of God and the faithful steward, to the coveted rose which grew up in spiritual dew and whose smell was fragrant to heavenly and mortal beings, from your servants and worshippers and those helped by your prayer continually, from Cosmas of the village Panir together with the deacons and readers and all the congregation and from the procurator (*epitropos*) and the veterans (*veteranus*) and all the village equally, all of us extol your great love in Christ, peace.

131. We make known our smallness to your greatness, our imperfection to you, our Father, concerning the precept of the fear of God which was laid on our imperfection by you. We are all writing

---

[286] 1 Cor 13:13.

to you in one perfect love concerning this. First we subscribe concerning Friday and Sunday, that they be kept purely and worthily; concerning measures, that we not make for ourselves two measures, but that we have one true measure and one honest weight; that we not change a man's boundary; that we not cheat a hired servant and a labourer of his wages; concerning usury, that half a percent[287] be collected on both old and new [debts]; about those small coins that are paid, that they be restored to their masters; that we administer honest judgement between the great and the small and that we show no favoritism; that we not accept a bribe, a man against his fellow-man; that we not slander one another and not associate with robbers and magicians, that we chastise evil-doers and transgressors of the law, and we remain in the congregation for the life of our souls. Surely no one will be presumptuous and transgress these laws, or plunder, or defraud, or bribe a judge, or plunder orphans and widows or the poor, or rape a woman. We will keep everything with great care. Whatever you command us we assent to and we rejoice and we will surely do. We swear by God and by his Christ and by his living and holy Spirit and the victory of our Lords, the Emperors: whoever dares to transgress these, let it be according to your word,[288] my Lord. We truly will chastise him; we will separate him from among us and we will not accept his offering in the congregation. His dead will not be accompanied to the grave. Whoever says, 'Because the interest is small I will not lend', he will hear what your love says and you will be his security that it is more advantageous to him to take half and have it be a blessing for him than to take all of it and have it be a curse to him.

132. Pray for us, my just, noble and true lord, that we be established and confirmed in what you have commanded us. We trust in Our Lord that if we do your words and keep your commandments and fulfill your laws we will be helped by Christ through your prayers. Pray for us, my lord, that we not be ashamed before you or found guilty by your Lord but that openly we will do these things in righteousness and we receive life from them. Pray for us,

---

287   That is, per month = 6% per year.

288   There is a large space in v before 'according to your word'. Bedjan supplied ḥrm, but there is really no need.

my lord, that we may always be helped by your prayers and that there may be upon the world mercy and hope and redemption by your prayers for ever. Amen. Amen.

133. Upon everyone who keeps [these], a blessing. Upon everyone who dares to transgress, a curse.[289] Let all the people say, 'Amen.' Here ends the letter sent by the priest Cosmas[290] with all his townsfolk to the enclosure of blessed Mar Simeon.

134. Praise to God the Creator, praise to the Son the Redeemer, praise to the Spirit the Paraclete, one deity, one Lordship, one power, one force which is incomprehensible, inscrutable, which cannot be grasped or apprehended but which is apprehended[291] through his grace according to his mercy by means of human nature for the sake of our redemption. To whom is owed worship for ever. Amen.

135. Let this be a good remembrance before God and his Christ for Simeon bar Apollo and for Bar-hatar, son of Adan, who undertook to compose[292] this book of the heroic exploits of blessed Mar Simeon. They composed it by the toil of their hands and the sweat of their brows to be a remembrance for their departed [relatives], to sustain them in their way of life, for the redemption of their souls and that they might find the new life in Christ and gain that portion allotted to the saints in the bright light which does not pass away nor be extinguished for ever. Amen.

136. This book of the heroic exploits of the blessed Mar Simeon was finished on the seventeenth of the month Nisan, on the fourth day of the week, in the year five hundred and twenty-one according to the Antiochene reckoning.[293] [It was done] in the time of the excellent and eminent doer of God's good deeds, the priest Mar Simeon, and in the time of his archdeacon Mar Cyrus. Let everyone who reads this pray for those who undertook to compose this book that God may grant them forgiveness of their sins forever. Amen. Amen.

---

[289] A word seems to be missing in the text.

[290] Something is rubbed out in v. An ' is visible at the end of the line.

[291] This word is rubbed out in v, but with Assemani supply *'tgśś*. An *ś* is legible at the end of the word.

[292] The word used is *'bd*. For this meaning of the word as 'compose', see C.C. Torrey, 'The Letters', 274–75.

[293] That is, 473 AD.

137. Let everyone who reads and does this pray for whoever wrote it out[294] and speak thus, 'May He who revived Job and gave him double of everything[295] answer the request for righteousness in this world and that, in the world to come, we may be worthy to receive life with the just and the righteous who pleased their Lord in truth and good deeds.' May you be firm in the Lord, and pray for me.

---

[294] The verb *ktb* is used here, not *'bd*.
[295] Job 42:10.

APPENDIX A

A SYNOPTIC CHART OF THE VERSIONS

Number	V	Assemani	B	M
1	1^1	268	508.6	$65a.13^2$
2	2.1.10	269.24	509.3	65b.15
3	3.1.8	270.7	509.15	66a.12
4	3.3.16	270.40	510.11	66b.15
5	4.1.2	271.17	511.1	67a.9
6	5.1.15	272.39	514.18	70a.15
7	6.1.6	274.12	515.17	70b.14
8	6.3.1	275.1	516.10	71a.8

---

[1] An explanation of the system of citations is as follows: Under V: These numbers refer to the folios of the Vatican text. Each folio has four columns, which I have numbered from right to left. So the first number is to the folio, the second to the column, the third to the line. Thus, 2.1.10 refers the reader to the second folio, the column farthest to the right, the tenth line.

Under Assemani: These numbers refer to the edition on the Vatican manuscript by Assemani in the second part of his *Acta sanctorum martyrum orientalium et occidentalium*. The first number refers to the page in Assemani, the second to the line. Thus, 269.24 refers to page 269, line twenty-four.

Under B: These numbers refer to Bedjan's edition of the British manuscript in the fourth volume of his *Acta Martyrum et Sanctorum*. The first number refers to the page 508, line six.

Under M: As discussed in footnote 2. Thus, 65a.13 refers to page 65 of the microfilm Professor Vööbus sent me, the right column, line thirteen.

[2] I have numbered the pages according to the order of the microfilm graciously sent to me by Professor Vööbus, numbering a-b from right to left. In his report on the manuscript, Professor Vööbus began numbering from fol.111b. However, the microfilm showed disorder in the pages: the life begins at page 65 and the narrative at page 86 continues without a break at page 1 to page 64a. At page 64b begins a life af Abba Evagrius, a deacon of Gregory Nazianzen. There has clearly been a dislocation of the folios. Professor Vööbus feels sure that his photographs of the manuscript are in the order in which he took them, and therefore the misplacement most probably occurred in the binding of the volume. Till the original manuscript can be inspected again, I thought it both prudent and most convenient to follow the page order of the microfilm.

9	6.4.3	275.19	516.17	71a.15
10	7.1.14	276.3	517.7	71b.8
11	7.2.10	276.17	517.14	71b.13
12	7.4.5	277.8	517.20	72a.4
13	8.1.7	277.26	518.3	72a.7
14	8.2.14	278.7	518.9	72a.15
15	8.4.3	278.34	519.1	72b.7
16	8.4.9	278.38	519.5	72b.10
17	9.1.6	279.11	519.9	72b.13
18	9.2.24	280.6	519.22-	73a.8–11;
19	9.3.21	280.24		74a.7
20	9.4.13	280.38	520.17	74a.13
21	9.4.17	281.2	522.4	74a.15
22	10.1.7	281.14	521.18	74b.1
23	10.2.4	281.31	522.9	74b.7
24	10.3.10	282.14	522.19	74b.16
25	11.1.27	283.28	524.1	75b.4
26	11.4.17	284.38	525.2	76a.9
27	12.1.12	285.15	525.10	76a.15
28	12.4.24	287.3	527.8	77a.13
29	13.2.10	287.40	528.6	77b.9
30	13.4.10	289.5	529.4	78a.7
31	14.1.7	289.25	529.14	78a.14
32	14.2.10	290.4	530.3	78b.6
33	14.3.1	290.16	530.10	78b.11
34	14.4.20	291.8	531.7	79a.9
35	15.2.4	291.32	531.21	79b.3
36	15.3.18	292.18	532.14	79b.15
37	15.4.11	292.32		
38	15.4.15	292.35	566.9	10a.7
39	17.3.16	295.17	569.6	12a.3
40	18.4.7	297.17	570.17	13a.12
41	19.1.17	298.2	571.2	13b.7
42	19.3.21	298.35	571.21	14a.5
43	20.2.15	299.36	572.20	14b.12
44	21.2.5	301.12	573.19	15b.12
45	22.1.23	302.27	574.20	16b.10
46	23.1.12	303.33	575.21	17b.7
47	23.4.6	304.31	576.19	18a.13

48	24.1.21	305.16	577.9	18b.12
49	25.1.4	306.22	578.7	19b.6
50	25.3.3	307.7	578.14	20a.4
51	25.4.25	307.33	579.1	20b.1
52	26.3.24	308.34	579.21	21a.10
53	27.1.12	309.15	580.11	21b.7
54	27.4.6	310.10	581.5	22a.15
55	28.1.7	310.25		22b.9
56	28.3.9	311.13	581.11	23a.11
57	29.4.13	313.16	583.3	24b.6
58	30.2.17	314.5	583.19	25a.7
59	30.4.18	314.36	584.9	25b.7
60	31.3.8	315.35	585.6	26a.11
61	33.2.3	318.24	587.21	28a.5
62	33.4.15	319.30	589.1	28b.11
63	34.1.6	320.1		28b.17
64	36.1.25	323.15	592.14	31a.10
65	37.2.22	325.23	594.18	32b.6
66	38.1.6	326.21	595.18	33a.12
67	38.3.23	327.19	596.20	33b.17
68	39.4.3	329.5	598.18	35a.5
69	41.1.9	330.39	600.21	36b.1
70	42.4.9	333.8	603.16	38a.10
71	43.1.1	333.18	604.3	38a.16
72	44.1.16	335.2	606.3	39b.8
73	45.1.23	336.26	607.20	40b.12
74	47.1.12	339.22	610.20	42b.7
75	47.2.1	339.31	611.4	42b.12
76	49.1.13	343.6	615.1	45a.7
77	49.4.2	344.8	545.9	86a.15–
78	50.4.13	346.3	547.12	1b.6
79	51.3.21	347.17	555.3	2b.3
80	52.2.24	348.28	556.13	3b.1
81	53.1.12	349.31	557.15	4a.9
82	53.4.24	351.9	559.4	5a.10
83	54.2.26	352.3	560.1	5b.13
84	55.1.3	352.36	561.1	6b.3
85	55.3.13	353.35	562.1	7a.7
86	56.1.20	354.34	562.18	7b.10

87	56.4.14	356.1	563.21	8b.4
88	57.2.14	357.6	565.1	9a.11
89	58.1.6	358.17	532.20	80a.4
90	58.3.9	359.10	533.17	80b.1
91	58.4.15	359.29	534.9	80b.11
92	59.1.12	360.3	534.19	81a.1
93	59.2.20	360.24	535.11	81a.7
94	59.4.27	361.25	536.13	81b.7
95	60.1.24	362.4	537.3	81b.15
96	60.2.13	362.15	537.10	82a.1
97	60.3.11	362.34	537.18	82a.7
98	61.1.10	363.35	539.4	
99	61.2.7	364.12	539.14	
100	61.3.1	364.29	539.21	
101	61.4.23	365.23	540.20	82b.5
102	62.1.20	365.39	541.10	82b.10
103	62.1.23	366.1	541.12	82b.7
104	62.2.14	366.12	541.15	82b.11
105	62.2.23	366.18	541.20	82b.15
106	63.2.4	367.35	543.16	83b.15
107	63.4.27	369.22	616.3	45b.14
108	64.3.17	370.21	617.6	46b.3
109	65.3.10	371.36	618.19	47b.4
110	65.4.22	372.18	619.12	48a.2
111	66.4.16	374.3	621.6	49a.4
112	67.4.18	375.29	623.4	50a.8
113	68.2.25	376.31	624.1	50b.16
114	69.3.17	378.27	626.10	52a.14–
115	70.3.6	380.12	628.7	56a.6
116	71.1.19	381.20	629.15	56b.15
117	72.1.8	383.6	631.12	58a.3
118	72.3.6	383.38	632.11	58b.6
119	73.2.14	385.22	634.5	59b.6
120	73.3.19	386.12	634.17	59b.17
121	74.2.7	387.30	636.5	52b.1
122	74.3.28	388.23	637.4	53a.3
123	75.1.2	389.8	637.17	53a.17
124	75.1.25	389.27	638.6	60a.9
125	75.4.24	390.40	639.16	61b.5

126	76.3.19	392.7	641.3	62a.13
127	77.1.11	392.39	641.21	62b.14
128	77.3.17	393.39	643.3	63a.17
129	77.4.21	394.21	644.13	
130	77.4.24	394.26		
131	78.4.16	396.5		
132	79.3.4	397.11		
133	79.4.3	397.26		
134	79.4.14	397.33		
135	79.4.26	398.3		
136	80.1.16	398.15		
137	80.2.8	398.27		

NARRATIVES FOUND ONLY IN B AND M

1. How Simeon saved his nephew from the Isaurians

M68a.13

B 512.14

When *the Isaurians made a raid, they entered* and plundered *Sis, a village in the region of Nicopolis* in the district subject to Antioch, a city in which there were many men of God. The saint was there among the people, and they *seized and took him* captive, *but the Lord freed him from their power.* They led away with them Thomas, a nephew who also relied on the Saviour of the world. Mar Simeon, trusting in the Lord, went to the camp of the raiding party. He carried with him documents which related that, for the redemption of his nephew, he brought gold which he would hand over for his release.

After this the Isaurians made a raid. They came and entered Sis, the village of the saint in the region of Nicopolis. The saint was present there and those Isaurians seized and took him, but the Lord freed him from their power. They captured many people, among them Thomas, the saint's nephew—a man who died after living a good, ascetic life. The saint pursued those taken captive and found them camped at Kastelen.

Approaching Kastelen where they were camped, he found them at meal. Those guarding the camp *held him securely and brought him before their leaders* whose names were Biswar and

When the camp guards saw him, they held him securely and brought him before their leaders, one of whom was named Bos and the other Altamadora. They asked him,

Tamidora. They interrogated him, saying, 'Why have you come here? Why did you not fear, and why was your heart not troubled that you were coming to where we dwell?' Then he answered them, '*I have come to redeem* a youth who is with you'. They saw by the documents he carried that he spoke the truth, as they related that forty dinars were sent by his hand for the redemption of the youth. But they only showed to the Isaurian leaders three darics, which they held out as he was standing before them.

When the chiefs saw this, *they were filled* with great wrath, *anger* ruled them and they were very emotionally excited as they said to him, 'In what do you trust that you mock us in our own territory? Instead of the forty darics mentioned in the documents you carry you want to give us only three.' They commanded that *his head* be lifted off *with a sword.*

One of those standing before them, also an Isaurian, lifted up his sword very menacingly and boldly brought it near to decapitate the blessed one when his right hand cleaved to his shoulder and fear and

'How have your dared to come here? Were you not afraid and did not your heart tremble?' He answered, 'I have come to redeem Thomas, my nephew, and these captives'.

On perceiving this they were filled with anger and they ordered his head to be taken off by a sword.

One of them drew his dagger to strike him and instantly his right hand cleaved to his shoulder. When they saw this, fear fell upon them and their leader.

trembling settled on the group because of this.

Their chief commanded, 'Let us order ourselves to go with all the captives *to another place'*. The saint heard this as he was kneeling and bowing down before him earnestly entreating him concerning the redemption of the youth.

The blessed one's *petition* was not accepted and immediately the man of God *lifted up his hand* upon Bosar, the chief of the Isaurians and *an evil spirit took possession* of his limbs. He bowed down before the saint as he entreated, *cried out and said*, 'What have I to do with you, *servant* of Christ?'

When all the camp saw *the sight*, fear and trembling fell upon them and their leaders *approached* and entreated the *blessed one*, saying, '*Tell us in truth if you are a Christian and the servant of* Christ.' The blessed one answered, '*I am a Christian*'. Then *the chief of the Isaurians as he stood in misery*, answered and swore by the sun which he worshipped as a god, '*My sins* today *were stirred up against me in your coming* to me, *but I beseech you to offer petition to God on my behalf.*'

Bos ordered them to set out for another place. When the saint saw that they would not grant his petition, he was strongly moved and he lifted up his hand against Bos.

Immediately an evil spirit took possession of him and before the saint he was in convulsions as he cried out and said, 'Woe! This comes from you, servant of Jesus Christ'.

When the Isaurians saw the sight they were exceedingly frightened. They drew near to the saint and said, 'Tell us in truth if you are a Christian and the servant of God'. He said to them, 'I am a Christian'. Then the chief of the Isaurians, as he stood in misery, said to the saint, 'My sins were stirred up against me in your coming, but I beseech you to offer petition to God on my behalf.'

Then the man of God, aroused in the spirit of God, answered, 'If you ask me *to offer petition to God on your behalf, release into my custody your captives* and sons will return to their fathers and fathers to their sons. *Behold, their crying has gone up before God, and he has sent this trial upon you.' Now the captivity numbered four hundred men* and children. *The chief of the Isaurians* answered the blessed one and said, 'Pray for me that I be set free of this trial, and I will release all this captivity *into your custody*'.

Then the man of God *knelt and prayed* and offered supplication on his behalf. *When he finished his prayer, he stretched out his right hand to him and said, 'In the name of Christ, be healed'. At that moment the unclean spirit departed from the man and he recovered; he released all the captivity into the custody of the blessed one. As he was leading the captivity away, the blessed one* commanded them that they should not tell anything of what their eyes had seen or their ears heard *that Christ had done by him to redeem them. Then he sent everyone home.*

As the blessed one was *travelling on the mountains* and leading *Thomas his nephew*, the

Then the saint answered, 'If you want me to offer petition on your behalf, release into my custody your captives. Behold, their crying has gone up before God, and he has sent this trial upon you.' Now the captivity numbered four hundred men and women. The chief of the Isaurians beseeched him to offer petition on his behalf and he released the captives into his custody.

The saint knelt and prayed. When he finished his prayer, he stretched out his right hand to him and said, 'In the name of our Lord Jesus Christ, be healed'. At that moment the unclean spirit departed from the man and he recovered; he released all the captivity into the custody of the blessed one. As he was leading the captivity away, the blessed one ordered them not to say anything to anyone about what Christ had done by him to redeem them. Then he sent everyone home.

As he and his nephew Thomas were travelling on the mountains, his nephew thirsted for

youth *thirsted for water* and was much afflicted. *The blessed one prayed and said,* 'Our Lord Jesus Christ, do not let him *whom you redeemed from captivity die of thirst.*' At that moment, *water burst forth and they drank. When their thirst was quenched, the water was sought but not found. He led the youth and brought him to the village of his kinsfolk.*

water. The blessed one lifted up his eyes and prayed and said, 'O Lord, do not let him whom you redeemed from captivity die of thirst.' At once water burst forth and they drank. When their thirst was quenched, the water was sought and not found. He led the youth and brought him to the village of his kinsfolk.

2. *Special Ascetic Exercises of Simeon*

M 73a.12

When he was forced *to sit* with the brethren, *he appeared* to eat with them *while really he did not eat* the food *at all. For he placed* the blessed morsel *that he received from the abbot underneath his couch. Without his wanting it, the brethren* came and *found it.*

After *night service* when *the brethren* were resting, *he would hang a weight* he had *on his neck all the time that his brethren were sunk in sleep.* When they were rising for morning service, he would take it off him secretly and nobody was aware of it. Once, as *the stone weight was on his neck, he was tempted by Satan and suddenly he fell mightily and his head was wounded. He took some of the dust from the place*

B 520.3

When he was compelled to sit at table, he appeared to eat while really he did not eat anything at all. For he placed the bounty that he received from the abbot with the brethren underneath his couch. Without his wanting it, the brethren found it.

Again, when the brethren finished night service and lay down to rest, he would hang a weight around his neck all the time the brethren were sunk in sleep. When it was time for them to rise, he would take the weight off his neck and stand up with them to pray. One night, when the stone weight was on his neck, he was tempted by Satan and fell asleep. Suddenly he fell

where he was standing, made the sign of the cross on it in the name of our Lord Jesus Christ, and *applied it* to the wound. Immediately *it was healed and he had no injury.*

mightily and his head was wounded. He took some of the dust from the place where he was standing, made the sign of the cross on it, and applied it to the wound. At that moment it was healed and he had no injury. Now a round piece of wood was there and he began to stand on it at night so that if he happened to fall asleep the wood would roll away from under him.

When the brethren saw his toil and his customs, *they wanted* to imitate him *but were not able.* All of them *planned* to drive him away from them, and *they proposed a calumny to a simple-minded brother* who was looked down on, 'Pour out some *cooked food* and take it and show it to the abbot and say to him, "I took this away *from Simeon when* I found him eating." *This fast he keeps is a sham* and pretence.' *The abbot called him and accused him.* He did not answer because he thirsted to be falsely accused and he was praying to God in the sight of all that he might attain to that beatitude that *our Lord said* to his disciples, *'Blessed are you when men speak against you all things in untruth.'* When the abbot saw that he did not want to tell the truth,

When the brethren saw his severe toil, they wanted to act like him but were not able. So they planned to bring a false accusation against him. They said to a simple-mimded brother of the monastery, 'Take a dish and put in it bits of bread and cooked food. Then go show it to the abbot and say to him, "I took this from in front of Simeon as he was eating it.

This fast he keeps is a sham." ' When he heard this, the abbot called him and accused him. But Simeon responded not a word about the matter for he longed to fulfill that word which our Lord said, 'Blessed are you when men speak against you all things in in untruth for my sake.' Then the abbot called him and said to him, 'Tell me

he put him under excommunication. Thus compelled, he told
him that these things *were said*
against him falsely and not
in truth.

if in truth this was accused
against you', and put him under excommunication. Then
he told him that these things
were said falsely.

3. Simeon's Clothing

B 538.19

His clothing consisted of
pieced-together stalks taken
from the roots which sprouted
up in front of him in the enclosure. Upon this he wrapped
around a hard rope. He stayed
clothed this way for seven
years. Then he made for himself a garment of goat-skin.
So the evil one with all his
forces was put to confusion
and Christ was triumphant in
his faithful servant.

4. Attacks by Satan and Seven Healings

M 84a.9

Again after these things as he
was confined *in the Lenten fast,
Satan appeared to him in the form
of a lion, and of a dragon and
stung him on* his left *foot.* His
Lord did not really turn away
from him, but that he might
manifest to him that he was
clothed in a *body.*

B 548.21

This then is the beginning of
the saint's life in the enclosure.
He stood on a stone in the
northwest corner of the enclosure. Every year during the
holy days of Lent he would
shut himself up in the enclosure and he was tempted by
the harmful enemy of humanity who envies the virtue of
the virtuous and hates righteousness. He appeared to
him in many forms, but he

remained firm and did not remove his gaze from heaven. In the Lenten fast Satan appeared in the form of a lion, and of a dragon which coiled itself round all his body and stung him on his foot. Not that he gained control over him but that his Creator might bring home to him that he was in a body.

In all this war he did not fall away *from his steadfastness and Satan from his discomfiture. 'What we received from Job is renewed to us in Simeon from Sis.' In all these Lenten fasts* he fought with him openly so that he might cease from his work. But he was occupied in his service and did not tremble and was not frightened by those visions.

In all this war and strife his strength was not weakened but Satan remained discomfited and cried out and wailed with the rest of his forces and said, 'Woe to us! The discomfiture that we received from Job is renewed to us in Simeon from Sis.' This often happened, yet he did not turn backwards but stood in continual prayer. Each year during Lent food such as men eat did not come near his mouth. Many who were brought in severe affliction were healed by his prayer.

There came to him a paralytic who could not move his legs. They carried him and brought and *placed him before him.* When he saw him, he *lifted his eyes to heaven* and prayed and said to him, 'In the name of our Lord Jesus Christ, rise up on your feet.' At that moment he stood and was going hither and thither before him as he *praised,* re-

There came to him a monk, a paralytic who could not move his legs. They carried him and placed him before the saint. He lifted up his eyes to heaven and, standing in prayer, he besought the Lord on his behalf. Immediately he could move his legs and he stood and leapt before him like a hart. He shouted out in a loud voice

joiced and *blessed God.*

praising and blessing God who had strengthened his enfeebled limbs, together with the rest of the people there.

After some time *a sickness fell* on *many people in Telneshe and many* died from it. *They assembled and went up and beseeched* the blessed one *to offer* prayers *on their behalf to God.* He was praying for a long time. Now there was a *certain stone cup placed in the recess* where the holy vessels are placed. As *all the people were standing, that cup was filled with water and overflowed on all sides to the ground. All of them ran and rubbed the water on and immediately they were healed* from their sickness.

Some time later many people in Telneshe were stricken by a severe outbreak of hard swellings that fell on them so that many died from the sickness. They all assembled and went up and beseeched him to offer petition on their behalf to God that they might be freed from the severe sickness sent upon them. As he stood in prayer, a stone eucharistic cup would be in the recess before him. As all the people were standing, entreating, beseeching, suddenly that cup was filled with water and overflowed on all sides to the ground. All of them ran and rubbed the water on themselves and immediately they were healed of their swellings.

From the west came a man of *noble family* who was in *severe* pain from *a flow of blood—for many years* it had been flowing and because of it he did not uncover himself. He would not let a doctor approach him and he beseeched the blessed one to petition God on his behalf. He *prayed* for him and *immediately* he was cured. *He*

From the west an important man of noble family who had heard of the saint was prostrate with a severe affliction, a flow of blood of many years' duration. This flow was a great trial to him as he could not put clothes on his prostrate body because of the flow of blood. It was kept a secret, however, not told to anyone because of

went home praising and blessing *God.*

the rank he held. He came
to the saint and besought him
to deliver him from this trial
upon him. He prayed to God
on his behalf and the stricken
one was delivered from his
affliction. He went home
rejoicing and praising God because healing had been bestowed on him through the
prayer of the man of God.

A *certain woman* had a demon
dwelling in her. He was tor-
turing her so that *blood flowed
from her mouth.* Her relations
led her and brought her to the
saint and they entered and informed him about her. The
blessed one said to one of his
disciples, "Take some of this
dust and go and apply it to
her and say to that demon, '*In
the name of our Lord Jesus Christ*
leave her and do not again torture her."' In that hour the
demon left and she was healed
and praised God.

Now a certain woman was
possessed by an evil spirit. She
was in severe torment, and
had not a single quiet moment
from the chastisement but was
convulsed by the devil so that
blood flowed from her mouth.
She came to the saint's enclosure, and when many saw
her they besought the saint
on her behalf to offer prayer
for her to God that she might
be healed of her severe torment. He prayed to God and
besought on her behalf, and
sent one of the men standing before him with a message to the devil who spoke
through the woman's mouth,
'In the name of our Lord Jesus
Christ I command you to be
silent and not to speak.' That
moment the unclean spirit left
her and she was healed from
her devil.

Again, a rich man from *Palestine* came to him in great

Again, an important man,
governor of one of the towns

affliction. *His head was placed on his breast* and his slaves carried him *on a litter*. They entered and placed him before the blessed one and he said to the blessed one, '*I will not depart* from before you and *from the door of God I will not remove* until I am healed from this sickness.'

of Palestine and a pagan, had his head bent with his neck placed on his breast so that he could not lift his head. He came to the man of God carried on a litter by two men. He petitioned him to beseech mercy from God, telling him that many doctors had seen him and he had spent a great deal on sorcerers and wizards, but his affliction was no better. He cried out and said in front of him as he clasped his feet and earnestly entreated him, 'I will not depart from you and I will not remove from the door of God until you lay your hands on my head.' While he so disputed, he did not allow the man of God to pray.

The blessed one said to him, '*A human cannot heal a human unless from God. But I entrust* your sickness *to God, who can heal you.*' As he spoke, he prayed and when he had finished his prayer, *he struck his foot upon* the anvil on which he was standing.

So the saint answered and said, 'I am a sinful human and the least of all humans. My hands are not confirmed like those of all the bishops and monks who laid hands on you. One thing I will say to you: a human cannot heal a human unless from God. I entrust you into the hand of the living God who created the world in his mercy and grace so that he may heal you from this severe affliction upon you.' Then he stopped holding the saint's feet. Now the saint's custom was that when he had finished his prayer he would strike his foot on a bench placed before the rock on which he stood. When the time came to end his prayer, he suddenly struck his foot and everybody kneeling before him moved and stood up.

At that moment the man stood up healed, *his head was lifted from his breast* and all the people there praised God when they saw it. *He offered much gold because of the healing*, but the blessed one did not wish to take it from him and *said* to him, '*I* do not need *gold* and silver. Instead of that gold, *I ask* you to receive *baptism* and *be enlightened in the knowledge of the truth, and to free those slaves who carried you.*' *He did as the blessed one commanded and he returned to his region* praising and blessing God.

At that moment the afflicted one stood up healed from his disease, his head lifted up from his breast. He praised God with all the people there because of the relief and healing he had received. He offered much gold to the man of God because of his healing but the saint answered and said, 'I do not need gold or silver, but I want the light of truth to enlighten you through holy baptism to the forgiveness of your sins and that you set free those servants carrying you so that by their freedom you may be set free from Satan.' When he heard the saint's words, he did everything enjoined. He returned home safe and sound, praising God because by means of his holy servant he had been healed of his affliction.

They brought to him *seven youths who* had been born *paralysed from their mothers' wombs.* They entered and *placed them before him and he looked at them and lifted his eyes to heaven* and said in his prayer, 'My Lord, into your hands I commit them.' When he finished his prayer he said to them, 'Rise up in the power of God.' Immediately they rose up and were walking hither and thither before him. All who saw gave *praise to God.*

Another time *there was a drought and the earth was nigh to not producing seed. A great crowd assembled* from every place and *came* to the blessed one *with petitions* and beseeched him *to ask God to give heed to the land.* He said to them, *"Turn away* from your *evil* ways and your hateful deeds and I trust in the Lord that he will again have mercy and give heed to the land." And he said to them, "Go." They went away *and did* as he had said to them, and the clouds poured rain and the cisterns were filled as usual. The reaper had a full harvest and the poor ate and were satisfied and they blessed God, the nourisher of all. The blessed one had previously made a vow that he would celebrate and offer the liturgy because God heard his prayer and sent down rain. He celebrated as he had said, and a great crowd

After a long time there was such a drought to the east and in the surrounding region that the earth was nigh to not producing seed because of the lack of water. A great crowd from the east and those who lived on the mountian assembled and came to the man of God with petitions and earnestly entreating him to ask God about this affair so that he be merciful and give heed to his creation. He answered and said, 'Turn to God and present an offering to the Lord your God. Turn from evil and do good, then he will quickly turn and have mercy on you.' They did as he commanded and the clouds gave abundant water and their cisterns were fill as usual. The reaper had plenty of sheaves, and the poor ate and were satisfied. They gave thanks and praised God their nourisher. The man of

gathered so that even the mountains were covered. They praised God for all that they had seen and heard.

God made a vow between himself and his God, 'Because you received the prayer which I offered on behalf of the poor and unfortunate I will appoint a commemoration and make an offering to you my Lord.' On the first commemoration he celebrated, an innumerable crowd gathered so that the mountains were covered.

Seven afflicted children came who from their mothers' womb had been paralysed and they were placed before him. He looked at them, then raised his eyes to heaven and prayed, entrusting them to God their creator. Immediately their limbs became strong, they stood up and danced for joy before him. All the people assembled there offered praise to God who gave such miracles to men.

5. Conclusion to the Saint's Life

M 63b.11

So the saint rested and the blessed and chosen one of God, Mar Simeon, was crowned. He completed his struggle and he received the crown of righteousness with a good name and an excellent life. There was rejoicing for all who serve Christ. His

B 643.15

So the holy and elect of God, Mar Simeon, rested and was crowned. He completed his struggle and received his crown in high repute and in righteous deeds. There was great joy to all who fear God. In the year 770, at the end of the *dodekate,* that is, the departure from this life was in the year 770 of the Greeks, in the numbering of Antioch in the year 507, at the end of the *dodeka* and the beginning of the *triskaidekate*, that is the thirteenth year, in the second of the month Elul on the fourth of the week. He was in his enclosure nineteen days from the time he died on the column, but he was there until the twentieth of the month because the numbering of the month began one day before the saint died. Therefore, he died on the second of the month Elul and he departed from the enclosure to go the city of Antioch on the twenty-first of the month Elul. He entered the city Antioch on the twenty-fifth of that month on a Friday into the holy Church. By the prayers and intercession of the blessed Mar Simeon may our Lord make tranquillity reign in the midst of his Church and his peace be throughout the world. May the poor and sinful man who wrote this and all the children of the holy Church receive mercy, now and at all times and forever. Amen.

Here ends the life of the holy Mar Simeon of the pillar. His prayer be with us. Amen. Amen.

twelfth year, and at the beginning of the *triskaidekate*, that is, the thirteenth year, on the second of Elul, on the fourth day of the week. After he died, he remained inside the enclosure in the coffin on the pillar nineteen days. It was the twentieth of the month because the month numbering began one day before the saint died. On the second of the month he died and he left the enclosure on the twenty-first of the month Elul. He entered the city of Antioch on the twenty-fifth of the month, on a Friday. For he left on a Monday and entered on a Friday, that is five days, amidst joy and great solemnity. May this memory be a blessing and his prayers be for the creation for ever. Amen.

6. The Good and the Evil Rich Men

M 53b

Again, there was a great affliction and an increase of famine during the days of the blessed one. Corn was so scarce that a daric was offered for three or four pecks of corn and none was available at that price.

There were two noblemen in the region of Edessa and each had a large barn full of corn. One of them had the custom of going up to pray and be blessed by the blessed Mar Simeon. When he saw him, he prayed and said to him, 'I beseech your holiness. I have a barn full of corn. Bless it with your prayer. I will go and open it up and sell it for half the price asked elsewhere.' Mar Simeon said to him, 'Take for yourself some ḥnana in the name of our Lord Jesus and make three crosses on the door of that barn. Then open it and sell and the Lord, he who makes his blessing dwell on your house and on your barn, will grant relief to everyone.

He went and did as the blessed one said to him. He opened and gave relief to all. He sold at a price to whomever had something, but those who had nothing he did not send away empty-handed. A huge innumerable crowd gathered and kept on growing—rich and poor, orphans and widows. He gave relief to everyone until the barn was empty and all used up. His servants had asked him to put aside and keep a little for them but he was not persuaded. He said to them, 'If we are reckoned like everyone else, let the Lord do whatever he wishes'.

As people kept appealing and the corn in the barn was all consumed, he said to his servants, 'Take brooms and gather what is there before everyone and share it out to everyone handful by handful and fistful by fistful.' His servants did as commanded, then they locked the barn and went away.

When our Lord saw his trust and wanted to validate the blessing of this righteous one, he worked a great miracle. For many again came to him appealing. Not to upset them he said to his servants, 'Go, open the door and show them the inside of the barn.' When they came, they were able to open the door only with difficulty because [the barn] was filled from top to bottom as if there had been no decrease. As he gave it out he granted relief to all both for a price and for free as long as our Lord granted. When the year began he again went and prayed and recounted these events to all and praised and thanked God for the gift he had done for him bv the prayer of the blessed one.

As for that other nobleman, many came and besought and requested him to sell to them or grant them relief but he did not want to as he only considered economics. One day a frightful judgement overtook him. A fire suddenly blazed up on his barn and the smoke went up as from a furnace. When he heard it he ran to see and his heart froze[1] as he opened and saw the black coals. The angel of the Lord struck him and he died a cruel and troublesome death.

---

[1] Literally, 'melted away', but this gives the opposite connotation in English.

APPENDIX C

NARRATIVES FOUND ONLY IN CERTAIN MANUSCRIPTS OF THE LIFE *BY ANTONIUS*

21a.[1] Certain unbelievers heard about the holy man and the marvels which God wrought through him. Unconvinced, they came during a severe winter to spy out whether he kept standing during the winter. As Scripture says, 'Bowing down they worshipped him'.[2] The blessed man said to them, 'It is good of you to come, children. Why have you come in such a winter?' While he was still speaking to them, they began to give account of the ways they had offended him. He prayed to the Lord God on their behalf so that they might be converted and he healed them of their condition. They besought him to pray for them always, and he sent them back home, saying, 'Go in peace'.

21b.[3] In those regions dwelt a leopard from some place or other, and it had devoured many men and animals. [The saint] was told about it, and he commanded some water mixed with soil to be sprinkled in that place; I myself went out and besprinkled the whole area. The next day the leopard was found dead at that very spot. They skinned it and brought the skin, and the righteous man ordered the skin of that leopard to be stuffed with chaff. When it had been stuffed, it was displayed there a long time and everyone who saw it glorified the God of heaven.

22.[4] A queen of the Arabs, who was sterile, came to him begging that she might bear children, for she was reproached every day by her husband. She was persistent in prostrating often and begging for many days at the column of holy Simeon. Then the

---

[1] This narrative is found only in manuscript C.
[2] Gen 43:28.
[3] This narrative is found only in manuscripts X and Y.
[4] The following six miracles are found only in manuscripts B, D and the Latin tradition.

saint sent a message to her, 'Go home, and the Lord is able to give you what is fitting.' Going back home, she had intercourse with her husband, straightway conceived and bore a daughter, but for five years [the child] neither spoke nor walked. The woman came weeping with her husband and child, and holy Simeon in answer said to them, 'Stay here and the Lord can help.' When seven days were up, nothing had happened and, saddened, they started to leave, saying, 'Clearly the Lord does not want to heal her.' They were on their way and had not gone far when they turned to look at the pillar of holy Simeon, and their daughter suddenly cried out, saying, 'Glory to you, holy Simeon.' When they saw it, the parents of the child glorified God because of holy Simeon.

23. Hear another mystery. One day when soldiers were on the march, a woman who greatly desired to see the face of holy Simeon asked herself how she could get to see him. She intended to make herself look like a man and to see him. One day, therefore, she saw many soldiers coming to the holy man to have him pray for them and she made herself look like a soldier and went along with them herself. When they arrived at the place where holy Simeon's pillar was, she said to the soldiers with her, 'Brethren, if you like, leave the animals with me and enter and be blessed by the righteous man. When you come back, I too will enter so that I may be deemed worthy to be blessed by the righteous man.' When they had entered and prostrated themselves, holy Simeon said to them, 'One of your soldiers has been left outside.' They said to him, 'Yes, master, he is guarding our animals.' The righteous answered them, 'When you go out, say to him: do not trouble yourself, for you have been heard and been blessed by the Lord.' When they went outside, they sent for him and inquired, 'What good have you done in God's sight? For the righteous man said to us, "Say to the soldier with you who remained outside: do not trouble yourself, for your prayer has been heard and you are blessed by the Lord."' She answered them and said, 'I confess to you, brethren, that I am a woman and I had a great desire to see the righteous man myself, for I am a sinner.' When the soldiers heard this they were astonished and blessed God on account of holy Simeon, and marched on in peace.

24. [Here is] another mystery, if you want to hear. When a large crowd came to be blessed, [the deacon came] with incense and as

usual called out to him, 'Servant of God, the people are waiting to receive your blessing. Give the command and send them away, for they have been waiting a long time and received no answer.' Now his spirit was not present. When I called out persistently and did not receive an answer, the deacon began to wail loudly beside the pillar, for he thought [the saint] was dead. When the crowd of people observed this, they began to be distressed and to grieve greatly lamenting their sins. But when his holy spirit returned after a suitable time, he answered and said to the people, 'Brethren, a great ship was tempest-tossed on the sea just now: it had on board about three hundred lives, and everyone cried out, summoning God, the Master. They called out to me with frightful oaths and, when I saw what was happening to them, I called on the God who is always long-suffering towards our sins to calm the sea, and I gave my hand to them and saved them all.' When they heard the mystery, the crowds of people glorified God on account of holy Simeon, and the righteous man blessed them and sent them away in peace.

25. A large growth came up on a female serpent and, because of her sufferings, she tried to leave for about one mile when the male, suffering her pains with her, took hold of the female, and they came to lord Simeon. When they arrived at his pillar, they separated from one another, for the female did not dare to be seen by the righteous man, but went into the women's section. The male came in the midst of that crowd and prostrated himself before the pillar, shaking his head up and down, and prayed to the righteous man. When the crowd saw the huge size of the snake, they ran away from it, but when he saw this holy Simeon said to the crowds, 'Do not run away, brethren, for he has truly come here to pray. His female is very ill and has gone into the women's section.' He said to the snake, 'Take up clay from the ground and carry it to your wife. Place it on [her] and breathe on it, and it will heal her.' The snake took some clay and went to his wife. When the crowds saw it they followed him to see what he would do. They saw the female standing upright outside the barrier, and she had a large growth. The [male] snake took the clay, placed it on [her] and breathed on her and, in the presence of all, it healed her. He then took her and went away, and when the crowds saw this mystery, they glorified God.

26. Another marvelous event occurred in his days. When the
great terrifying threat swept over all the inhabited world, all the
East and Antioch came to him, imploring him to entreat God.
Many buildings were collapsing and many people died, and even
the righteous man with his pillar was shaken like a reed by the
wind. Weeping with them he said to the crowds, 'Brethren, all
have turned aside, together they have gone wrong, there is not
even one.[5] You do not listen to me, but your fornications and
your injustices have so increased that everyone defrauds everyone
else. Truly, brethren, I say to you: it is easier for me to talk with
the Master than with you unbelievers.' Commanding them to stop
their entreaties he began to pray, but once more the threatening
condition which shook everything was continuing among them.
He then allowed them to call out, 'Lord, have mercy', and while
they continued for several hours to cry out, 'Give us peace', he
was praying greatly. When he had finished the prayer, he said
to the people, 'Brethren, truly I say to you: no one of all this
multitude was heard except for one person. To prove it to you
I will bring him into the middle.' He commanded him to come
before everybody and asked him, 'Brother, believe what I say:
among all of these only you were heard. But satisfy us all and tell
us what good you have done.' He however did not want to speak
and said, 'I am a sinner, let me be'. As much pressure was being
put on him, a voice from heaven came to him saying, 'Your prayer
has been heard.' So the rustic stood in the midst of all the people
and began to tell his story.

'I am a farmer, and it is my custom to divide into three parts
the wages[6] I get on whatever day I work. First I put aside the
portion for the poor, then the state taxes, and finally the portion
for my own expenses. I have not stopped acting in this way right
up till now.' Then everyone was greeting him with respect and
each person was excitedly pressing around the man to see him.

27. There was a certain man called Julian who belonged to
Ardabur, and he was constantly annoying Ardabur, saying, 'Give
me permission and I will go and take him down from his pillar

---

[5] Ps 14:1 = Romans 3:12.
[6] *kopos* = labor, here with the meaning of 'fruit of my labor'.

and beat him up, for he is an impostor and leads people astray.'[7] So Julian rushed towards [the saint], placed a ladder against the pillar, and started to climb up, expecting to bring Simeon down. When he reached the third rung, the ladder moved away from the pillar and was suspended about four cubits from the ground and hung in the air. Everybody was astonished at the sight, but Ardabur was annoyed and tried to draw his bow to shoot [the saint] and immediately his hand grew numb and he could not let fly the arrow. Until his death he had gout not only in his hands but also in his feet.

---

[7] Lietzmann notes that there is a section missing from manuscript B from "and beat . . ." I have followed the Latin manuscripts and manuscript D.

BIBLIOGRAPHY

Adam, A. 'Rezension von A. Vööbus: History of Asceticism, in the Syrian Orient', *Göttingische Gelehrte Anzeigen* 213 (1960) 127–145.

Alexander, Paul J. *The Oracle of Baalbek. The Tiburtine Sibyl in Greek Dress.* Washington: Dumbarton Oaks, 1967.

Amadou, R. 'Chôrêveques et périodeutes', *L'Orient Syrien* 4 (1959) 233–240.

Attridge, H.W. and Oden, R. *The Syrian Goddess*, Texts and Translations SBL 9. Missoula: Scholars, 1976.

Assemani, S.E. *Acta sanctorum martyrum orientalium et occidentalium in duas partes distributa.* Rome: Collini, 1748.

Bedjan, P. *Acta Martyrum et Santorum.* 7 vols. Paris/Leipzig: Harrassowitz, 1890–97.

Blersch, H.G. *Die Säule in Weltgeviert.* Sophia: Quellen östlicher Theologie 17. Trier: Paulinus, 1978.

Bouché-Leclercq, A. *Histoire de la divination dans l'antiquité.* Paris: Leroux, 1879–82.

Brock, S. 'Early Syrian Asceticism'. *Numen* 20 (1970) 1–9.

―――. *Syriac Perspectives on Late Antiquity.* London: Variorum Reprints, 1984.

Brown, P. 'The Rise and Function of the Holy Man in Late Antiquity'. *Journal of Roman Studies* 61 (1971) 80–101.

―――. *The Cult of the Saints.* Chicago: University of Chicago, 1981.

Cameron, R. and Dewey, A. *The Cologne Mani Codex.* Texts and Translations SBL 15. Missoula: Scholars, 1979.

Canivet, P. *Le monachisme syrien selon Théodoret de Cyr.* Theologie historique 42. Paris: Beauchesne, 1977.

Chaine, M. *La Vie et Les Miracles de Saint Syméon Stylite l'Ancien.* Bibliothéque d'Études Coptes 3. Cairo: L'Institut Français d'Archéologie Orientale, 1948.

Chestnut, Glenn. *The First Christian Histories*. Theologie historique 46. Paris: Beauchesne, 1977.

Cross, F.M. *Canaanite Myth and Hebrew Epic*. Cambridge: Harvard University Press, 1973.

Cumont, Franz. *Astrology and Religion Among the Greeks and Romans*. New York/London: Putnams, 1912.

Delehaye, H. *Les Saints Stylites*. Bruxelles: Société des Bollandistes, 1923.

――――. 'Les Femmes Stylites'. *Analecta Bollandiana* 27 (1908) 391–92.

――――. 'Les recueils antiques de miracles des saints'. *Analecta Bollandiana* 43 (1925) 49–57.

Devos, P. 'La structure de l'Histoire Philothée de Théodoret de Cyr. Le nombre de Chapitres'. *Analecta Bollandiana* 97 (1979) 319–335.

Doran, Robert. 'Compositional Comments on the Syriac Lives of Simeon Stylites'. *Analecta Bollandiana* 102 (1984) 35–48.

Downey, G. *A History of Antioch in Syria: from Seleucus to the Arab Conquest*. Princeton: Princeton University Press, 1961.

Draguet, R. 'La Christologie d'Eutyches, d'après les Acts du Synode de Flavien, 448', *Byzantion* 6 (1931) 441–457.

Drijvers, H.J.W. *Cults and Beliefs at Edessa*. Leiden: Brill, 1980.

――――. 'Spätantike Parallelen zur altchristlichen Heiligenverehrung unter besonderer Berücksichtigung des syrischen Stylitenkultes'. *Aspekte frühchristlicher Heiligenverehrung*. Oikonomia: Quellen und Studien zur orthodoxen Theologie 6. Erlangen: Universität Erlangen, 1977, 54–76.

――――. 'The 19th Ode of Solomon: Its Interpretation and Place in Syrian Christianity'. *Journal of Theological Studies* 31 (1980) 337–355.

――――. 'Hellenistic and Oriental Origins'. *The Byzantine Saint*. University of Birmingham Fourteenth Spring Symposium of Byzantine Studies. San Bernardino, CA: Borgo, 1983. 25–33.

――――. 'Odes of Solomon and Psalms of Mani. Christians and Manichaeans in Third-Century Syria'. *Studies in Gnosticism and Hellenstic Religions*. Festschrift G. Quispel. Leiden: Brill. 117–130.

――――. 'Die Legende des heiligen Alexius und der Typus des Gottesmannes im Syrischen Christentum'. *Typus, Symbol,*

Allegorie bei den östlichen Vätern und ihren Parallelen im Mittelalter. Eichstatter Beiträge 4. Regensburg: Pustet, 1981 187–217.

Eliade, Mircea. *Shamanism and Archaic Techniques of Ecstasy.* Princeton: Princeton University Press, 1964.

Festugière, A.M. *Antioche Païenne et Chrétienne. Libanius, Chrysostome et les moines de Syrie.* Paris: Boccard, 1959.

Fowden, G. 'Bishops and Temples in the Eastern Roman Empire A.D. 320–435', *Journal of Theological Studies.* 29 (1978) 53–78.

Frank, S. *Aggelikos Bios.* Münster: Aschendorff, 1964.

Frankfurter, David T.M. 'Stylites and *Phallobates*: Pillar Religions in Late Antique Syria', *Vigiliae Christianae* 44 (1990) 168–198.

Frend, W.H.C. *The Rise of the Monophysite Movement.* Cambridge: CUP, 1972.

Garrite, G. *Vies géorgiennes de S. Syméon Stylite l'ancien et de S. Ephrem.* CSCO 171–172. Louvain: L. Durbecq, 1957.

Gregory of Tours, *Opera.* Monumenta Germaniae Historica, Scriptores Rerum Merovingicarum 1. Hanover: Hahn, 1885.

Harvey, Susan Ashbrook. 'The Sense of a Stylite: Perspectives on Simeon the Elder'. *Vigiliae Christianae* 42 (1988) 376–394.

Hendriks, O. 'La vie quotidienne du moine syrien oriental'. *L'Orient Syrien* 5 (1960) 293–330; 401–431.

Henrichs, A. and Koenen, L. 'Ein griechischer Mani-Codex'. *Zeitschrift für Papyrologie und Epigraphik* 5 (1970) 141–149.

Jonas, Hans. *The Gnostic Religion.* Boston: Beacon, 1958.

Jones, A.H.M. *The Later Roman Empire 284–602.* Oxford: Blackwell, 1964.

Klijn, A.F.J. *The Acts of Thomas.* Leiden: Brill, 1962.

——. *Seth in Jewish, Christian and Gnostic Literature.* Supplements to Novum Testamentum, 46. Leiden: Brill, 1977.

Lane Fox, Robin. *Pagans and Christians.* NewYork: Knopf, 1987.

Lent, F. 'The Life of St. Simeon Stylites: A Translation of the Syriac Text in Bedjan's Acta Martyrum et Sanctorum, Vol. IV'. *Journal of the American Oriental Society* 25 (1915) 103–198.

Leroy-Molinghen, A. 'A propos du texte de l'Histoire Philothée de Théodoret de Cyr'. *Zetesis Album amicorum.* Festschrift E. de Strycker. Antwerp/Utretch: De Nederlandsche Bockhandel, 1973. 732–735.

Lietzmann, H. *Das Leben des heiligen Symeon Stylites.* Texte und Untersuchung 32, 4. Leipzig: Hinrichs, 1908.

Life of Genofeva. Monumenta Germaniae Historica, Scriptores Rerum Merovingicarum 3. Hanover: Hahn, 1896.

MacMullen, Ramsay. *Christianizing the Roman Empire (A.D.100–400)*. New Haven: Yale University Press, 1984.

Martindale, J.R. *The Prosopography of the Later Roman Empire. Volume II A.D. 395–527*. Cambridge: CUP, 1980.

Murray, R. *Symbols of Church and kingdom. A Study in Early Syriac Tradition*. Cambridge: CUP, 1975.

———. 'The Characteristics of the Earliest Syriac Christianity'. N. Garsoian *et al.* edd. *East of Byzantium: Syria and Armenia in the Formative Period*. Washington: Dumbarton Oaks, 1982. 3–16.

Nagel, P. *Die Motivierung der Askese in der alten Kirche und der Ursprung des Monchtums*. Texte and Untersuchung 95. Berlin: Akademie, 1966.

Nasrallah, J. 'Le Couvent de S. Simeon L'Alepin [=Stylite]. Témoinages littéraires et jalons sur son histoire'. *Parole de l'Orient* 1 (1970) 327–356.

Nedungatt, G. 'The Covenanters of the Early Syriac-Speaking Church'. *Orientalia Christiana Periodica* 39 (1973) 191–215, 419–444.

Nestorius. *The Bazaar of Heracleides*. Trans. G.R. Driver and L. Hodgson. Oxford: Clarendon,1925.

Nöldeke, T. *Sketches from Eastern History*. Beirut: Khayats, 1963.

Parke, H.W. *The Oracles of Apollo in Asia Minor*. London: Croom Helm, 1985.

Peeters, P. *Orient et Bysance: le tréfonds oriental de l'hagiographie byzantine*. Bruxelles: Société des Bollandistes, 1950.

Peña, I. *et al. Les Stylites Syriens*. Milan: Franciscan Printing Press, 1975.

Quasten, J. *Patrology*. Antwerp: Spectrum, 1960.

Robinson, James M., ed. *The Nag Hammadi Library*. San Francisco: Harper & Row, 1977.

Rousselle, A. 'Du sanctuaire au thaumaturge: La guérison en Gaule au IVᵉ siecle'. *Annales* 31 (1976) 1085–1107.

Schuler, P.L. *A Genre for the Gospels*. Philadelphia: Fortress, 1982.

Segal, J.B. *Edessa 'The Blessed City'*. Oxford: Clarendon, 1970.

Stroumsa, Gedaliahu A.G. *Another Seed: Studies in Gnostic Mythology*. Leiden: Brill, 1984.

Tchalenko, G. *Villages antiques de la Syrie du Nord*, Vol. I. Paris: Geunther, 1953.

Theodoret of Cyr. *Histoire des Moines de Syrie* 2 Vols. Sources Chretiennes 234, 257. Paris: Cerf, 1977–79.

————. *A History of the Monks of Syria*. Translated by R.M. Price. Kalamazoo, MI; Cistercian, 1985.

Torrey, C.C., 'The Letters of Simeon the Stylite'. *Journal of the American Oriental Society* 20 (1899) 253–276.

Towner, W. Sibley. 'Form-criticism of Rabbinic Literature'. *Journal of Jewish Studies* 24 (1973) 101–118.

————. *The rabbinic 'enumeration of scriptural examples'. A Study of a rabbinic pattern of discourse with special reference to Mekhilta d'R. Ishmael*. Leiden: Brill, 1973.

Trimingham, J. *Christianity among the Arabs in Pre-Islamic Times*. New York: Longman, 1979.

Vööbus, A. *A History of Asceticism in the Syrian Orient*. 2 Vols. Corpus Scriptorum Christianorum Orientalium 184,197. Louvain: Secretariat du CSCO, 1958–1960.

————. 'Discovery of New Manuscript Sources for the Biography of Simeon the Stylite'. C. Laga *et al.*, edd. *After Chalcedon. Studies presented to Professor Albert van Roey*. Louvain: Peeters, 1985, 479–484.

West, M.L. 'Oracles of Apollo Kareios. A Revised Text'. *Zeitschrift für Papyrologie und Epigraphik* 1 (1967) 183–187.

Widengren, G. *Mani and Manichaeism*. New York: Holt, Rinehart and Winston, 1945.

Williams, M. *The Immoveable Race: A Gnostic Designation and the Theme of Stability in Late Antiquity*. Leiden: Brill, 1985.

————. 'The *Life of Antony* and the Domestication of Charismatic Wisdom'. *Charisma and Sacred Biography*, Michael A. Williams, ed. JAAR Thematic Studies.

Wright, G.R.H. 'The Heritage of the Stylites'. *Australian Journal of Biblical Archaelogy* 1 (1970) 82–107.

Wünsche, A. 'Die Zahlenspruche im Talmud und Midrasch'. *Zeitschrift der deutschen morgenländischen Gesellschaft* 65 (1911) 57–100; 395–421; 66 (1912) 414–459.

SCRIPTURE INDEX

HEBREW SCRIPTURES

APOCRYPHA

CHRISTIAN SCRIPTURES

NAME AND SUBJECT INDEX

239

Ethiopians 69
Eusebius of Teleda 26, 27, 71
Eusebona 71, 109
Eusebonas see Eusebona
Evagrius 30–31, 35
Ezekiel 40

F

Festiguière, A.M. 17 n. 5, 27, 35, 55
    n. 87, 71 n. 8, 73 n. 10, 92 n. 8,
    93 n. 9, 93 n. 10, 97 n. 16, 100
    n. 22

G

Gabula 111
Gaul 19, 29, 75
Gindaris 22, 23, 143
Gospel of Thomas 24, 26

H

Harvey S. 37, 38
Heliodorus 71
ḥnana 19, 120, 123, 124, 141, 142,
    144, 151, 152, 167, 222
Homerites 19, 75
Hosea 40, 57, 58, 180

I

Iberians 19, 75, 77
Isaiah 57, 180
Isaurians 107, 167, 207, 208, 209,
    210
Ishmaelites 19, 40, 41, 77, 81
Italy 75

J

Jacob 70
James of Nīsībis 20, 26
James the Persian 26
Jeremiah 40, 57–58, 180
Jesus 42, 52, 177–78
Jews 19, 83, 189, 190
Jezebel 126
Job 42, 51, 94, 131, 195, 198
John, Bishop of Antioch 38–39, 65,
    189
Jonah 179
Jones, A.H.M. 18 n. 7, 92

Joseph 70, 93
Joshua 195
Julian 228, 229
Julian Saba 26, 27, 38

K

Kastelen 207
Kyriakos 156
Kings see Emperors

L

Lebanon 141
Leo 194
Lietzmann H. 55, 59, 94 n. 12, 97 n.
    16, 229 n. 7
Lucian of Samorata 29–30

M

Mara 111, 112
Mar'ash 166
Maris 17, 28, 117, 119
Martha 107
Martyrius 98
Maru 193
Medes 69
Meletius 41, 74
Merope 99
Micah 70
Moses 51, 52, 58, 70, 72, 125, 126,
    128, 176, 177, 184, 195
Mount Ukhama 167
Murray R. 24–25, 33

N

Naaman 146
Nicopolis 16, 103, 137, 207
Noah 58, 180

O

Odes of Solomon 23
Oracles 20–21

P

Palestine 216
Panir 18, 22, 23, 194–95
Parents of Simeon 16, 42–43, 70, 88,
    104; mother 30, 43, 92–3; father
    87

CISTERCIAN PUBLICATIONS, INC.
TITLES LISTINGS

CISTERCIAN TEXTS

THE WORKS OF BERNARD OF CLAIRVAUX

Apologia to Abbot William
Five Books on Consideration: Advice to a Pope
Grace and Free Choice
Homilies in Praise of the Blessed Virgin Mary
The Life and Death of Saint Malachy the Irishman
Love without Measure. Extracts from the Writings
  of St Bernard (Paul Dimier)
The Parables of Saint Bernard (Michael Casey)
Sermons for the Summer Season
Sermons on the Song of Songs I - IV
Steps of Humility and Pride

THE WORKS OF WILLIAM OF SAINT THIERRY

The Enigma of Faith
Exposition on the Epistle to the Romans
The Golden Epistle
The Mirror of Faith
The Nature and Dignity of Love

THE WORKS OF AELRED OF RIEVAULX

Dialogue on the Soul
The Mirror of Charity
Spiritual Friendship
Treatises I: On Jesus at the Age of Twelve, Rule for
  a Recluse, The Pastoral Prayer

THE WORKS OF JOHN OF FORD

Sermons on the Final Verses of the Song of
  Songs I - VII

THE WORKS OF GILBERT OF HOYLAND

Sermons on the Songs of Songs I-III
Treatises, Sermons and Epistles

OTHER EARLY CISTERCIAN WRITERS

The Letters of Adam of Perseigne I
Baldwin of Ford: Spiritual Tractates I - II
Gertrud the Great of Helfta: Spiritual Exercises
Gertrud the Great of Helfta: The Herald of God's
  Loving-Kindness
Guerric of Igny: Liturgical Sermons I - II
Idung of Prüfening: Cistercians and Cluniacs: The
  Case of Cîteaux
Isaac of Stella: Sermons on the Christian Year
Serlo of Wilton & Serlo of Savigny
Stephen of Lexington: Letters from Ireland
Stephen of Sawley: Treatises

MONASTIC TEXTS

EASTERN CHRISTIAN TRADITION

Besa: The Life of Shenoute
Cyril of Scythopolis: Lives of the Monks of Palestine
Dorotheos of Gaza: Discourses
Evagrius Ponticus:Praktikos and Chapters on
  Prayer

The Harlots of the Desert (Benedicta Ward)
Iosif Volotsky: Monastic Rule
The Lives of the Desert Fathers
Mena of Nikiou: Isaac of Alexandra &
  St Macrobius
Pachomian Koinonia I - III
The Sayings of the Desert Fathers
  Spiritual Direction in the Early Christian East
  (Irénée Hausherr)
The Syriac Fathers on Prayer and the Spiritual Life
  (Sebastian Brock)

WESTERN CHRISTIAN TRADITION

Anselm of Canterbury: Letters I - [III]
Bede: Commentary on the Seven Catholic Epistles
Bede: Commentary on the Acts of the Apostles
Bede: Gospel Homilies I - II
Bede: Homilies on the Gospels I - II
Cassian: Conferences I - III
Gregory the Great: Forty Gospel Homilies
Guigo II the Carthusian: Ladder of Monks and
  Twelve Mediations
Peter of Celle: Selected Works
The Letters of Armand-Jean de Rance I - II
The Life of Beatrice of Nazareth
The Rule of the Master

CHRISTIAN SPIRITUALITY

Abba: Guides to Wholeness & Holiness East & West
A Cloud of Witnesses: The Development of
  Christian Doctrine (D.N. Bell)
Athirst for God: Spiritual Desire in Bernard of
  Clairvaux's Sermons on the Song of Songs
  (M. Casey)
Cistercian Way (André Louf)
Fathers Talking (Aelred Squire)
Friendship and Community (B. McGuire)
From Cloister to Classroom
Herald of Unity: The Life of Maria Gabrielle
  Sagheddu (M. Driscoll)
Life of St Mary Magdalene and of Her Sister St
  Martha (D. Mycoff)
The Name of Jesus (Irénée Hausherr)
Penthos: The Doctrine of Compunction in the
  Christian East (Irénée Hausherr)
Rancé and the Trappist Legacy (A.J. Krailsheimer)
The Roots of the Modern Christian Tradition
Russian Mystics (S. Bolshakoff)
The Spirituality of the Christian East (Tomas
  Spidlék)

MONASTIC STUDIES

Community & Abbot in the Rule of St Benedict
  I - II (Adalbert De Vogüé)
Beatrice of Nazareth in Her Context (Roger
  De Ganck)
Consider Your Call: A Theology of the Monastic
  Life (Daniel Rees et al.)
The Finances of the Cistercian Order in the Four
  teenth Century (Peter King)
Fountains Abbey & Its Benefactors (Joan Wardrop)
The Hermit Monks of Grandmont (Carole A.
  Hutchison)

TITLES LISTINGS

In the Unity of the Holy Spirit (Sighard Kleiner)
Monastic Practices (Charles Cummings)
The Occupation of Celtic Sites in Ireland by the
 Canons Regular of St Augustine and the
 Cistercians (Geraldine Carville)
The Rule of St Benedict: A Doctrinal and Spiritual
 Commentary (Adalbert de Vogüé)
The Rule of St Benedict (Br. Pinocchio)
Towards Unification with God (Beatrice of Nazar-
 eth in Her Context, II)
St Hugh of Lincoln (D.H. Farmer)
Serving God First (Sighard Kleiner)

CISTERCIAN STUDIES

A Difficult Saint (B. McGuire)
A Second Look at Saint Bernard (J. Leclercq)
Bernard of Clairvaux and the Cistercian Spirit
 (J. Leclercq)
Bernard of Clairvaux: Man, Monk, Mystic
 (M. Casey) Tapes and readings
Bernard of Clairvaux: Studies Presented to Dom
 Jean Leclercq
Christ the Way: The Christology of Guerric of Igny
 (John Morson)
Cistercian Sign Language
The Cistercian Spirit
The Cistercians in Denmark (Brian McGuire)
The Cistercians in Scandinavia (James France)
The Eleventh-century Background of Cîteaux
 (Bede K. Lackner)
The Golden Chain: Theological Anthropology of
 Isaac of Stella (Bernard McGinn)
Image and Likeness: The Augustinian Spirituality
 of William of St Thierry (D. N. Bell)
An Index of Cistercian Works and Authors in the
 Libraries of Great Britian I (D.N. Bell)
The Mystical Theology of St Bernard (Etiénne
 Gilson)
Nicholas Cotheret's Annals of Cîteaux (Louis J.
 Lekai)
The Spiritual Teachings of St Bernard of Clairvaux
 (J.R. Sommerfeldt)
Wholly Animals: A Book of Beastly Tales (D.N.Bell)
William, Abbot of St Thierry
Women and St Bernard of Clairvaux (Jean Leclercq)

MEDIEVAL RELIGIOUS WOMEN
Lillian Thomas Shank and John A. Nichols, editors

Distant Echoes
Peace Weavers

STUDIES IN CISTERCIAN ART AND ARCHITECTURE
Meredith Parsons Lillich, editor

Studies I, II, III now available
Studies IV scheduled for 1992

THOMAS MERTON

The Climate of Monastic Prayer (T. Merton)
The Legacy of Thomas Merton (P. Hart)
The Message of Thomas Merton (P. Hart)
Thomas Merton: The Monastic Journey
Thomas Merton Monk (P. Hart)
Thomas Merton Monk & Artist (Victor Kramer)

Thomas Merton on St Bernard
Thomas Merton the Monastic Journey
Toward an Integrated Humanity (M. Basil
 Pennington et al.)

CISTERCIAN LITURGICAL DOCUMENTS SERIES
Chrysogonus Waddell, ocso, editor

The Cadouin Breviary (two volumes)
Hymn Collection of the Abbey of the Paraclete
Molesme Summer-Season Breviary (4 volumes)
Institutiones nostrae: The Paraclete Statutes
Old French Ordinary and Breviary of the Abbey of
 the Paraclete: Text & Commentary (2 vol.)
The Twelfth-century Cistercian Psalter
The Twelfth-century Usages of the Cistercian Lay-
 brothers

STUDIA PATRISITICA
Papers of the 1983 Oxford patristics conference
edited by Elizabeth A. Livingstone

XVIII/1 Historica-Gnostica-Biblica
XVIII/2 Critica-Classica-Ascetica-Liturgica
XVIII/3 Second Century-Clement & Origen-
 Cappodician Fathers
XVIII/4 *available from Peeters, Leuven*

Cistercian Publications is a non-profit corporation.
Its publishing program is restricted to monastic
texts in translation and books on the monastic
tradtion.

North American customers may order these books
through booksellers or directly from the warehouse:
 Cistercian Publications
 St Joseph's Abbey
 Spencer, Massachusetts 01562
 (508) 885-7011
 fax 508-885-4687

British and European customers may order these
books through booksellers or from:
 Brian Griffin
 Storey House, White Cross
 South Road, Lancaster LA1 4QX
 England

Editorial queries and advance book information should be
directed to the Editorial Offices:
 Cistercian Publications
 Institute of Cistercian Studies
 Western Michigan University
 Kalamazoo, Michigan 49008
 (616) 387-8920

A complete catalogue of texts in translation and studies
on early, medieval, and modern monasticism is available
at no cost from Cistercian Publications.

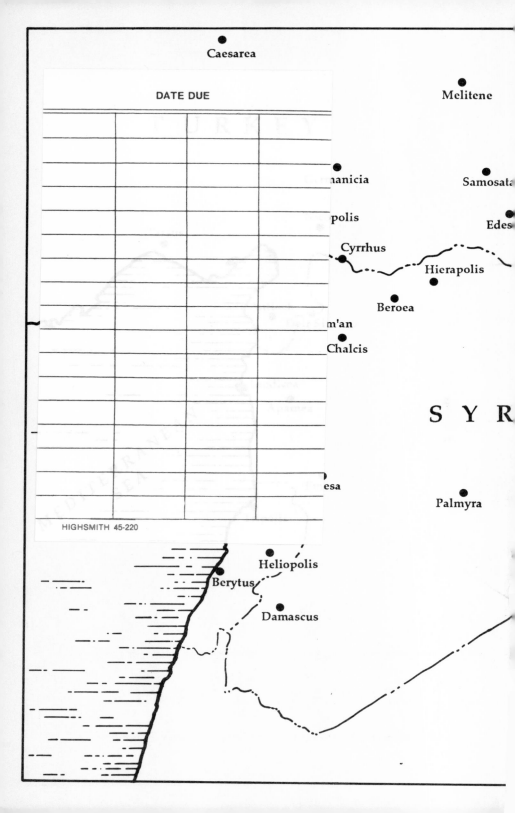